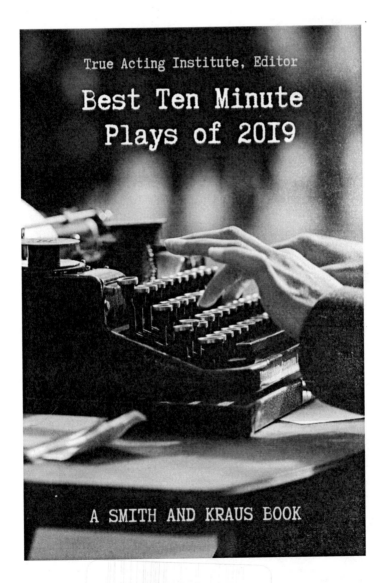

True Acting Institute, Editor

Best Ten Minute
Plays of 2019

A SMITH AND KRAUS BOOK

A Smith and Kraus Book
177 Lyme Road, Hanover, NH 03755
editorial 603.643.6431 To Order 1.877.668.8680
www.smithandkraus.com

The Best Ten-Minute Plays 2019 Copyright
© 2019 by Larry Silverberg
All rights reserved.

Manufactured in the United States of America

ISBN: 978-1-57525-933-8
Library of Congress Control Number: 2018915109

All plays appearing here are by permission of playwright.

Typesetting and layout by Elizabeth E. Monteleone
Cover design by Larry Silverberg

For information about custom editions, special sales, education and corporate purchases, please contact Smith and Kraus at editor@smithandkraus.com or 603.643.6431.

TABLE OF CONTENTS

INTRODUCTION

Welcome to our new book of ten minute plays, chosen for you by the team at True Acting Institute. For the first time, the content of this classic book was chosen as a result of a playwriting competition with three winning categories. We had thousands of submissions. Yes, thousands. The first place winners have their plays presented here in the book along with details about the playwright and the producing theatre. Second place winners are plays that were produced and third place winner have yet to be produced. For more information about any of the plays in this book, and for production inquiries, please contact the playwright directly. Enjoy the book!

The team at True Acting Institute.
For more information about us, go to: www.trueactinginstitute.com

1st Place

The Standing Ovation Award

HAMLET INVESTIGATIONS, INC.
ELLEN ABRAMS

BEST 10 MINUTE PLAYS 2019

THE PLAY:

Hamlet Investigations, Inc.

THE PLAYWRIGHT:

Ellen Abrams

SYNOPSIS:

Although everyone knows Prince Hamlet as the Melancholy Dane, he is also a curious, excitable student, zealous about sussing out cant and hypocrisy. Now, flush with the ambivalent thrill of discovering that his uncle killed his father, he has temporarily gone into the private investigation business to help others solve their own vexing, personal mysteries. Annette, a woman from our own time, hires the prince to utilize his amateur detecting gifts to help with a vexing romantic conundrum.

ABOUT THE PLAYWRIGHT:

Ellen's full-length play Intentions, was chosen as a semi-finalist by both the O'Neill Playwrights Conference and the New American Voices Reading Series. Her short play *Hamlet Investigations, Inc.* won first-place in the True Acting Institute's Best Ten-Minute Plays, 2019 competition, and was presented in October 2018 by the Emerging Artists Theatre's (E.A.T.) New Work Series (NYC), as was a reading of her one-hour, one-act play *Handsome*, about Rock Hudson's brief marriage in the 1950s, told through the eyes of his ex-wife, Phyllis Gates. In August 2018, her short play, *Eulogy(s)* was produced at Rhino Theatre's One-Act Jamboree (Pompton Lakes, NJ). In July 2018, her short play, *Metonym Or the Almost Completely False Story Behind the Creation of Roget's Thesaurus* was produced at the Secret Theatre (Long Island City, NY) as well as at the Manhattan Repertory Theatre in October 2017 (NYC). In March 2018, her short play, *Relations*, was presented by E.A.T., as was a reading of a full-length comedy, *The Ransom of Rona.* Another play, 30 minutes long, *On the Couch*, was produced as a reading by E.A.T. in October 2017.

This play is dedicated to my parents who taught me to love language and Shakespeare, and to Kevin, for everything, always.

CONTACT: abramse85@gmail.com

THE THEATRE:

Emerging Artists Theatre

15 West 28th Street, 3rd floor
New York, NY 10001-6439

MISSION:

To act as an incubator for new voices from the page to the stage.

ABOUT:

Emerging Artists was one of the first companies in NYC to begin programming for developing solo works for both female and male performers and for short and full-length musicals in our New Works Series. Emerging Artists also has a great reputation for its Off Broadway premieres that have garnered a Drama Desk nomination, the American Theatre Wing's grant award for Sustained Excellence in Theatre and Top 10 Critics Picks from both the *New York Times* and the *New York Post*.

CONTACT:

Paul Adams
EatTheatre@gmail.com
212-247-2429

WEBSITE:

emergingartiststheatre.org

PRESENTING THE PLAY:

Hamlet Investigations, Inc.

CAST OF CHARACTERS:

HAMLET: An entrepreneurial 17th century college student, home for the holidays, who has correctly determined that his uncle killed his father and subsequently married his mother. He has temporarily set himself up in business to help others solve the mysteries in their lives. He is quite gloomy and distracted by grief.

ANNETTE: Perplexed 21st century woman in her 30s seeking answers about her betrothed.

TIME: Today.

SETTING: Simple office, with desk, a scroll of writing paper, and a quill pen, skull, two chairs, an hourglass, perhaps a lute in the background.

At Rise: HAMLET, in medieval hat and poet's shirt, sits at the office desk.

HAMLET: *(stares into space, hand rests on side of face)* Ah, me. My heart is cloakéd deep in inky grief. If only I could cast off this knighted colour as with a doublet outgrown.

ANNETTE: *(tentatively peeks into office)* Uh, hello?

HAMLET: Enter, do, I beseech ye, shrew. Seat yourself and betray your burdens with honest speech.

ANNETTE: Um, okay. I heard from Horatio that you solved the mystery of your father's murder. Which, first—WOW! Congratulations! That couldn't have been easy—And second—

HAMLET: —'Twas mine Uncle Claudius who betrayed mine own father true. And then mine mother—

ANNETTE: Right, heard all that from Horatio. My problem is different. But your price is right. And I don't have much time, soooo…

HAMLET: Have you entered into vile quarrel with the villainous brother of your lamented father?

ANNETTE: Not exactly.

HAMLET: Might your love-weak mother have blackened her soul with bedchamber betrayal?

> *(pauses)*

Frailty, thy name is woman!

ANNETTE: Have you tried meditation?

> *HAMLET raises his forefinger, pauses a moment.*

> *ANNETTE opens her mouth to speak.*

HAMLET: I shall recover anon.

> *(ANNETTE opens her mouth to speak.)*

HAMLET: Hasten me not. My dear father, the King, did recent expire. Weak am I yet with sentiments dire.

ANNETTE: Sure, that's a tough thing for anyone.

> *(pauses)*

ANNETTE: *(Cont.)* You all right now, Mister?

> *(HAMLET recovers)*

HAMLET: I am called Prince Hamlet.

ANNETTE: Hamlet? Like an omelet? But with ham?

HAMLET: Might I enquire why it be meet that we meet?

ANNETTE: It's my boyfriend. Full disclosure—my fiancé.

HAMLET: You are his lady, you are his love?

ANNETTE: I thought so, but now I'm not so sure. Which is where you come in.

HAMLET: Forsooth, I would fain prove so.

> *(takes out scroll and quill to write)*

Name?

ANNETTE: That's the issue, right there. I think he's given me a fake one.

HAMLET: What manner of knave dares capture a gentle lady's heart with sham and falsehood?

ANNETTE: Right? Purely by accident, I happened to see this picture of him on a dating site a few months after we became engaged. But he was using a different name than the one he told me was his.

HAMLET: Foul cur invokes foul deed!

ANNETTE: We're supposed to be getting married later this month, and I'm not actually sure what his real name is!

HAMLET: Why did thou not simply loiter until the utterance of the vows and the pealing of the wedding bells before seeking my aid?

ANNETTE: Are you being sarcastic? I don't care for sarcasm.

HAMLET: *(pats her hand)* Not a bit of it, ladybird. I gage thou my earnest exertions. But I needs must apprehend more afore I commence my purpose on your behalf.

ANNETTE: He told me his name was Jerry. Thing is, on the site he calls himself Jason. Plus, he told me he is a software designer. But on this dating site, he claims to be an international business-man. Can you find out who he really is before we tie the knot?

HAMLET: Knots be not knots/when they be untangled whatnots.

ANNETTE: I don't take your meaning.

HAMLET: Describe his mien, his attributes, his visage so I might be apprised as for whom I search.

ANNETTE: *(thinks)* Do you know that actor who was in that movie with that girl from the TV show?

HAMLET: The image of same has quick vanish'd from my mental sights.

ANNETTE: I have a likeness of him here. In *People* magazine.

(pulls out magazine from her purse)

This is what he looks like.

HAMLET: *(peers at the photo, reads name)* Armie Hammer. 'Tis a handsome warrior and young. Much victorious in battle? His name befits such merit.

ANNETTE: I am not engaged to Armie Hammer. Jerry/Jason just looks like him. Only shorter. Fuller in the face. And a lot less handsome.

HAMLET: *(bitter)* Beauty is not all there is to recommend a man. Sweetest things turn sourest by their deeds; Lillies that fester smell far worse than weeds.

ANNETTE: Truth is, we live together. But he's so secretive he won't even trust me with his computer passwords.

HAMLET: Co-habitation? Mine own Ophelia would ne'er perpend a kiss of even the most cousinly sort 'pon her roseate lips, lest I seal a marriage contract in the doing.

ANNETTE: I didn't think there were girls like that anymore.

HAMLET: She was a glorious maiden with maidenhead complete withal.

ANNETTE: Um, that is like way TMI.

HAMLET: *(holds his head in his hands)* It was I, alas, who, in my own wretched, mad grief, unwittingly ripped her soul from spirit, and left only distraction in its stead.

ANNETTE: Bummer. Can we get back to my problem? You might want to write this down.

HAMLET: *(writes)* Marry, I attend. I inscribe. The Hammer. Jason. Jerry.

ANNETTE: He's about 5'5", wears tiny, round wire frame glasses for his beady little eyes—

> *(interrupts herself)*

—Say, do you think my Jerry could maybe be a prince, like you? Only in disguise or something? And that's why he maintains two identities?

HAMLET: Hiding his true self behind a merry mask of knavery—to test your love, perhaps—?

ANNETTE: Could be....

HAMLET: Do you suspect of him murder most foul?

ANNETTE: I suspect he's a freelance louse who wants to sponge off my health insurance by marrying me.

HAMLET: Mine Uncle Claudius also took advantage of a lady— Gertrude, my mother. A witch who tumbled with much dexterity into incestuous sheets—

ANNETTE: *(interrupts)*—So how do you plan on detecting what Jason/Jerry's real name is?

HAMLET: *(thinks)* Behold, mine thoughts follow a cunning train! He prays behind the arras, yes?

ANNETTE: Behind the—what now?

HAMLET: Pay heed. I cogitate a mirror of the plan I will force onto mine own uncle and depravéd mam.

ANNETTE: Just how does that go?

HAMLET: A theatrical that I will write so as to portray his perfidy. It will not fail to ensnarl him unawares and provoke an unwitting, but true, accounting of his intentions.

ANNETTE: I don't know about that. He's a pretty clever guy.

HAMLET: Mine uncle was clever enough to win mine mother's love from her true lord, my noble father.

ANNETTE: Where would you even find actors for this crazy self-produced play?

HAMLET: Players abound the countryside.

(points out members of the audience)

Look, there's one. And another. And yon, still two more. They are everywhere near.

ANNETTE: What makes you think your little skit will work on both your uncle and my Jason/Jerry?

HAMLET: I am but mad north-northwest; when the wind is southerly I know a hawk from a handsaw.

ANNETTE: Uh-huh.

HAMLET: I will find/Where truth is hid, though it were hid indeed/ Within the center.

ANNETTE: Know what? Maybe I'm asking too much of a guy who just lost his dad and is coping with some nasty mother issues—

HAMLET: Stay yourself, gentle distaff-tender. Attend. Behind the arras doth Polonious—I mean Jerry/Jason!—lurk. With one speedy Phhwwwft, he shall be dispatched. With ne'er time spare for his soul to fly heavenward.

ANNETTE: Look, I don't need you to kill him. Just confirm what I already suspect. Then I'll kill him. Just kidding.

HAMLET: Stay your own violent delights. Lean instead on the helm of my bare bodkin and I'll see the thing done in a singular slice.

(smiles invitingly)

You are a most comely lass whose honor I desire to serve.

ANNETTE: Maybe this was a mistake.

(attempts to leave)

HAMLET: (stops her) We men are arrant knaves, are we not? From prince to fishmonger. Believe none of our eloping endearments.

Get thee to a nunnery.

ANNETTE: I'm not even Catholic. Why would I—?

HAMLET: I say we will have no more marriages. 'Though affairs of the heart may be too customary to forbid.

ANNETTE: Are you married, by the way? You're kind of cute—in an antique-y sort of way.

HAMLET: No mouse-hunter, I. My darling Ophelia who I thoughtlessly and by method wild, did spurn—

ANNETTE: —So I heard. For some reason, she thought it would be hilarious to chuck rosemary, pansies, fennel, columbine and rue into the river, crooning all the while.

   (shudders)

Creepy.

HAMLET: The fault lies on mine own poll. I did cozen the dear lady into thinking me mad, which explains the junction with vegetation that you make reference to.

ANNETTE: You do have quite the effect on the ladies, don't you?

HAMLET: Life is a twisting snake, with neither wit nor order.

ANNETTE: A-men to that, brother.

HAMLET: *(gazes at HER appraisingly)* Wouldst thou have a brother? Prithee tell. One inclined to enigmatic yet explosive anger?

ANNETTE: Actually I do.

HAMLET: Might he be the sort of fellow to take arms against a sea of troubles—or even against one who dallied with his sister—and by opposing end him?

ANNETTE: Are you suggesting that you and I might . . . dally?

HAMLET: Attend not my manner nor my speech, it is disordered and at frazzle. Father dies, mother turns aunt, ghostly apparitions—

ANNETTE: You're not really serious about the bodkin business, are you?

   (SHE mimes cutting HER neck.)

HAMLET: Let us together conceive another infant, then. Something with more cunning than art, more body than blood, more claw than kitten—

ANNETTE: *(enough with the words, already, Hamlet)* What've you got in mind?

HAMLET: Alas, 'twould appear that but one circumstance has of late taken hold of me.

ANNETTE: 'Twould appear that way to me too. What the heck happened?

HAMLET: The case was revealed in a foggy moon-full night at the Castle Elsinore, where the weird laid siege to the senses.

ANNETTE: And you heard…something?

HAMLET: It spake to me close, though I knew within what it would utter afore the discourse.

ANNETTE: So I should listen to what my own inner voice is spaking?

HAMLET: You have been warned by your unsettled soul to cast aside this loathsome Romeo. And it is in this voice you must stake your trust.

ANNETTE: Cancel the wedding, then?

HAMLET: *(passionate)* Call me but your love and I'll be new baptized.

ANNETTE: We hardly know each other.

> *(considers)*

But…you *are* single now. And a Wittenberg U. student, I hear.

> *(SHE appraises HIM.)*

You look like you work out.

HAMLET: Rosencrantz and Guildenstern will vouchsafe it.

ANNETTE: Except they both got the shiv. Thanks to you.

HAMLET: They are not near my conscience; their defeat/Doth by their own insinuation grow.

ANNETTE: Thou doth protest too much, methinks.

HAMLET: Touché.

ANNETTE: On the other hand, you might want to slow down. Mourn your recent losses before you go seeking new relationships.

HAMLET: Sensitive utterance forsooth.

(checks his hourglass)

Alas, I fear I must make all haste.

ANNETTE: Still, you and I could possibly comfort the other, and put heartbreak behind us.

HAMLET: Thinkest thou it would work?

ANNETTE: Just between us, I don't suppose that Jerry/Jason was really right for me. What about you? Might you truly banish Ophelia from your heart?

HAMLET: Peering into your deep, expressive eyes, those orbs that reveal your soul and wit, makes me almost believe it possible.

ANNETTE: It is, it is possible! My orbs are witty and soulful. And my kisses are exquisite.

(grabs HIM; THEY kiss)

HAMLET: *(flustered)* But what of my mousetrap, the clever plot I have meticulously labored o'er to ensnare my father-uncle and mother-aunt?

ANNETTE: Isn't it enough that *you* know? And what about us? Think of the merry music we might make 'pon Cupid's pallet.

HAMLET: Revenge, I fear, is too sweet to ignore. Even if it means depriving myself of the luscious meal your mouth offers my starving soul.

ANNETTE: Maybe you should give it some more thought. Killing family members almost never works out.

HAMLET: But my vitriol-poisoned blood refuses to cool.

(ANNETTE kisses HIM again.)

HAMLET: *(pauses)* You make an excellent point, my sweet.

ANNETTE: I know I can love the bloodlust out of you.

HAMLET: To abandon the bloodlust or not to abandon the bloodlust. That is the question.

ANNETTE: I think you know the answer.

HAMLET: I do. Do I? I should. Or should I?

ANNETTE: You're not the most decisive guy, are you?

HAMLET: 'Tis a fault long credited to me.

ANNETTE: Forget the play thing for now. Look at it this way: Is there ever a wrong time to avenge your father's death and your mother's untimely marriage?

HAMLET: I suppose you're right.

ANNETTE: Of course I am.

HAMLET: But my actors await.

(SHE kisses HIM again.)

ANNETTE: Let 'em await.

(HE pulls HER into another kiss.)

END OF PLAY

DANCING IN THE ELEVATOR
DOROTHEA CAHAN

BEST 10 MINUTE PLAYS 2019

THE PLAY:

Dancing In The Elevator

THE PLAYWRIGHT: Dorothea Cahan

SYNOPSIS:

Kate, desperately unhappy after being spurned by her married lover, encounters Marushka, an exotic tea leaf reader, in their apartment building elevator. Marushka visits Kate, reads the details of her life in a teacup, and declares that someone who should love Kate has put a curse on her. Who this person is and how the curse is lifted are revealed to us by the play's end.

ABOUT THE PLAYWRIGHT:

Dorothea Cahan is an acting teacher, director, and writer of historical novels and of plays, both comedies and dramas. Her plays have been produced all over the United States and in England, and have won international playwriting awards. When not writing, she might be painting or sculpting.

Dorothea enjoys doing research for each of her plays, For *Dancing In The Elevator*, she studied tassomancy until the character of Marushka emerged. Then, conjuring up her opposite, Kate, the story evolved.

CONTACT:

djcahan@gmail.com
561 369-5936
215 673-1082

THE THEATRE:

Old Academy Players
3534 Indian Queen Lane, Philadelphia PA 19129

MISSION:

Old Academy Players is a diverse and inclusive non-profit volunteer organization with the mission and vision to enrich the theater experiences of our patrons by providing extraordinary and enjoyable theater at an affordable price, draw upon the talents, strengths and individualism of our members and volunteers who are invited to be a part of our productions, promote social activity among the membership and foster charitable and community activities. OAP welcomes all interested in theater to join us in accomplishing our mission.

ABOUT:

The Old Academy Players is a non-profit community theater established in 1923 and located in the East Falls section of Philadelphia. The theater's home is the charming, historic Old Academy building, where Grace Kelly and Robert Prosky began their acting careers. Every year the theater presents an all-comedy Summer One-Act Bonanza.

CONTACT:

oldacademyplayers@gmail.com
215-843-1109

WEBSITE:

oldacademyplayers.org

Presenting the Play:

Dancing in the Elevator

Cast of Characters:

KATE: a naïve young woman

MARUSHKA: a fortune teller of indeterminate age

Time: The present.

Scene: A shabby, city studio apartment. KATE is speaking on the phone.

KATE: Hello. Is this Marushka? .... This is Kate Norris. We met yesterday You gave me your business card. Do you remember me? ... Yes. The one who was crying on the elevator... I'm feeling better today. Thank you … The reason I'm calling … I see it says on your card that you do divination .... and I'm not exactly sure what that is ... Oh! ... Uh huh ... You foretell the future ... Specifically my future. Oh, Marushka, that is what I need. That is exactly what I need ... Would you do that?... Wonderful! ... I'm in 4C. ... You want me to boil water. Am I to be reborn? ... No, that was meant to be a joke.... See you shortly. Thank you. Thank you, Marushka.

(She disconnects the phone and sets a kettle on a hot plate on the table, then picks up the phone and punches in a number, pacing as she speaks.)

KATE: Hello. This is Kate Norris again. I wondered if he is still in the meeting... I see ... What a long meeting!.... It's only that I've been calling for three hours. Has he been getting my messages?... Yes, I'll hold. .... Yes? ... He's gone? You mean he's left for the day?... Well, did you give him my messages? ... All right, I'll hold.

(She sits on a chair, phone to her ear. Gradually her body slumps and shudders. We hear a dial tone. The phone slips to the floor. There is a knock at the door. Enter MARUSHKA, dressed in a slapdash approximation of gypsy garb. She holds a tambourine above her head and strikes it sharply.)

MARUSHKA: I am here! Here is Marushka!

KATE: Welcome. You look … nice.

MARUSHKA: These clothes special for divination. So now we will sit. Drink tea like old friends.

KATE: Okay.

MARUSHKA: What kind of tea you have?

KATE: Orange pekoe. Tea bags.

MARUSHKA: No good. Leaves all smashed up. No good for tassomancy.

KATE: Tassomancy? What is that?

MARUSHKA: Is the art of divination by tea leaves. Never mind. I bring good tea.

(She retrieves a vial from her bosom.)

KATE: The water is boiling.

MARUSHKA: You have big cup?

KATE: How about these?

MARUSHKA: Okay. Now I put in leaves. You pour water … Good. Now, wait two minutes.

KATE: Would you like a cookie?

MARUSHKA: No. You have small piece pumpernickel?

KATE: I'm afraid not. I have English muffins.

MARUSHKA: No good... . So. Your soul is in torment?

KATE: Yes... I would say so.

MARUSHKA: Hmm... Would you have maybe a little piece of herring?

KATE: No, I'm sorry. Would you like some tuna fish?

MARUSHKA: No good. Okay. We drink tea now. Then we see what will the tea leaves tell us.

KATE: Does that really work?

MARUSHKA: That depends who is doing the reading. You have Marushka. I have special gift. Also, I was taught by my grandmother, the great Grushenka who is revered in Romania.

KATE: Wonderful! I was lucky you spoke to me in the elevator. You were very kind.

MARUSHKA: You have great sadness in your eyes.

KATE: Oh, yes, Marushka. I am frantic with sadness. Can you help me?

MARUSHKA: We shall see. Drink. Drink … Okay. No more. Stop! … Now lift up the cup and swirl. Swirl, swirl. To the left. Three times. Good. Let me see. Mmm.

KATE: What do you see?

MARUSHKA: Ahh!

KATE: What is it?

MARUSHKA: Very interesting. You see this man?

KATE: Where?

MARUSHKA: Just here. A man with long legs. He is very bad man. Beside him a spade. Means danger. Over here a triangle pointed down. Means big trouble.

KATE: Oh, no!

MARUSHKA: You know this man?

KATE: It must be Charlie. He's been so mean to me.

MARUSHKA: For Charlie you are crying in the elevator?

KATE: In the elevator. In the subway, in the shower, in line at Starbucks ...Oh, Marushka, I am a crying fool. I make a spectacle of myself.

MARUSHKA: *(peering into the cup)* I see flowers. You met in Spring. You fell in love.

KATE: It was beautiful. Dinner by candlelight. Kisses in the moonlight, concerts in the park. He was my first love.

MARUSHKA: You didn't mind that he was married?

KATE: Gosh! You can see all that in the cup?

MARUSHKA: Of course.

KATE: Where?

MARUSHKA: Just over here. Beside him.

KATE: That chunky little blob?

MARUSHKA: His wife. Yes.

KATE: He told me he was finished with her. He was my boss. I believed everything.

MARUSHKA: Of course. You are innocent young girl.

KATE: I was head over heels. What did I know? He brought me caviar and pomegranates. He said we would marry. He seduced me.

MARUSHKA: Ah, poor little one.

KATE: In a month he grew bored.. He stopped calling me every night. He avoided me. Then he used a silly excuse – he said I had stolen paper clips, which was true – and he had me fired.

MARUSHKA: Oh, he is evil!

KATE: Then things got worse, Marushka. The more he rejected me, the more I became obsessed. I couldn't leave him alone. I waited for him outside the office building, but he walked quickly by, not turning his head. It was so painful, Marushka.

MARUSHKA: Oh, he is cruel!

KATE: Now, I telephone him six, eleven, nineteen times a day. I can't stop myself. I am ashamed. I am humiliated, but I can't stop. Do you understand?

MARUSHKA: Yes. Someone has put a curse on you.

KATE: So that's it! Can you help me?

MARUSHKA: We shall see. *(Peering in the cup)* Ah, look here. I see something! Do you see this bird in flight?

KATE: What does that mean?

MARUSHKA: A trip!

KATE: Really? Does it say where?

MARUSHKA: I am searching. Ah, yes. An island.

KATE: An island! Great! Does it say which island?

MARUSHKA: One moment. Hmm … It is either Catalina or Madagascar.

KATE: Wow! I've never been anywhere.

MARUSHKA: This is interesting. Look. Do you see many tables in a great hall set for a feast? And look here. Do you see beautiful white dress, strapless, in mermaid style?

KATE: Where?

MARUSHKA: Just here. Only Marushka knows how to read the spaces between the tea leaves.

KATE: That's amazing. Are you saying what I think you're saying? You see a wedding dress for me? Am I going to meet somebody?

MARUSHKA: Absolutely.

KATE: But how? I never meet anyone.

MARUSHKA: You do, but you do not recognize him.

KATE: Then, how am I to recognize him?

MARUSHKA: You will look deeply into the eyes of everyone you meet. And even if he has the face of a bulldog or a frog …

KATE: Eww!

MARUSHKA: … if you search his eyes and they are pools of love, then he will be transformed and become beautiful.

KATE: That is a little hard to believe, Marushka.

MARUSHKA: Yes, I know. Try it for one month.

KATE: A month? But what if I start to think about Charlie?

MARUSHKA: Trust in Marushka. The curse will be lifted. But wait! Here is important new information. You see? Just near the rim. It is the sun!

KATE: You mean this little soggy lump?

MARUSHKA: This the best news. This wonderful omen. Means joy! And look where it is! At the top of the cup. Bottom of the cup means future. Rim of the cup means now!

KATE: Now? What do you mean?

MARUSHKA: Soon. Who knows? Maybe tomorrow.

KATE: Tomorrow! I don't think I'm quite ready for joy tomorrow!

MARUSHKA: First we wash away curse. You have bath tub?

KATE: Yes.

MARUSHKA: *(retrieving vials from her bosom)* Put these in bath water to prevent curse. Two drops oil of lavender and cinnamon, three drops essence of rosemary. Next morning, no more obsession. Obsession finished.

KATE: I can hardly believe it.

MARUSHKA: It is guaranteed.

KATE: Fantastic!

MARUSHKA: Tomorrow, no more telephone. No more crying in elevator. Only dancing. Dancing in elevator.

> *(MARUSHKA picks up her tambourine. slaps it against her hip, dances joyously and hands the tambourine to KATE)*

MARUSHKA: Now you. Dance. Dance!

(KATE jingles the tambourine, twirls, laughing while MARUSHKA claps her hands.)

KATE: Suddenly I feel so light … so light that I can just float away. It feels as though a great weight has been lifted from me.

MARUSHKA: It is the curse leaving your spirit.

KATE: But Marushka, who would have done that to me? Who would have put such a dark curse on my spirit?

MARUSHKA: Someone who should love you.

KATE: But who? Who would torture me and torment me?

MARUSHKA: You don't know? It was you, dearest girl. It was you, yourself.

(Fade lights)

END OF PLAY

KAMASUTRA

TOM COASH

THE PLAY:

KAMASUTRA

THE PLAYWRIGHT: Tom Coash

SYNOPSIS:

The question of sex raises its head when Doris and Harold, a nice older couple from Hackensack, visit the Chandela Temples in India, famous (or infamous) for the erotic carvings celebrating the Kamasutra religious rituals. Amidst the highly suggestive surroundings, Doris and Harold reexamine their love and marriage.

ABOUT THE PLAYWRIGHT:

Tom Coash is a New Haven, Ct. playwright, director, and teacher. Prior to New Haven, he spent three years in Bermuda and four years teaching playwriting at The American University in Cairo, Egypt. Coash has won numerous playwriting awards including the American Theatre Critics Association's "M. Elizabeth Osborn Award", the Clauder Competition for New England Playwrights, an Edgerton Foundation National New Play Award, and The Kennedy Center's Lorraine Hansberry Award. His plays have been produced around the world including such theaters as: Barrington Stage, Portland Stage, InterAct Theatre, Abingdon Theatre, Ensemble Studio Theatre, Bailiwick Theatre, West Coast Ensemble, and many more. Coash currently teaches playwriting for the University of Southern Maine's Stonecoast Creative Writing MFA Program.

CONTACT:

thomascoash@sbcglobal.net

WEBSITE:

newplayexchange.org/users/156/tom-coash

THE THEATRE:

> Barrington Stage Company
> 122 North Street, Pittsfield, MA 01201

MISSION:

Barrington Stage Company (BSC) is a not-for-profit professional theatre company with a three-fold mission: to produce top-notch, compelling work; to develop new plays and musicals; and to find fresh, bold ways of bringing new audiences into the theatre, especially young people.

ABOUT:

Barrington Stage Company is the fastest growing arts venue in Berkshire County, attracting more than 58,500 patrons each year. BSC continues to gain national recognition for its superior quality productions and comprehensive educational programming. Barrington Stage has produced several award-winning plays and musicals, beginning in its inaugural year with The Diary of Anne Frank, which won the Elliot Norton/Boston Theatre Critics Award. Barrington Stage gained national prominence in 2004 with the world premiere of The 25th Annual Putnam County Spelling Bee by William Finn and Rachel Sheinkin. The musical, a runaway hit at Barrington Stage, later moved to Broadway and won two Tony Awards. In June 2013, BSC produced Leonard Bernstein, Comden, and Green's On the Town, directed by John Rando and choreographed by Joshua Bergasse. A Broadway production opened in October of 2014 to rave reviews. The show received four Tony nominations, including Best Musical Revival.

Every February, Barrington Stage hosts the 10x10 Play Festival in their St. Germain Theater. Barrington selects ten 10-minute plays out of nearly 300 script submissions. The festival typically runs three weeks, but will add an extra week in 2019 due to overwhelming demand. For more information, please contact the literary department at Barrington Stage Company.

CONTACT:

> Branden Huldeen, Artistic Producer
> literary@barringtonstageco.org

WEBSITE:

> barringtonstageco.org

Presenting the Play:

Kamasutra

Doris and Harold, an older American couple, are sitting on a bench at the famous kamasutra temples in India. They are over-dressed in typical American tourist gear. Doris is reading aloud from a guidebook. Harold is grumpy and continually attacked by bugs. She has no bug problem.

DORIS: Kamasutra...an ancient Sanskrit text giving rules for sensual pleasure, love, and marriage.

HAROLD: Rules! *(Slaps mosquito.)*

DORIS: The rules of love..of desire. From Kama..the God of Love plus sutra, the sanskrit word for string.

HAROLD: Where is that tour bus?!

DORIS: *(Pause)* There was a time when I thought of you as the God of Love.

HAROLD: Ten thousand dollars!

DORIS: Then you took up golf.

HAROLD: Ha, ha!

DORIS: *(Back to book.)* Built in the 10th century, India's Chandela Temples contain stunning examples of the Kamasutra art of love.

HAROLD: Porno.

DORIS: ...I beg your pardon?

HAROLD: Porno temples!

DORIS: It's not porno.

HAROLD: Airfare..five thousand dollars...

DORIS: What you've got in the garage is porno.

HAROLD: ..five star hotels..five thousand dollars..

DORIS: This is art. Capital A, capital R, capital T.

HAROLD: ..porno temples..priceless!

DORIS: Art, you old fart!

(They glare at each other.)

HAROLD: Where's that damn bus! *(Slaps bugs away.)*

DORIS: You should have sprayed.

HAROLD: I should have stayed in Hackensack!

DORIS: *(Reads...)* There are more than 85 buildings in the Chandela Temple complex.

HAROLD: And not one of them a toilet. *(Slaps several bugs)* Ow! Ow! Jesus!

> *(She just watches him.)*

They're not biting you?!

DORIS: You should have brought the spray.

HAROLD: I should have brought a gas can!

DORIS: Gas can?

HAROLD: So I could immolite myself! Isn't that what they do in these "temples"? Light themselves on fire.

DORIS: Harold!

HAROLD: I can see why, these bugs! Gotta sleep under nets for christ sake!

DORIS: I like the nets! They make me feel romantic.

HAROLD: They make me feel like Charlie the Tuna!

DORIS: Just like that movie..with what's her name and Robert Redford? Africa something...

HAROLD: We're in India, Doris!

DORIS: Out of Africa! He died in that plane crash!

HAROLD: Out of India is all I want.

DORIS: So romantic.

HAROLD: That and a cold beer!

DORIS: Harold, please?

HAROLD: *(Slaps leg)* Our big anniversary celebration and we can't even get a cold beer.

DORIS: I thought this would be fun. Try something new.

HAROLD: Like what? Malaria?!

DORIS: Fine! You old poop!

HAROLD: *(Looks at her, she ignores him. Looks for bus..no bus..)* Ok, ok, read me your book! Sheesh!

(Doris looks at him, a bit sadly turns back to her book..reads silently..then..)

DORIS: ...the grouping on the north side...*(looks up)*..north side...

(Looks at sun, looks around, looks at Harold. He ignores her. She licks her finger and holds it up, testing the wind in some kind of attempt to find north...or maybe just testing Harold.)

HAROLD: *(Can't take it..)* This is the north side!

DORIS: Thank you...the grouping on the north side..

HAROLD: Groping.

DORIS: I beg your pardon?

HAROLD: Should be the groping on the north side!

DORIS: *(Gives him a look, then continues..)* The group groping on the north side...

(He gives her a look.)

..is thought to represent the "Chakra-Puja" ritual of opening and entering..*(Harold snorts)*..basic to the awareness of seeing the world and connecting with it.

HAROLD: They're connected all right.

DORIS: Better listen to this Harold. The Chakra-Puja ritual aids in bringing peace and harmony to the practitioner.

HAROLD: And maybe a disease.

DORIS: The prominent figure on the north side..and his..linga..are said to symbolize the "Tree of Life". What's a linga?

HAROLD: Don't look at me.

DORIS: You always think you know everything.

HAROLD: I'm a mobile home dealer from New Jersey, not the Encyclopedia Britannica. *(Slaps ear)* Ow!

DORIS: You should have...

HAROLD: All right! Give me the goddamn spray!

(She looks at him questioningly.)

I know you brought it just so you could say I told you so!

(She gets spray from purse and hands it to him. He sprays himself all over while she calmly watches.)

Ok, I'll tell you what it is! Vulgar!

DORIS: What?

HAROLD: You know what! You'd be shocked if I said it. Or maybe you wouldn't since you're the one who brought us to this Hindu mosh pit.

(He doesn't know what to do with the spray...she holds her hand out for it as they're talking..he hands it to her, she puts it away in her purse.)

DORIS: Vulgar as in the magazines you hide in the garage vulgar? Or is it me that's vulgar?

HAROLD: Vulgar is as vulgar does is what it means.

DORIS: Might not be a bad idea.

HAROLD: What?

DORIS: We're here..might as well do as the natives do.

(Waves her hand indicating the temple.)

HAROLD: What?!

DORIS: Immo-late, Harold...Come on baby light my fire?

HAROLD: *(Pause, he looks at her, she looks back.)* Doris, you made a joke.

DORIS: I did, didn't I?! *(Quite pleased with herself.)*

HAROLD: A ten thousand dollar joke.

DORIS: Burning, burning love?

HAROLD: A ten thousand out of our retirement fund joke...

DORIS: I feel my temperature rising...

HAROLD: A ten thousand, money we'll never get back joke...

DORIS: All right! I..GET..IT!

(They glare. He sits, turns away. She defiantly opens her book. He is starting to feel uncomfortable digestion-wise, puts hand on stomach. Doris pulls binoculars from her bag and focuses on the temple.)

HAROLD: Binoculars! You brought binoculars!!

DORIS: I didn't want to miss anything. Only now I see I've been missing something for years.

HAROLD: What's that supposed to mean?

DORIS: I'm finding this very educational.

HAROLD: Where in god's name is that bus?!

(Adjusting trousers, looking uncomfortable.)

DORIS: Delhi belly?

HAROLD: No!

DORIS: You should have...

HAROLD: It's not Delhi belly!

DORIS: *(Pause)* So, you do know what it means.

HAROLD: What?

(She points at temple with binocs, he explodes..)

I don't know what it means! All I know is that we spent a fortune to come half way around the world to spend two weeks sitting on the damn toilet! Seven shots we have to get! Just to stay alive!

DORIS: Well, I'm sorry!

HAROLD: What were you thinking of, Doris?!

DORIS: You! I was thinking of you!

HAROLD: Me?!

DORIS: You! The way you used to be. The way you used to love me.

(Starts crying, pulls rumpled tissue from sleeve.)

It's been three years, Harold!!

(Harold is shocked.)

I thought this might be romantic! I thought that maybe we could pick out a good one and try it!

HAROLD: Doris!

DORIS: I thought maybe we could start with that one right there!

(She points!)

HAROLD: *(Harold looks.)* They're just holding hands.

> *(No answer.)*

Doris, they're just...

> *(Pause...he takes her hand. She pulls it back. Pause...)*

I'm sorry.

> *(No answer. He takes her hand again, this time she lets him. She dabs eyes with tissue.)*

DORIS: I know I don't look like I used to.

HAROLD: Doree..

DORIS: I sag.

HAROLD: So what? So do I!

DORIS: What is it then!? Tell me.

HAROLD: I..I don't know.

DORIS: Harold, please?

HAROLD: I..I'm old, Doris.

DORIS: You're not old.

HAROLD: I've let you down.

DORIS: What are you talking about?!

HAROLD: I sell mobile homes for not much of a living...

DORIS: You're very successful!

HAROLD: I'm not even a manager. We get by.

DORIS: We get by very well!

HAROLD: You always said you married me for my potential..and what have I done with it? Sell Airstreams and double-wides.

DORIS: What's wrong with that?

HAROLD: The South Sea cruise with your sisters and their lawyer-doctor husbands.

DORIS: I don't...

HAROLD: The cruise I should have taken you on.

DORIS: We couldn't afford it.

HAROLD: I should've borrowed the money! Hocked my damn golf clubs!

DORIS: Harold, that was...

HAROLD: Three years ago. *(Pause)* We went to Palm Harbour and you hated it.

DORIS: I didn't hate it.

HAROLD: Mr. Can't Take His Wife on a Cruise.

DORIS: You're wrong.

HAROLD: Am I?

DORIS: I didn't hate it. I was just..disappointed.

HAROLD: Is that what you call it?

DORIS: Ok, I was a little mad.

HAROLD: I knew it.

DORIS: Mad at you. Mad at my sisters. But mostly mad at myself..

HAROLD: I was being an old poop.

DORIS: ..for feeling that way.

HAROLD: And who wants to make love to a cheap, old poop?

DORIS: You had a pulled groin!

HAROLD: I didn't.

DORIS: From your backswing!

HAROLD: I lied.

DORIS: Why?

HAROLD: *(Shrugs)* You had a headache, I had a groin.

DORIS: Oh Harold..

HAROLD: I saw it in your eyes.

DORIS: Saw what?

HAROLD: That I let you down...

DORIS: You didn't..

HAROLD: I did! And I'm sorry!

DORIS: Stop! Just stop..please?

HAROLD: But..

> *(She slaps his neck..)*

Ow!

DORIS: *(Looks at her palm..)* Got him!

HAROLD: Oh. Thank you.

> *(She giggles)*

Don't laugh!

> *(She smiles)*

Doree I...

DORIS: Harold, look! *(She points at sculptures.)*

HAROLD: What?

DORIS: Mr. Can't Take a Hint.

> *(He looks at temple, then back at her, then kisses her. A good kiss, then she pulls back...)*

You want to know why I really married you?

HAROLD: You were pregnant.

DORIS: And very happily thank you!

> *(Holding his hand.)*

Remember our first night...at the drive-in?

HAROLD: Yes.

DORIS: When you touched me, I thought I was going to melt into a little puddle right there on the back seat.

HAROLD: Doris!

DORIS: You have the warmest, softest, strongest, most knowing hands of any mobile home dealer on the face of this planet.

> *(Looks in his eyes.)*

You made me a happy woman, Harold! We were connected! We were connected right from the start. And we didn't need any Chakra-Puja to do it!

> *(He kisses her. It's a good kiss. She rests her head on his shoulder. Dabs with the tissue...)*

HAROLD: What are you thinking?

DORIS: Priceless. *(They kiss again.)* What are you thinking?

HAROLD: *(Romantically)* Where's that damn bus?

   (Lights down.)

END

THE NEW CLIENT

PAUL DONNELLY

THE PLAY:

The New Client

THE PLAYWRIGHT:

Paul Donnelly

SYNOPSIS:

A small-town attorney who is lesbian faces a threat to her relationship for taking on a controversial client, a homophobic baker. The New Client depicts two principled women grappling seriously with an ethical and personal dilemma. It has the added advantage of passing the Bechdel test.

ABOUT THE PLAYWRIGHT:

My life as a "trailing spouse" has included stops in Washington DC, Atlanta, Honolulu, and Tallahassee. My work has won the Source Theatre Company National 10-Minute Play Contest, the Larry Neal Writers Award for Drama, the Virginia Playwriting Prize, and twice been nominated for a Helen Hayes Award. I had pieces in the 2015-2017 Atlanta One-Minute Play Festivals and my romantic comedy, Falling Off the Edge, was produced in Atlanta in January 2018. My newest full-length play, Memorial Day, received a reading in Kumu Kahua Theatre's Dark Nights series in Honolulu in March 2018 and was named a Finalist (one of eight out of 1,243 entries) for the first Moss and Kitty Carlisle Hart New Play Initiative. I am a member of the Dramatist Guild, the Klunch, the New Play Exchange, the Playwrights' Center, and Working Title Playwrights.

The New Client was written for a legal continuing education workshop, Courtroom Drama: A Creative Look at Legal Ethics through Original Comedic Plays, presented by Actors Express, Georgia Lawyers for the Arts and Working Title Playwrights in Atlanta in February 2017.

CONTACT:

paul@pauldonnellyplays.com
808-465-0602

WEBSITE:

pauldonnellyplays.com

THE THEATRE:

Santa Cruz County Actors' Theatre

MISSION:

Serving Santa Cruz County since 1985, Actors' Theatre supports, champions, and provides an outlet for the performing arts, with an emphasis on the theatrical arts: Provides resources for theater artists to explore their creativities and develop their crafts. Presents new and established works by local, national, and international authors. Cultivates and maintains audiences for the theatrical arts. Collaborates and partners with other groups to create a stronger presence for theater. Holds playwriting contests for 10-minute format and full-length plays, bringing the winners' plays to life on the stage. Sponsors the Actors' Theatre Award for Theatre Excellence at Cabrillo College by awarding an annual scholarship to an outstanding student. Started in 2016, the inaugural recipient was Cabrillo Theatre Arts student Malia Machado.

ABOUT:

The theatre serves the Monterey Bay Area, has been in operation for over 35 years and is a 90-seat house. It is used by Actors' Theatre as well as being a performance space for poetry, improv workshops and new works in theatre.

The 8Tens@8 Festival has been a landmark theatre production every January-February for almost 25 years. (S&K published our first anthology "30 Plays from the SC Actors' Theatre 8 Tens@8 Festival") and has become the official herald of the theatre season in the Santa Cruz Area. To date we have launched the world premieres of over 100 short plays, produced over 250 ten-minute plays, worked with over 75 directors and hundreds of actors from the entire Bay Area. Our playwrights have come from almost every state in the U.S. as well as many foreign countries. We consider the festival, which was the first ten-minute festival on the West Coast, to be a way of connecting with and honoring the talents of so many playwrights and the art of playwriting.

CONTACT: Bonnie Ronzio, ronziob@gmail.com, 831-335-4409

WEBSITE: sccat.org

PRESENTING THE PLAY:

The New Client

CAST OF CHARACTERS:

MARGARET HENSON-MITTENDORF – 40's. A small town attorney in a two-person firm in north Georgia. Margaret is not from Georgia. She settled in this small town because it is Lee-Ann's hometown. They have been a living together in the town for four years and a couple for much longer.

LEE-ANN HENSON-MITTENDORF – 40's. Proprietor of a yoga studio, surprisingly successful for a small town in north Georgia. She and Margaret moved back to her hometown four years ago, after the death of her father.

SETTING:

The den of the comfortable home shared by Margaret and Lee-Ann Henson-Mittendorf in a small town in northwest Georgia.

TIME:

The present.

At rise: Close to 9 p.m. Sunday. Margaret Henson-Mittendorf is seated on a sofa with an open laptop and stacks of file folders on a coffee table in front of her. Margaret's attention moves from a legal pad on which she is writing to typing on her laptop and back. She is concentrating deeply.

There is an unseen television downstage. It is on, but muted. Lights might suggest the flickering screen.

The alarm on Margaret's cell phone rings. She is startled, but immediately grabs the phone and silences the alarm.

MARGARET: Heck. Already?

MARGARET glances to the television, then begins shutting down her laptop, straightening the folders and returning them to her briefcase.

MARGARET: *(calling off)* Hey Lee-Ann! It's almost time.

MARGARET exits quickly and returns with two bottled beers which she places on the coffee table.

MARGARET: Lee-Ann!

MARGARET picks up and points the remote and clicks off the mute button. We hear the unmistakable strains of the theme to "Game of Thrones."

MARGARET: Lee-Ann, it's starting!

LEE-ANN HENSON-MITTENDORF enters. She is coiled, poised between fury and betrayal.

MARGARET: I got your beer.

LEE-ANN glares at her, unmoving.

MARGARET: *(turning and seeing LEE-ANN)* What?

LEE-ANN continues glaring.

MARGARET: *(gesturing to the television)* Can't you let it go for an hour?

LEE-ANN continues glaring.

MARGARET: *(hitting the mute button)* For god's sake.

LEE-ANN: It's completely unacceptable.

MARGARET: It's also completely non-negotiable.

LEE-ANN: How can you say that?

MARGARET: Since when do you get to review my client list?

LEE-ANN: Oh come on … this is …it's beyond the pale. This isn't just some random client I'm objecting to.

MARGARET: No.

LEE-ANN: It's going to have a huge impact on our lives.

MARGARET: Probably.

LEE-ANN: Then how can you not give me some say …

MARGARET: I'm sorry. It's too late. I've said yes.

LEE-ANN: And tomorrow you can go back and tell them no.

MARGARET: I can't …

LEE-ANN: You can tell them … You can tell them … that your marriage is more important than standing up for bigots.

MARGARET: Lee-Ann …

LEE-ANN: Or whatever they're paying you.

MARGARET: Wait a minute …

LEE-ANN: Or that you had momentarily taken leave of your senses and now you're in your right mind.

MARGARET: Look. You don't have to agree with me. You don't have to support me … although that would be nice. But you do have to accept that I am going to represent Shelley and Mark and the bakery.

LEE-ANN: I don't have to accept anything.

MARGARET: *(after a beat)* No. No, you don't. But your not accepting isn't going to change anything.

LEE-ANN: *(after a beat)* Does Bert know?

MARGARET: Excuse me?

LEE-ANN: Does Bert know?

MARGARET: Do I have permission from my male partner? Is that what you're asking? Are you serious?

LEE-ANN: Does he?

MARGARET: Yes.

LEE-ANN: So, you discussed this with him but not with me.

MARGARET: Y'know I frequently discuss business with Bert that I don't discuss with you. I don't typically discuss things like the color to paint the guest bathroom or where my wife and I should go on vacation with him; and I don't typically discuss whether or not I'm going to take a case with you.

LEE-ANN: This isn't a typical case! They're bigots ... hate-mongers ...

MARGARET: Who have the right to counsel.

LEE-ANN: Maybe. But why do you have to be that counsel?

MARGARET: Because they asked.

LEE-ANN: And you couldn't say no?

MARGARET: Shall we tease out the levels of meaning in that question.

LEE-ANN: Don't ...

MARGARET: Are you suggesting that I should deny them service because of what they believe?

LEE-ANN: That's not ...

MARGARET: Or for who they are?

LEE-ANN: They wouldn't serve you!

MARGARET: That is immaterial.

LEE-ANN: No, it isn't!

MARGARET: If Shelly turned up at your studio tomorrow night for the 5:30 Stretch Away Your Day class would you turn her away?

LEE-ANN: She wouldn't.

MARGARET: But if she did ...

LEE-ANN: They wouldn't bake a cake for a child's birthday party because his mothers ... because he has two mothers.

MARGARET: I know the particulars of the case.

LEE-ANN: Two women like us. Two women who are friends of ours … or who will be until they find out you are defending the bakers who wouldn't bake a cake for their son's birthday! How … how can you … what kind of internalized horseshit would allow you to think those people were right?

MARGARET: I don't think they're right.

LEE-ANN: You're defending them.

MARGARET: I am exploring the possibility that they may have a legal right to be wrong.

LEE-ANN: Oh my god, what does that even mean in English? No. Never mind. I don't want to hear your brief! Don't make this an abstraction. You were at that party. You know that child. You've known him his whole life. You held him when he was four days old … and now you can somehow justify defending people who wouldn't bake him a birthday cake? Really? At no point does simple human decency come into play for you?

MARGARET: I can see you're angry.

LEE-ANN: Oh, don't do that. Don't patronize me.

MARGARET: Okay … then give me a little credit.

LEE-ANN: For what?

MARGARET: Oh that's great.

LEE-ANN: What?

MARGARET: Nothing.

> *LEE-ANN glares.*

MARGARET: Since there's nothing else to say … *(picks up the remote)*

LEE-ANN: I would appreciate it if you didn't do that.

MARGARET: I would appreciate it if you would support me in this.

LEE-ANN: There's no way.

MARGARET: I haven't mentioned this once in the last four years, but don't you really owe me your support?

LEE-ANN: I can't.

MARGARET: I gave up a partnership for you. I moved to Dogpatch for you. I gave up WBNA season tickets. I have to drive nearly two hours to see a baseball game. I did all of that willingly … because I share my life with you and you needed to be here for your mother. Because your mother couldn't leave Dogpatch. Oh no. God forbid!

LEE-ANN: What's your point?

MARGARET: A little quid pro quo?

LEE-ANN: No. This isn't about a little career disruption …

MARGARET: Oh my god …

LEE-ANN: This isn't about a few life-style sacrifices …

MARGARET: You really want to stop …

LEE-ANN: This is a matter of pure and clear right and wrong. These people are wrong. Being on their side is wrong.

MARGARET: Then maybe you'd be happier moving in with your mother until this blows over.

LEE-ANN: Maybe I should...

(There is a long moment of silence.)

MARGARET: Okay then.

LEE-ANN: That's it? That's all you have to say? You would let me move out?

MARGARET: That is entirely your choice to make.

LEE-ANN: Can you at least tell me why …

MARGARET: I was calling their bluff.

LEE-ANN: What?

MARGARET: Shelley and Mark came into my office expecting me to say no. Expecting to be able say "See, the lesbian lawyer wouldn't take our case. Oh, the hypocrisy!" I'm sure there was conference room full of high-priced talent up at Jones-Day who soiled themselves when the call came in that I said yes.

LEE-ANN: And you're not going to represent them all that effectively!

MARGARET: What? Do you really have no respect for me at all?

LEE-ANN: That would at least make sense.

MARGARET: No, it wouldn't. I am going to give this my best shot.

LEE-ANN: That's appalling.

MARGARET: Oh, I'm likely to lose. While Shelley and Mark are now stuck with little ole' me, Dee and Kelli have the HRC and millions of dollars' worth of real legal talent on their side. And our case is weaker. We'll probably do okay in Georgia, but we'll get our clocks cleaned in Federal court.

LEE-ANN: But meanwhile you'll be all over the news …

MARGARET: And think of the cognitive dissonance it would cause if the bigot baker's lawyer had her wife standing at her side during all those press moments.

LEE-ANN: There's no way …

MARGARET: Think about it.

LEE-ANN: I couldn't …

MARGARET: Sometimes infiltration can be as effective as confrontation. The optics will kill. Time and time and time again.

LEE-ANN: And millions of people will think what's wrong with those two? What kind of self-hatred would let them …?

MARGARET: I do worry about getting lumped in with the Log Cabin losers.

LEE-ANN: Exactly.

MARGARET: Think of it as taking one for the cause. A big one, I'll grant you.

LEE-ANN: I can't. I guess I don't have your moral sophistication or something. I have to say wrong is wrong and I won't be a party to it.

MARGARET: I'm sorry you feel that way.

LEE-ANN: It will define us for the rest of our lives … the traitors

… the champions of bigotry!

MARGARET: But we'll know better.

LEE-ANN: That's not enough. For me. I can't live a life of lonely virtue for thirty or forty years.

MARGARET: I can't make you stand with me.

LEE-ANN: Are you really going to do this? In spite of how I feel about it? In spite of what it's going to do to my life without my agreement?

MARGARET: Yes.

LEE-ANN: That's it? "Yes"?

MARGARET: Yes. You're always asking me to "speak English." So here it is, clearly and unequivocally: Yes. I am going to defend the right of the Sitton Family Bakery to refuse to make a birthday cake for the son of two lesbians.

LEE-ANN: No matter what it does to me.

MARGARET: Yes.

LEE-ANN: *(after a long beat)* Wow.

LEE-ANN turns to walk out of the room.

MARGARET: Where are you going?

LEE-ANN: I'll let you know when I decide.

LEE-ANN exits.

MARGARET picks up a beer and sits. She sits holding the beer and thinking for a beat. She takes a sip, then picks up the remote as lights fade to black.

End of Play.

DOING LUNCH
ANNE FLANAGAN

THE PLAY:

Doing Lunch

THE PLAYWRIGHT:

Anne Flanagan

SYNOPSIS:

A shy playwright fights to maintain the integrity of her play after it catches the attention of a slick agent and an aging movie star. Both Hollywood elites adore the script, but want just a few teeny, tiny changes.

ABOUT THE PLAYWRIGHT:

Anne Flanagan's plays include Lineage, Artifice, First Chill, Skirts, Dark Holidays and Death, Sex & Elves. Her work has been produced throughout the US and internationally. Anne is the recipient of several writing awards and zero sports trophies. Publications include her comedy Artifice (Dramatic) as well as many short play and monologue anthologies.

Anne has taught public school in New York's South Bronx and LA's South Central. She's worked as a Private Investigator on the mean streets of Los Angeles (and the not so mean streets of Sherman Oaks). She's climbed Machu Picchu, used hot coffee as a weapon, had a gun pressed to her forehead, spied on thieving bartenders, built a house alongside Jimmy Carter, got lost in Watts holding a giant pineapple, and never mastered the metric system.

CONTACT:

AngryTimmyPresents@yahoo.com

WEBSITE:

AnneFlanagan.net

THE THEATRE:

Donna Scott Productions at the Charlotte Arts
League Theater Center
4100 Raleigh St, Charlotte NC 28206

MISSION:

Our mission is to provide Charlotte audiences, artists and collaborating partners with unique and diverse opportunities for creative experience and expression through storytelling.

ABOUT:

Donna Scott Productions is a theatre and production company focused on storytelling through theatre, film, special events and digital content. We seek to amplify and embolden the voices of women and girls through our projects and produce in non-traditional spaces while supporting local businesses. Our ten minute play festival supports our mission by amplifying the voices of women and girls through storytelling. 2018 was our first year.

CONTACT:

Donna Scott
donnascottproductionsinfo@gmail.com

WEBSITE:

donnascottproductions.com

PRESENTING THE PLAY:

Doing Lunch

The scene is inside a swank Beverly Hills cafe. Two women are seated at a table. JEMMA, mid 50s, is a slick Hollywood Agent. SUE, 30s, is a playwright.

JEMMA: When I read your play, I knew I had to represent you! It's so intense! You're so intense! Why look at you now, you're positively glaring at the menu!

SUE: I forgot my glasses.

JEMMA: I know, I know, The Ivy is so cliched, but I live for their chopped salad! I assume you're vegetarian—

SUE: No, actually I —

JEMMA: Beans! Sprouts! How cute. And politically correct. As is your script! The story of a female forest ranger - What a talent! Here's to you! I need a real drink— where is that waiter? Oh - you do drink don't you? Of course you do! Alone in a seedy bar, observing the dregs of mankind no doubt. Just don't go overboard. I'm sick of meeting clients at Betty Ford - the food is dreadful! - where is that waiter?! - Darling, we are going to turn your little play into a big, big movie. I predict wealth and fame! But don't let it change you - you must keep that New York edge.

SUE: I'm from Kansas.

JEMMA: Not any more you're not. Oh, I know Carrington will love you! She's salivating to play Katie.

SUE: Don't you mean Katie's mother? She's too old for Katie—

JEMMA: Let's get her excited about the project first and then we - Oh! Here she comes. You had better move, dear. Carrington'll want to sit across from the mirror.

SUE: How do you know?

JEMMA: She's an actress isn't she?

CARRINGTON LARUE joins them at the table. In her in her late 40s, she is desperately trying to appear twenty years younger.

JEMMA: Darling!!

CARRINGTON: Jemma! Honestly, it's been too long!

JEMMA: Here she is! My little genius! Sue Soomer!

SUE: Summer. Sue Summer. It's so great to meet you, Ms. LaRue! I'm a fan of your work - well, what little I seen—and your Father's work, of course!

JEMMA: That's right, your father was -

SUE: Martin LaRue - a Hollywood Legend!

CARRINGTON: Ahh. My father, the Great Director. The next Houston, the new Welles. He began molesting me when I was twelve and that summer, we got a flat tire on the 405. Daddy got out to fix it and was flattened by a bread truck. Blam! Exploded like a fire cracker.

SUE: How awful!

CARRINGTON: It was the happiest day of my life.

SUE: Oh....well... nice to meet you.

CARRINGTON: I need a drink.

JEMMA: Who doesn't? I've practically sent up flares for the waiter. OHHHH! Light Bulb!!

(She grabs a cell phone from her purse.)

Cecil, pick up! NEVER hire an actor as a personal assistant.

Cecil - it's me. Look - I've got an idea. A rouge painter drives cross-country with his personal trainer, who's black, and they have an altercation with the mob—

CARRINGTON: Jemma. Bad news. I just came from Steven's office and they're talking about the exact same thing.

JEMMA: Damn. Hmmm - ok, Cecil, change the black guy to a woman, a young woman. Hot. Make the painter a spy with Touretts. You work out the rest and have a synopsis on my desk by morning. Ciao!

(Jemma makes another call.)

Hello, yes. I'd like to order. Not, not for delivery, I'm here, sitting in your restaurant, and I'd like a friggen' waiter!

(A waiter appears.)

JEMMA: Thank you.

WAITER: Yes?

JEMMA: Scotch, neat.

WAITER: And to eat?

JEMMA: I'll have the Greek pizza.

CARRINGTON: Me too, but without the cheese.

JEMMA: I'll take her cheese.

CARRINGTON: And no olives/

JEMMA: I'll take her olives.

CARRINGTON: And no crust/

JEMMA: I'll take her crust.

CARRINGTON: And a margarita, no tequila.

SUE: I'll take her tequila!

WAITER: And to eat?

SUE: Umm... the soup and salad?

(The Waiter nods, then leaves abruptly.)

CARRINGTON: Jemma, you were right! She's precious! Absolutely precious! Just look at her, her little hair —that little book bag. Sue Soomer!

SUE: Summer—

CARRINGTON: And what you're wearing, this ensemble, it's adorable. What is it? What?!

SUE: Uh, it's just my ... clothes?

CARRINGTON: Priceless!

JEMMA: Uh Oh! Idea!

(She grabs her cell)

Cecil, pick up damnit! I tell young mothers, don't despair if your child is born retarded. They can always be a personal assistant.

Cecil! Listen - a married couple sails across the Pacific on a raft, just like the pilgrims, but he's schizophrenic.

CARRINGTON: Sorry to piss on your parade, Girl, but that was the Lifetime movie last night.

JEMMA: Damn! Ok, Cecil. Make the woman a dog. A young dog. Hot. Change the Pacific to the Ozarks and add a vampire. You work out the details. Have a full treatment on my desk by morning. Ciao!

(The waiter crosses. Carrington snags his/her sleeve.)

CARRINGTON: Are our drinks ready yet?

WAITER: Probably.

(The Waiter exits.)

CARRINGTON: Asshole.

JEMMA: Probably some actor I passed on.

CARRINGTON: You'd remember?

JEMMA: Lord no! I only remember the ones I represent or screw.

CARRINGTON: Which in your case is one and the same.

JEMMA: Touché! Sooo!

CARRINGTON: Soooo!

SUE: So?

CARRINGTON: Sue Soomer.

SUE: Summer.

CARRINGTON: Your script. I love it! Raves!

SUE: Thanks —

CARRINGTON: Of course, I have some teeny tiny changes if I'm to play Katie.

SUE: Actually, you are —

JEMMA: Let's hear them! There are always changes when we go from stage to screen.

CARRINGTON: Yeah - from boring to not boring.

SUE: What? Theatre is a pure art form that dates back to -

CARRINGTON: The Greeks, I know, I know. They wore masks and everyone had to sit outside.

JEMMA: Speaking of which, where the hell's my Greek pizza?

CARRINGTON: About my playing Katie -

SUE: See, that's a problem because -

JEMMA: Yes! Your ideas, Carrington! We're all ears and baited breast.

SUE: Breath.

JEMMA: Mint? Here!

CARRINGTON: Well! I'm not feeling the whole 'forest ranger' thing. It's not sexy and I never wear flannel. I think Katie should be a hooker, but with a heart of gold, or perhaps a stripper - I've been taking pole dancing classes! Now, Katie needs a lover. A young lover. Hot. But edgy, like maybe that rapper who beat up Rhianna? Katie's mother seems too healthy, why not throw in a tumor or something? And Katie should adopt a kid from India. Everyone's going Asian these days. Of course, we'll cut all the nature stuff because it's just too - "naturey." We should set it in Vegas. Celine Dion could cameo! Or, wait - even better! She could play my Mother! We'll sing a duet!

SUE: Yeah, I don't think that's —

JEMMA: Ah! ah! News Flash!

(She grabs her phone)

Cecil - picture this. Maine. Autumn. Fiery red leaves and apple cider. There is a woman - quiet, reserved - but young. Hot. She has a spiritual awakening when she saves a deer —

SUE: Hey! That's MY script!

JEMMA: Oh? Oh. right. Never mind, Cecil.

CARRINGTON: I also think Katie should live in a unique space, a loft maybe.

SUE: She wouldn't.

CARRINGTON: Or a warehouse!

SUE: No -

JEMMA: A Geodesic dome!

CARRINGTON: An underground cave!

JEMMA: A giant, plastic pod that looks like an egg!!

SUE: No!

CARRINGTON: Brilliant!!

JEMMA: I know!!

SUE: Whoa - hold on! The play I wrote is about a woman's relationship to nature, so I can't just cut all the 'nature stuff'. Katie's not a stripper, she's not a whore, and she's doesn't adopt "L'il Ganges" just because he's 'in'! Her mother doesn't have cancer because that's not what the story is about and they don't live in a giant egg because that is just stupid! We're not going to Vegas and we're not casting freakin' Celine Dion and you are not playing Katie because I'm sorry, but you are too old - way, way too old, and my name is Sue SUMMER!!

(Beat. Carrington begins to applaud.)

CARRINGTON: Oh, she's good!

JEMMA: Didn't I tell you?

CARRINGTON: Really good!

JEMMA: Didn't I?!

SUE: But I —

CARRINGTON: Where did you find her?

JEMMA: One of the flyover states.

CARRINGTON: I will use her as a model for Katie!

JEMMA: You must! Have your people call mine —

CARRINGTON: Will do! This afternoon!

JEMMA: You too, dear.

SUE: But —

JEMMA: Kiss Kiss!!

CARRINGTON: Kiss Kiss!!

(The two women exit, each talking on their cells.)

SUE: Oh.

(The waiter enters with a tray of food.)

WAITER: They've gone.

SUE: Yes.

WAITER: Does Madam still wish to eat?

SUE: I guess.

WAITER: Bon! Now, Madam ordered the soup and salad, but really –that is so cliché!! I made a few changes. I present for you an effervescent goat cheese pilaf with a shitake/arugula garnish, hand picked heirloom tomatoes charmingly dressed in essence of roses, a gluten free brioche infused with truffle oil and...

(Over the waiter's continuous litany of exotic foods, the lights FADE TO BLACK.)

THE LAST BOX
JON FRASER

BEST 10 MINUTE PLAYS 2019

THE PLAY:

The Last Box

THE PLAYWRIGHT:

Jon Fraser

SYNOPSIS:

An older lesbian packs the remaining boxes of a home that she shared with her lover. Her brother is there to help, but she's reluctant to go, and her lover wants her to stay. But is the lover there?

ABOUT THE PLAYWRIGHT:

Jon Fraser is a playwright and director who began his theatrical life as an actor. As a writer, his first play, Crimes Against Nature, was a finalist in the New York State Council on the Arts CAPS program and won him an Edward Albee Fellowship in Playwriting. Plays include Kid Napper; Black Forest; Bungee (The Phoenix Ensemble); as well as Heavens to Betsy, Falling From Grace, Voyage, and Vert Gallant, all produced by Circle East Theatre Company. Circle East, the grandchild of the famous Circle Repertory Theatre in New York, is now the New Circle Theatre Company, where Jon is Co-Artistic Director. For New Circle, Jon wrote The Last Box (The Playroom Theatre) and Palace of Secrets (The Gene Frankel Theatre). He is also a screenwriter, and his screenplay The Cadaver Synod won Best Historical Drama in the Cannes Screenplay Contest.

Jon is a Professor of Theatre & Director of Graduate Studies at LIU Post, where his plays Red; White; And Blue; Heavy Mettle ; and Happily Ever After, have been produced. His has also written biographical essays on Edward Albee, William M. Hoffman, Mart Crowley, and Jean Claude van Italie, in The Gay and Lesbian Theatrical Legacy, published by University of Michigan Press.. MFA in Dramatic Writing, New York University.

CONTACT:

jfraser212@gmail.com

WEBSITE:

jon-fraser.com

The Theatre:

New Circle Theatre Company
140 West 44th St, #2, New York, NY. 10036

Mission:

The New Circle Theatre Company's (NCTC) mission is to create theatre that illuminates and questions the world in which we live, by supporting and promoting the voice of the playwright. We are a company of writers, actors, directors and designers working together to nurture the journey of a play through all stages of development, from original concept to production. We celebrate our history of excellence established by giants of the American theatre by offering a compassionate and inspirational environment to our artists so that they can safely experiment and grow. We foster diversity and parity as essential factors to achieve our mission. NCTC's objective is to stimulate, educate, and inspire our audience and our community by creating theatrical productions of the highest caliber that can elevate the human spirit, and address the challenges of the 21st Century.

About:

New Circle Theatre Company is a company of actors, writers and directors, many of whom have worked together for decades with a dedication to develop and foster new American plays.

New Circle Theatre Company is producing a multi-year event called The Inferno Project, in which writers are asked to write short plays based on specific circles of hell in Danté's Inferno. In 2017, 10-minute plays were presented about "Limbo;" in 2018, short plays were presented about "Lust" and "Gluttony." The circles for 2019 are "Wrath" and "Greed."

Contact:

David Kronick, Executive Director
dkronick@newcircletheatrecompany.org
646-863-0005

Website:

newcircletheatrecompany.org

Presenting the Play:

The Last Box

Setting:

An almost empty middle-class living room in an apartment/home. Open packing boxes are scattered about; odd and ends that need packing sit beside them. A lone rocking chair is next to the front door.

AT RISE:

BEA, mid-50's with battle scars to prove it, enters from the kitchen, wearing jeans, a man-tailored shirt untucked, a kerchief, and sneakers. She's carrying a packing tape gun, attempting to load it with packing tape. The gun is not co-operating.

She thinks she's got it: she attempts to tape a box, and it doesn't work. She rips the tape out of the gun and flings the gun against the wall.

BEA: Sonofa...BITCH!

MARIA, mid-late 50s, enters from the kitchen, dressed smartly.

MARIA: What was that?

BEA: The tape thing. The wall wanted to meet it, so I made introductions.

MARIA: Let me help you.

She goes to get the tape gun.

BEA: I don't need or want your help, thank you. I'm perfectly capable of taping the boxes.

MARIA: Apparently not.

BEA: This one is just defective, is all. Where'd you buy it, at the Dollar Store?

MARIA: Yes, as a matter of fact.

BEA: Cheap piece of shit.

MARIA: Let me load it for you.

BEA: No! I can do it!

MARIA: Oh really?

BEA: Watch me.

Bea tries to do it, fails, and in frustration, pulls a piece of tape from the roll, which instantly gets tangled. She throws the gun and the tape on the floor. Maria laughs.

BEA: I'm not done packing that one anyway.

MARIA: Sorry. Looks pretty full to me.

BEA: Well it's not. Okay? It's not.

MARIA: What's in there?

BEA: None of your business. Look, could you just like go somewhere else?

> *Maria takes a strap-on dildo out of the box.*

MARIA: Well well well, looka here. You're taking this?

> *BEA tries to grab the strap-on from Maria.*

BEA: Yes. Why shouldn't I?

MARIA: It's probably rusted.

BEA: It doesn't rust. It's silicon.

MARIA: Ooh, are these cobwebs?

BEA: Give it to me.

MARIA: That's what you always used to say when I wore it.

BEA: You're not funny.

MARIA: You used to think so.

BEA: When? When did I ever laugh at one of your pathetic stupid jokes.

MARIA: Whenever I made one.

BEA: In your dreams. Look, get out of my way, would you?

MARIA: Sorry. I'll be in the kitchen if you need me.

> *Maria exits. The front door opens simultaneously, and DANNY, 40s-50s, and rugged, wearing a white tee shirt and jeans, enters. He's sweating and breathing heavily.*

DANNY: Damn! That muthafucker was a bitch! You should'a thrown it away.

BEA: I know, I know, I'm sorry, but I couldn't. It would be like throwing away an old friend.

DANNY: A dead friend, you mean. How old is that piece of shit?

BEA: Bought it when I moved in here, so, thirty years?

DANNY: You can't fix that sort of thing, you know. We should just leave it on the curb.

BEA: You know how I am, I can't do that.

DANNY: Besides, there's not much room left in the truck. You might have to get rid of something to make room for the rest of your shit.

BEA: Let me think about it.

DANNY: Yeah, think about it. I'm going to the bathroom.

DANNY exits. Maria enters from the kitchen.

MARIA: You're going to throw it out, aren't you?

BEA: No, I just said...

MARIA: You should.

BEA: What? We bought that together.

MARIA: So? We're not together anymore. It's just another souvenir of bad times.

BEA: They weren't all bad times. At least not until you/

MARIA: What? Not until I what?

BEA: I'm not discussing this with you now.

MARIA: Fine. Avoid the topic.

BEA: I have to finish.

MARIA: Don't let me stop you.

BEA: You are. You're doing this deliberately. Why don't you just leave me alone?

MARIA: I'll go check the bedroom.

BEA: Don't bother. I cleaned it out. I checked.

MARIA: Doesn't hurt to check again.

Maria exits. DANNY enters, zipping up his fly.

DANNY: What next?

BEA: These two boxes.

DANNY: What about that rocker?

BEA goes to the rocker and feels the wood.

BEA: Leave it for the moment.

DANNY: Okay. Not sure how we're going to fit it in, though.

> *DANNY grabs the two boxes and lumbers out the front door. BEA sits in the rocker. Maria enters.*

MARIA: The bedroom was empty. Except for this.

> *Out of her pocket she takes a string thong with a frilly heart on the front.*

BEA: Oh god.

MARIA: You left it in the closet on the top shelf.

BEA: You bought that for me one Valentines day.

MARIA: I remember. You pretended to like it.

BEA: And you made me prance around the house in it.

MARIA: You looked sexy in it.

BEA: I looked ridiculous, what are you talking about?

MARIA: Sexy and ridiculous. A win-win.

BEA: And the heat was busted and it was freezing in here and you wouldn't let me wear anything else.

MARIA: That's not true! You didn't want to. You liked teasing me.

BEA: Throw it out.

MARIA: You might get some use out of it yet. Needs a washing, I don't think you ever washed it.

BEA: I thought I threw it out. Throw it away. I don't want it.

MARIA: I think you have room in the box for it.

> *She throws the thong into the box. Bea goes to the box, takes it out, and throws it at Maria.*

BEA: I said I DON'T WANT IT!! And I DON'T WANT YOU! I don't want anything to do with you! Don't you get it? Get the fuck out of my LIFE!

MARIA: You don't mean that.

BEA: The fuck I don't! Get out!

MARIA: Any beer left in the fridge?

BEA: Jesus! Yes, but not for you! It's for my brother. Don't drink it!

Maria exits into the kitchen as she says:

MARIA: But I'm thirsty.

BEA: Then drink water!

MARIA: *(O.S.)* There are no glasses in here.

BEA: That's right. They're packed!

Danny enters, breathing hard.

DANNY: You would choose to move on the hottest day of the year.

BEA: Yes, I waited for the weather report. As soon as they said "heat wave," I said "let's go!"

DANNY: If you weren't my sister, no way I'd be doing this.

BEA: I'm bronzing your metal as we speak.

Maria appears in the doorway holding a beer. Danny's back is to her so he doesn't see her. Bea sees her.

DANNY: You're welcome. Got any beer left?

Maria waves the bottle above her head as she exits into kitchen.

BEA: I don't think so. No. Sorry. Water. You should probably drink some water. Let me get you some water.

She exits into the kitchen. As she does:

DANNY: I'd prefer beer if you got it.

BEA: *(O.S.)* Let me see.

Danny sits in the rocker and surveys the room.

DANNY: I always liked this place. It's a real shame you have to move. It's got character. Kinda sad, though, to see it so bare, without anything. Kinda eerie.

Bea enters with half a bottle of beer. She hands it to him; he chugs it.

BEA: I drank half. You have to drive the truck.

DANNY: Oh, thanks. Half a beer. So thoughtful of you.

BEA: Only thinking in your best interests.

DANNY: So what's left? Is that the last box?

BEA: Yeah.

DANNY: Ready for it to go?

BEA: No. I'm not finished.

DANNY: *(looks around)* There's nothing left to pack.

BEA: Take the rocker first. I'll bring out the last box when I'm done.

Danny picks up the rocker, pauses, then puts it down again.

DANNY: Bea, you know, you don't have to do this. You don't have to move. I can bring all the stuff back in here, you call the landlord, and you figure something out.

BEA: Why would you say that? No, if I stay here I'll never leave. I'll die here. I can't die here. Enough. I have to go.

DANNY: You don't have to go clear across the country. You could rent something new here.

BEA: Yeah, but no, Danny, I have to go. This is all I've ever known, all I've ever loved. If I don't go now, I won't know anything else, won't love anything else.

DANNY: I doubt that.

Danny picks up the rocker and puts it down again.

DANNY: I don't know if this is going to fit in the truck. Let me go see if I can make room.

BEA: Okay.

He exits. Maria enters.

MARIA: Is he gone?

BEA: Yes.

MARIA: It's so empty in here.

BEA: Yes. It is.

MARIA: Our home. Thirty years.

BEA: Thirty-five.

MARIA: I'm so sorry, Bea.

BEA: Me, too.

MARIA: Don't go. Stay with me.

BEA: I can't.

MARIA: We can make it work.

BEA: How? I don't...

MARIA: I love you. I always have.

BEA: Stop. It's too late.

MARIA: Is it? I don't think so.

> *Bea goes to the box and looks inside. She takes off a ring from her ring finger, looks at it, and throws it into the box. Then, she begins to tape up the box.*

MARIA: That ring was my grandmother's.

> *Danny enters on Maria's next line, unseen by her.*

BEA: Yes, I know.

MARIA: Probably worth something. You should sell it if you don't want it.

BEA: Maybe I will.

DANNY: Uh, hello, who are you talking to?

> *Bea turns to him. Maria slips away.*

BEA: Nobody.

DANNY: You're not losing it now on me, are you sis?

BEA: No. No, I'm fine. What about the rocker? Will it fit?

DANNY: No. But we can come back and pick it up later.

BEA: *(sighs)* Fine.

> *Danny grabs the last box.*

DANNY: Okay. This it?

BEA: Yes. That's the last box.

DANNY: Let's go, then.

BEA: Go ahead. I'll be with you in a minute.

> *Danny exits. Bea walks around the room, ending at the rocker. She stares at the rocker for a moment, and then pushes it so it rocks. Then, she exits. A light shines on the rocker.*

> *Rock rock.*

> *Rock rock.*

> *Lights fade.*

End of Play.

LAST DRINKS
GREG GOULD

BEST 10 MINUTE PLAYS 2019

THE PLAY:

Last Drinks

THE PLAYWRIGHT:

Greg Gould

SYNOPSIS:

Mel's partners keep dying. Ben can't die, no matter how hard he tries. Did destiny bring these two lost souls together?

ABOUT THE PLAYWRIGHT:

Greg Gould is a Canberra playwright. His short plays have been performed in festivals throughout Australia, New Zealand, the United States, India, the United Arab Emirates, and the Philippines. Some of them have even won awards! His first full length play "The Inheritance" was produced by Budding Theatre in 2017.

CONTACT:

greg@nowordfor.com

WEBSITE:

nowordfor.com

THE THEATRE:

Short+Sweet Canberra
PO Box 462, Newtown NSW 2042 Australia

MISSION:

The Short+Sweet family is committed to building a more creative world, 10 minutes at a time. The platform provides an accessible and enjoyable theatrical experience to individuals from all walks of life and gives them the opportunity to connect with creatives from all over the world.

ABOUT:

Short+Sweet has been running in Canberra since 2009, and this has grown to become a major event for the city's artistic community. Each year over 100 people contribute to the festival over two weeks at the Canberra Theatre Centre, making this the largest annual collaboration of performing artists in the national capital.

CONTACT:

Trevar Alan Chilver (Festival Director)
info@shortandsweet.org

WEBSITE:

shortandsweet.org

PRESENTING THE PLAY:

Last Drinks

(A shabby pub. BEN sits at the bar nursing a beer. He's contemplating life – as people do in bars. Suddenly he pulls out a bottle of pills, takes one out, washes it down with a swig of beer. Then he sits, waiting.

MEL enters. She's agitated, distraught, and wearing a wedding dress. She sits at the other end of the bar.)

MEL: Vodka. Straight up.

(The drink arrives, and she downs it.)

MEL: Keep 'em coming.

(MEL notices BEN looking at her, intrigued. MEL looks away, wants to be left alone.)

MEL: Don't.

Beat.

BEN: I got to ask.

MEL: No. It's not my wedding day.

BEN: *(Confused)* Right.

Beat.

BEN: So ...?

MEL: Really?

BEN: What?

MEL: You're really gonna do this?

BEN: Bride in a bar. *(Shrugs)* Got to ask.

MEL: If you must know, I've been at a funeral.

BEN: Funeral?

MEL: Yep. *(Downs another drink)*
    Beat.

BEN:That only raises more questions.

MEL: You asked.

BEN: Why would you wear a wedding dress to a funeral?

MEL: Last request.

BEN: Hell of a last request.

MEL: Wasn't exactly made under the best of circumstances.

BEN: Who would want that?

MEL: James would. My husband. Or at least he was going to be my husband. He didn't quite make it.

BEN: *(Understanding)* Right.

MEL: Yep. Dropped dead right at the altar. Ceremony hadn't even started. By the time I got to him he was all but gone. But he held on. Said he wanted to see me in my wedding dress. Said I was the most beautiful bride in the world. Then he said the other thing: "Keep the dress on, babe. Wear it at the funeral."

BEN: Jesus.

MEL: I know. The doc reckons it was the endorphins talking. Probably didn't he even know what he was saying.

BEN: But you did it anyway?

MEL: Of course. It was his last request. And everyone heard it. The priest. The best man. The bridesmaids. Shit, even his mother heard it. Old bat's deaf as a door nail, but she hears that fucking request from three rows back.

BEN: So how...?

MEL: Heart attack. At 34. Who the fuck has a heart attack at 34?

BEN: *(Envious)* Son of a bitch.

MEL: You know the messed-up thing? I wasn't going to do it.

BEN: Do what?

MEL: The wedding. I was halfway across the parking lot when they found me. Gone. But then this. God, I'm such a bitch.

BEN: You weren't to know.

MEL: Still. It's so low. I was just going to leave him standing there. Like a schmuck. He was so excited. Been asking me to marry him for years. But I kept knocking him back. Finally, I say yes, and this happens. Maybe he knew. Maybe that's why …

BEN: Nah, shitty timing is all. Chances are he died happily oblivious.

MEL: That's even worse.

BEN: Bah, you're being too hard on yourself. You didn't want to get married, so you acted. End of the day you were trying to do the right thing.

MEL: Till he died.

BEN: Bad luck. Nothing more.

MEL: I just can't believe this happened again.

BEN: You've been married before?

MEL: No. I mean the death thing. This is the fourth guy I've been with that's keeled over.

BEN: You're shitting me?

MEL: Nope. The first was Ivan Taylor. High school boyfriend. He lived two towns over. One night he borrowed his dad's car to come see me and BAM, t-boned by a semi. Dead. Second guy was Glen Walsh. Nice guy. Met at uni. Went on a romantic weekend to Thredbo and BAM, he skis straight into a snow machine. Dead.

BEN: Accidents. Could happen to anyone.

MEL: Then there was Jason Mills. Met at work. He fell out of a hot-air balloon.

BEN: Bullshit.

MEL: True story. He took me up for my 25th. 2000 feet in the air, he leans out to take a selfie ... and ... gone. Landed on power lines below. Burnt to a crisp.

BEN: That's pretty unlikely.

MEL: I swear, I'm cursed. You know what they call me? 'The Widow Maker'. So stupid. Doesn't even make sense.

BEN: Surprised the cops didn't get suss on you. Three boyfriends. Three deaths.

MEL: Oh, they did. That how I met James. He was a detective.

BEN: Fuck off!

MEL: I tried to tell him. I warned him. But he wouldn't listen. Said

I was being superstitious. He even sent me to a shrink. She said I was paranoid delusional. Guess I proved them both wrong.

BEN: How is this even possible?

MEL: Dunno. Must've fucked over the wrong person in a past life or something.

BEN: I'm so sorry.

MEL: Not your fault. I should never have said yes. Big mistake. But everyone kept saying "It'll be fine, Mel. It'll be fine." What do they know? I'm destined to be alone. Destined to die alone. Destined to ... get shit faced. *(Downs a drink)*

BEN: No. I mean I'm sorry you have to be here for this.

MEL: For what?

BEN: For this. My death. I've come here to die. To have my last drink.

MEL: You've lost me. Jesus, how many of these have I had?

BEN: I took a pill. I should be dead any minute. Actually, I should be dead now. Supposed to be quick.

MEL: You're serious?

BEN: Yep.

MEL: Jesus! Should I call someone? An ambulance?

BEN: No, don't. I've thought about this. A lot. I've tried many times.

MEL: How many?

BEN: Twelve.

MEL: Twelve?! Fuck, you mustn't be very good! *(Cringes)* Sorry. That came out really bad. I'm just saying after so many tries, maybe this isn't what you want.

BEN: No. I'm certain of it. Things just keep getting in the way.

MEL: What kind of things?

BEN: All sorts. Odd things. Last week I drove my car off a cliff. 100-foot drop straight into the ocean. Walked away with nothing but a bruised collarbone.

MEL: How?

BEN: Police Rescue squad was training on the beach below.

MEL: Get out.

BEN: Last year I tried the whole connect-the-hose-to-the-exhaust-pipe thing. Everything was going great. Car was full of fumes. Head was spinning. Then a truck crashes through the garage door. Driver had a stroke or something. I wake up in the hospital. Clean bill of health.

MEL: No way!

BEN: I know. It's crazy. Nothing works. I'm like the Frank Spencer of suicide attempts. Stupid shit just keeps happening. You name it, I've tried it.

MEL: Gun?

BEN: Faulty ammunition.

MEL: Electrocution?

BEN: Took the toaster into the bath. Whole block went dark. I didn't feel a tingle.

MEL: Slit wrists?

BEN: Went out bush. Was miraculously found by the SES who happened to be searching for a lost bushwalker. They still haven't found him.

MEL: Drug overdose?

BEN: Jehovah witness.

MEL: *(Confused)* What?

BEN: They came knocking at the door.

MEL: Base jump?

BEN: Leapt from a sixth-floor window, landed in a trailer full of mattresses.

MEL: Fuck off! That doesn't happen. Not in real life.

BEN: It happened.

MEL: What about stepping in front of bus?

BEN: Broken arm the first time, broken leg the second. Otherwise fine.

MEL: Hanging? No, let me guess. Rope snapped.

BEN: Actually no. But the beam I tied it to did. Brought down the entire first floor of my sister's apartment. Walked away without a scratch.

MEL: Get fucked!

BEN: I know. It's absurd. I even paid a professional hit man to take me out. Dickhead went to the wrong house. Killed my neighbour instead.

MEL: Jesus. You're like Bruce Willis in that movie. The one where he's all invincible.

BEN: Unbreakable.

MEL: Nah. The other one. With the ghosts.

BEN: I'm pretty sure you mean Unbreakable.

MEL: Whatever. You're totally that guy. Un-killable. It's insane.

BEN: Glad you find it entertaining.

MEL: Not just entertaining. I am in awe. The sheer persistence of it. It's admirable.

BEN: You know the weird thing? This is what I live for now. It's the only reason I get out of bed in the morning. I need to know. You know? I need to find out how it ends. (*Picks up the pill bottle*) What the fuck is wrong with these things? Should kill a horse.

MEL: Aren't we the pair? The Widow Maker and the Invincible Man. Destiny, I salute you! You've got one fucked up sense of humour. (*Another drink*)

>*Beat.*

BEN: You believe in that stuff? Destiny? Fate?

MEL: Only explanation. I don't give a shit what anyone says. Co-incidence can only explain so much.

BEN: So, you think we're supposed to be here? To meet? Like this?

MEL: Makes sense. Who knows? Perhaps all the men in my life

died just so I would meet you.

BEN: And maybe that's why I'm can't die.

MEL: There is a kind of poetry to it. A sick, depraved kind of poetry. But poetry none the less.

BEN: Would explain the impotent pills.

MEL: And why I'm wearing this stupid dress. You wouldn't have talked to me otherwise.

BEN: You do look beautiful.

MEL: Thanks. You're not too bad yourself. For a manic depressive.

BEN: Says the paranoid delusional.

(They laugh. There's a beat filled with attraction.)

BEN: So, what now?

MEL: You like hot air balloons?

BEN: Never been on one.

MEL: Maybe you should. Maybe instead of trying to kill yourself all the time, you should live a little.

BEN: And maybe you should stop feeling guilty about things you can't control. Let go a little.

MEL: Maybe I should.

(Beat. More attraction. They move closer.)

MEL: We should kiss.

BEN: You think?

MEL: I dunno. It feels right. *(They lean in close)* Though I should warn you. This doesn't usually end well.

BEN: Don't worry. I'm invincible. Remember?

(They share a lingering kiss.)

MEL: Wow. That was actually pretty good.

BEN: Thanks.

(Beat as they smile stupidly at none another. They lean in to kiss again ...)

(BEN drops dead.)

MEL: Oh, c'mon. Really? Really?!

Beat.

(MEL picks up a drink, downs it.)

MEL: Another!

PLAY ENDS

LENDING A HAND
CRAIG GUSTAFSON

BEST 10 MINUTE PLAYS 2019

THE PLAY:

Lending a Hand

THE PLAYWRIGHT:

Craig Gustafson

SYNOPSIS:

Oak Park, Illinois; the present. An Irish woman undergoing a terrifying ordeal has an Unusual Request for her boyfriend. The type of story we might have had if Rod Serling's *Night Gallery* had gone in for comedy.

ABOUT THE PLAYWRIGHT:

After years of writing newspaper columns, radio and children's shows, writer/actor/director Craig Gustafson was content writing the occasional sketch or song parody *(Not Getting Naked Today, If I Had a Meltdown.)* for a local awards show. Then, early in 2018 a loved one unexpectedly passed away and when resurfacing from grief, Craig's reaction was, "Hmm… maybe time isn't infinite," and he began writing his ass off, shortly producing sixteen (and counting.) 10 minute plays, most of which have been produced and/or won contests, including Lending a Hand, A Cheap Maid in Chasteside, Soul Custody, Curse of the Hoo Ha, Dracula's Significant Others and Torquay Holiday.

Craig lives with his wife Margie in Lombard, Illinois.

CONTACT:

GustafsonPlays@comcast.net

WEBSITE:

Bozolisand.com/GustafsonPlays

THE THEATRE:

The Acorn
107 Generation Drive, Three Oaks, MI 49128

MISSION:

To offer a broad range of high-quality entertainment that nurtures cultural experience, participation and community engagement among residents and visitors of all ages, and enhances the economic vitality of the region.

ABOUT:

The Acorn is Southwest Michigan's Harbor Country center for live performances, home to well over 100 events per year, entertaining thousands in a village of only 1600 residents. We provide a venue for entertainment and pride ourselves on nurturing new talent. The Acorn encourages original works through a singer songwriter competition in July and a 10-Minute Play Writing Competition in November.

The Acorn Spectacular Tournament of Playwrights is set for its fourth annual competition of 10-Minute Play Writing. Submissions are due May 31, with performances of the top six plays in November. Judges with experience in the industry select first place and runner-up. The Acorn audience selects People's Choice.

CONTACT:

Sandra Thompson, Executive Director
Sandra@acorntheater.org
269-756-3879

WEBSITE:

acorntheater.org

PRESENTING THE PLAY:

Lending A Hand

CAST OF CHARACTERS:

KATHLEEN MALLOY – mid-20s; a lanky redhead with the face of a champion smartass. Has a thick Irish accent. She's in a pretty foul mood right now, as a result of pain and fear.

OLIVER O'CONNOR – late 20s; a presentable ginger with an unfortunate attempt at a mustache. He also has an Irish accent, but he has lived in Chicago longer than Kathleen and the brogue really shows up only in times of stress.

TIME: The present

PLACE:

Oak Park, Illinois. Living room of Kathleen's apartment.

(A vintage apartment in Oak Park, Illinois. Built in the 1920s, it has high ceilings and ornate molding. A bay window displays the tops of some beautiful elms and a street lamp. There are framed family pictures and a theater poster: "Titus Andronicus." Front door up left, kitchen door right. Furniture matches the room. A large sofa with coffee table. The table is littered with junk food bags, beer cans and a half-empty bottle of Irish Mist. Down right: two bentwood chairs, placed next to each other. The stage right chair has a small cat carrier on it.

OR

A couch, a coffee table and two bentwoods with a cat crate.)

(Kathleen Malloy is stretched out on the sofa, pointing a remote out front, at an off-stage TV. She is flipping channels. We go past a couple of late-night TV shows/commercials, before pausing at an old horror movie, The Beast with Five Fingers. We hear a bit of the soundtrack as Kathleen sips a glass of Irish Mist.)

PETER LORRE: *(Soundtrack recording.)* The hand... I caught it. I locked it up.

ROBERT ALDA: *(Soundtrack recording.)* That's fine.

PETER LORRE: *(Soundtrack recording.)* The Horrible Hand. Can't escape anymore. Now it can't get out. It *can't*.

(Kathleen sips her drink and looks sourly at her right hand, which is heavily bandaged.)

ROBERT ALDA: *(Soundtrack recording.)* Of course, it can't. Now, go to bed.

(There is a knock at the door. Kathleen clicks off the TV. She doesn't rise.)

KATHLEEN: Well, it's unlocked, isn't it. Get in!

(Oliver O'Connor enters, laden with a huge bouquet and two bottles of Irish Mist. Barely able to see past the bouquet, he staggers to the kitchen.)

OLIVER: I brought you some flowers, Kathy. To cheer you up.

KATHLEEN: Kathleen. Plunk them in a vase, then.

OLIVER: I will. Don't get up.

KATHLEEN: I won't.

(Oliver exits into kitchen. Re-enters a moment later, empty handed.)

OLIVER: Where are your vases kept?

KATHLEEN: They aren't.

OLIVER: Ah.

(He hurries to the sofa to fill Kathleen's glass from the open bottle. She grudgingly sits up to let him sit beside her.)

OLIVER: The Irish Mist was on sale. Do you need more? Are you still in pain?

(She takes the glass as he finds a used glass and pours himself a drink.)

KATHLEEN: It's been a week. How much pain could I be in over one little finger? I'm made of tougher fabric, Oliver O'Connor.

(They drink in silence for a while.)

OLIVER: *(Exaggerating his Irish accent.)* Your conversation gets rather traditional when you're hurting, doesn't it, Kathleen Malloy?

KATHLEEN: *(Exaggerated Chicago accent.)* Sorry, Mr. My-Kind-of-Town. I'll try and talk more Chicago, so's ya can unnerstand me. *(Mutters.)* Marblemouth.

OLIVER: Not to poke my nose where it isn't wanted, but are you comfortable talking about it yet?

KATHLEEN: *(Starts silently counting to ten to check her fury. Stops. Sighs.)* I'm not. But there's a connected matter we need to discuss. So... you've seen my cat at some point, right? He hides when people come over, but you've seen him?

OLIVER: Pussy McPussyface? Sure.

(Kathleen rises and saunters behind the sofa, eventually ar-

riving at the two bentwoods and sitting in the left one.)

KATHLEEN: Last week, I took Pussy McPussyface to the vet. He had an eye infection. Doctor Heidi gave him an antibiotic shot...

OLIVER: In the eye?

KATHLEEN: ... what?! No, not in the eye. In his great hairy bum, you plank.

OLIVER: Well, that's a relief. A shot in the eye - that gives me the willies. *(Off of her look.)* I'll shut up now.

KATHLEEN: See that you do. Dr. Heidi told me to bring him back in two weeks. No big deal.

(She is sitting on the chair. Lighting special on the chairs, which become Kathleen's car. She drives with her left hand. With the right, she does as she describes.)

KATHLEEN: *(Continued.)* Pussy McPussyface was quiet but worn out on the way home, so while I drove, I stuck a finger in the crate for him to nuzzle. I'd switch fingers every once in a while, because the grating is small and it was kind of awkward. We were stopped at Madison and Harlem, waiting to turn left. MeTV-FM was playing "Put Your Hand in the Hand" by Ocean...

OLIVER: Really? I haven't heard that in years – *(Kathleen is glaring at him. He shuts up.)*

KATHLEEN: ... Anyway... my right pinky finger was in the crate and Pussy McPussyface was rubbing his chin on it. This S.U.V. comes tearing up in the straight lane, and at the last second, the thick melter changes his mind and decides to turn left without bothering to see if anyone else was there first. Rear-ended me...

OLIVER: *(Unintentionally snorts.)*

KATHLEEN: *(Beat.)* Really?

OLIVER: Sorry.

KATHLEEN: ... rear-ended me at about thirty-five, forty miles an hour and smacked me into the car ahead of me. At that, I was pretty lucky. The windshield shattered into such tiny pieces that it coated my hair and face, but I didn't get any bad cuts. But my pinky finger in the crate snapped right off and I fainted from the pain and shock.

OLIVER: Oh, my god. Oh, my god.

KATHLEEN: I woke up in hospital, powdered with glass like a masochist's doughnut, my pinky finger lost forever.

OLIVER: Forever? Why couldn't they dig it out of the crate and reattach it?

KATHLEEN: Because by the time anyone saw what happened to me and thought to look for the finger, the cat had eaten it.

OLIVER: What?! What?! *(Stunned pause.)* All of it?

KATHLEEN: Well, not the bone, of course. That gave him something to play with. They had a hell of a time getting it away from him.

OLIVER: And they couldn't do anything?

> *(Lighting special fades out as Kathleen crosses to sofa, grabs her drink and sits.)*

KATHLEEN: What's to do? You can't reattach a bone. No flesh to hold the stitches on. And why would you? It'd just look creepy. So they soldered it up, kept me for a day and sent me home.

OLIVER: ... Really. Really?

KATHLEEN: *(Holding up her right hand.)* Pinky swear.

OLIVER: Ugh! *(He gets up and paces.)* You poor thing. What an awful thing to happen. That's the worst thing I've ever heard...

KATHLEEN: You've not heard the worst of it.

OLIVER: *(Beat.)* I've not?

KATHLEEN: Hell, no.

OLIVER: *(Beat. Takes a drink.)* What's the worst?

KATHLEEN: Pussy McPussyface decided he likes the taste. He wants more.

OLIVER: Oh, come on now!

KATHLEEN: *(Raises her right hand again.)* Hand to god!

OLIVER: Okay, stop that.

(She shrugs. Drinks.)

OLIVER: *(Continued.)* What makes you think that...? Has Pussy McPussyface attacked you?

KATHLEEN: Not yet. But it's only a matter of time. Two nights in a row, I've awoken to find Pussy McPussyface standing on my chest. Stroking my head with his paw. No claws, mind you. Just... petting me. And I can see the look in his eyes: *(The voice of a psychotic cat:)* "I love you, Kathleen I really do love you. But a cat's got to eat. Doesn't he?"

(Pause. Severely freaked out, they simultaneously drain their glasses. Oliver pours them each another one.)

KATHLEEN: *(Continued.)* Tonight will be the third night. I don't think he's going to wait much longer.

OLIVER: I just... this is so hard to believe...

KATHLEEN: Why? You've wanted to nibble on my flesh often enough!

OLIVER: Not to consume it, for heaven's sake.

KATHLEEN: What's good enough for you is good enough for my cat.

OLIVER: If you think you're in danger, why don't you get rid of him?

KATHLEEN: *(Frostily.)* It's plain to see that you are not a cat person. It's fortunate I found you out in time.

OLIVER: For god sake, Kathleen is he eating his normal food?

KATHLEEN: He's ravenous.

OLIVER: Then why would he want to eat you?

KATHLEEN: Well, I'm a delicacy, amn't I? Fancy Feast doesn't quite cut it for him anymore. He's become enamored of human flesh. I don't know what to do. I need time to figure this out, and I don't have any time.

(She is near tears. Oliver sits with her.)

OLIVER: Kathleen, you know how much I love you, right? *(She nods.)* I'd do anything in the world for you. *(She nods.)* Tell me what I can do to relieve your terrible distress.

(She gulps. Smiles bravely. A romantic moment just might ensue.)

KATHLEEN: I want your finger.

OLIVER: *(Beat.)* What?

KATHLEEN: Not necessarily the pinky. You pick. *(Stands, crosses right.)*

OLIVER: You want my finger?

KATHLEEN: *(Exiting into kitchen.)* He's already had one of mine. I need to conserve.

(Oliver sits there, stunned. Tries to work out in his head what's going on. Kathleen returns. She has a large knife and a box of SpongeBob band-aids, which she puts on the coffee table. She sits and offers Oliver the knife.)

KATHLEEN: Do you want to carve or shall I?

OLIVER: *(Gets up and strides to the other side of the room.)* Kathleen, you aren't serious.

KATHLEEN: Of course, I am. It's your finger. The choice should be yours.

OLIVER: I mean, you can't be serious about all of this. You can't expect me to cut off my finger.

KATHLEEN: I see. And all that fine talk about how you'd cut off an arm for me. Just a lot of flummery, wasn't it, you randy blatherskite!

OLIVER: It's a saying, damn it! Nobody really means that!

(Kathleen begins pursuing Oliver around the room, knife in hand.)

KATHLEEN: You infamous worm! You give me that finger right now or so help me Hannah, I'll never have to do with you again! You wanted to marry me! You asked for my hand and I said, "Yes, Oliver Yes. You can have my hand." And all I want from you is one finger!

OLIVER: Kathleen, be reasonable!

KATHLEEN: "Reasonable," is it? You cad! If you asked me, I'd give you all my fingers! From both hands!

OLIVER: And what would I be wanting that for? You haven't got a full set!

(Kathleen screams and chases Oliver about the room. He tries to leap over the sofa, but she catches his leg and he is stretched out on the sofa. She leaps on top of him, knife in hand, held over OLIVER They are panting. The moment becomes passionate and they kiss, at length. Kathleen comes up for air, sobbing.)

KATHLEEN: I don't know what else to do.

(They sit up. Oliver has an arm around Kathleen, comforting her as she cries. A long moment.)

OLIVER: *(Finally.)* Give me the knife.

KATHLEEN: *(Gives it to him.)* It goes by the sink. Right hand drawer.

OLIVER: No. *(Beat.)* We'll have to get me to the E.R. afterwards. What we'll tell them, God only knows. *(She looks at him, startled.)* I have to keep my word, don't I?

(Kathleen kisses him ardently. Then Oliver clears a space on the coffee table. Puts his left hand down. Slowly raises the knife.)

KATHLEEN: Be sure to pluck the hairs from your knuckles.

OLIVER: *(Beat.)* Why?

KATHLEEN: Choking hazard.

OLIVER: *(Sighs. Raises knife. Pause.)* In view of our engagement, I would like to keep the ring finger.

KATHLEEN: Oh, that is entirely up to you, my love.

(Oliver raises the knife. Slowly brings it down to his pinky finger. Pause. Kathleen can't bear the suspense. She gets up and paces frantically.)

OLIVER: Here goes.

KATHLEEN: *(Pause, then:)* NO!!!

(She rushes to Oliver, takes the knife, runs to the kitchen and tosses it in, then turns to him with a phony laugh.)

KATHLEEN: *(Continued.)* Well. You've certainly passed that test, young swain.

OLIVER: Test?

KATHLEEN: Certainly. You didn't believe all that guff about a flesh-eating cat, did you? Ha ha. Ha ha ha. Ha.

(Oliver rises and starts for her, angry and puzzled. She steers him to the front door.)

KATHLEEN: *(Continued.)* Listen, it's been a hell of a day. Week. Why don't you head on home, and you can come back tomorrow. *(Kisses him.)* We'll play Strip Yahtzee.

OLIVER: *(Not satisfied; not pushing it.)* All right. You know now how much I love you. Right?

KATHLEEN: And how I love you! Good night. I'll deal with Pussy McPussyface.

(They kiss briefly. Oliver exits. Kathleen shuts the door and presses her back to it. Pause. We hear the low, menacing growl of a cat on the hunt. Kathleen's eyes widen in terror as the noise gets louder. Lights fade out.)

END OF PLAY

MAE THE MAGNIFICENT
MARGO HAMMOND

THE PLAY:

Mae the Magnificent

THE PLAYWRIGHT:

Margo Hammond

SYNOPSIS:

Mae Young, legendary champion of women's professional wrestling, faces her greatest challenge: going to the dentist. Can mild-mannered Fred provide her the extra courage she needs?

ABOUT THE PLAYWRIGHT:

Margo's plays have been produced in London, Milan, NYC and at various theatres across the U.S. Mistress Marlene received a production at The Unrestricted View Co in London and at Theatre 54 in NYC. It has been published in Smith & Kraus' "Best Ten-Minute Plays of 2015". Margo's other plays have been presented in NYC at 78th St. Theater Lab, Soho Playhouse, Theater 54, CAP21, Little Church Around the Corner, Directors Co and Workshop Theater Co. Her play, Look Me In the Eyes was produced in Colorado Springs, CO at Six Women Playwright's Festival and in San Diego, CA at North Park Playwright Festival. Margo is the grateful 1st Place recipient of the 2016 Jerry Kaufman Award for Excellence in Playwriting. Let Maisy Rest In Peace has been accepted into Barter Theatre's 2019 Appalachian Festival of Plays and Playwrights. Dramatist Guild member & AEA, SAG/AFTRA.

CONTACT:

margoham@comcast.net

WEBSITE:

margohammond.com

The Theatre:

ANDTheatre Company
250 West 90th Street, NYC, NY 10024

Mission:

To develop and present new theatrical works in fully staged productions that ignite the theatergoer's mind, heart and imagination and set out in artistic new directions; to build and sustain a community of theatre artists and their collaborators, to provide that community with artistic and technical resources from inspiration to production, to explore and expand the possibilities of improvisation as a performing skill and as a means of creating scripted works.

About:

Founded in 1984 as Artistic New Directions, ANDTheatre Company explores the bridge between improvisation and scripted material. This takes the form of workshops in improvisation, playwriting, acting and physical comedy. Currently our workshop in creating scripted material from improvisation (Improv-to-Script) has been used to create full plays as well as many 10-minute plays seen in our own Festival as well as others. Our performance series, Without-a-Net, regularly presents a scripted play which is performed with actor/improvisors creating instant relationships while performing together for the first time on stage. It is the ultimate of our bridging of the two worlds of improv and script.

Throughout the past eleven years, AND's "Eclectic Evening of Shorts: Boxers and Briefs" has presented over 124 new plays by authors from the well-known to the soon-to-be-known. Published in short play anthologies are FAMILY OF FLECHNER by Gregory Fletcher; LUNCHTIME AT WESTFIELD HIGH by Nicole Pandolfo and MISTRESS MARLENE by Margo Hammond.

Contact:

Rebecca Shafer, Managing Director
info@artisticnewdirections.org
646.450.9487

Website:

andtheatrecompany.org

PRESENTING THE PLAY:

Mae The Magnificent
(or, Piss & Vinegar to you)

CHARACTER BREAKDOWN:

MAE YOUNG: A retired champion female wrestler, preferably over 60 (strong, flamboyant, cocky and full of "piss and vinegar" – with a heart)

FRED TURNER: An innocent bystander, gentle, unobtrusive (yearning to be stronger)

(MAE and FRED are sitting in a dentist's waiting room. FRED is minding his own business. MAE, true to form, is boisterously commanding the room, talking to herself and perhaps thousands of imaginary fans.)

MAE: Damn it, my face aches. And contrary to popular belief, I did not bite my ex-husband's dick off.

(FRED looks over at MAE.) No, that was somebody else. Hah!

FRED: I'm just wait—

(MAE addresses Fred)

MAE: —I'll tell you something, back in the day, that crowd loved to hate me. (laughs) And I love to be hated! Hell, yes.

FRED: I'm just waiting for—

MAE: —The women in my business are tough. Okay?

FRED: Okay.

MAE: Organizers used to shield the ring with chicken wire to protect me from the rotten eggs and cabbage people were throwing. *(Mae commands Fred)* Look at me! *(FRED obeys)* You always gotta have an "angel" but you also gotta have a "heel".

(FRED stares incredulously at MAE.)

What am I talkin about? I'll tell ya! Ok, "Angel" is the baby face. Anybody can be a baby face, what we call a clean wrestler. She's all dolled up. She don't have to do nothin'. Now, I was the "Heel". I've always been the heel and I wouldn't be anything but.

FRED: You're a wrestler?

MAE: I could beat your ass.

FRED: Oh dear.

MAE: You think I'm too old?

FRED: No, I was just—

MAE: —I may look like an old lady to you—

FRED: —I didn't say—

MAE: —but in my day, I was the world champion. The Champ! Multiple titles. I'm in the Wrestling Hall of Fame, for Christ's sake.

FRED: I don't want any trouble mam.

MAE: Mam? Are you kidding? Look at these. *(she shows her biceps)*

FRED: Thank you.

MAE: I was invited into the ring with The Fabulous Moolah. I smashed a guitar over her head and then proceeded to put her right into the figure-four leglock. Oh yeah. After that I began appearing regularly on the televised wrestling shows. They even named video games after me. What have you done?

FRED: I'm not... I can't, ah...

MAE: You can't talk?

FRED: I don't want to start anything.

MAE: What's your name?

FRED: Huh?

MAE: Your name. You have a name.

FRED: Yes. *(pause)* Fred.

MAE: Fred. Okay. Well, I'm Mae. Mae Young. Mae the Magnificent!

FRED: Okay.

MAE: I'll let you in on a few things Fred. Rule Number 1: The heel's the one who carries the whole show! That's me. I carried the show.

FRED: Uh huh.

MAE: I *(pointing to herself)* I had moves! Oh, yeah – choke hold, spike bump, joint locks - the works. Of course, drop kicking was my forte', ya know what that is don't ya?

FRED: Ahh?

MAE: Ya jump up in the air and with both feet you just kick the hell out of her, so she falls back into a fetal heap. Whadaya think happens next Fred?

FRED: Ah, she... gets pinned down on the mat?

MAE: That's right! Good. You got the picture. Oh, yeah, that was some fun stuff! And I created most of it myself. I was the only one doin a "short arm scissor lift".

FRED: Scissor Lift.

MAE: Short arm scissor lift! You lift her up with her legs scissored atop your shoulders. Look at me. She's your propeller now. You got her hooked up there and… Hey, you want me to show you?

FRED: No.

MAE: You can be the angel.

FRED: No thank you.

(She pulls FRED up from his seat.)

There's furniture here. Lamps and—

MAE: —I said angel, not baby. Are you a baby? Freddy the baby?

FRED: Yes.

MAE: What? Nah, here, I'll just do the super spin. *(She tries to haul FRED onto her shoulders, but he only makes it half way and slides down.)*

FRED: Oh my God!

MAE: You're a light weight. We can do this.

(FRED is breathing heavily.)

FRED: NO!

(FRED pulls himself free.)

MAE: You don't want to?

FRED: I need to sit down.

MAE: Can't take the heat huh? (laughs) Here. *(MAE quickly grabs her bag, pulls out an ice pack and hands it to FRED.)* This works for me.

(FRED happily applies it to his face.)

FRED: Oohh. Ahh.

(MAE feels sorry for Fred but feels compelled to finish her story.)

MAE: Well, anyway. *(pause)* I took her up above my shoulders, spun 5 or 6 times and then, no place to go but down, Splat! She went flat on her back. That was an amazing maneuver and it was legal.

FRED: It was?

MAE: *(Confidentially)* In the ring, if the referee didn't see me, it was legal. Hah! Yeah, I could dish it out.

FRED: *(referring to his tooth)* Ow.

MAE: But I could take it too. In Kansas City, Elvira Snodgrass busted one of my teeth. You could hear it crack. Audience loved that. I groaned. They laughed.

FRED: Ha ha.

MAE: Yup.

FRED: I don't know how you do it. *(referring to tooth)* I can hardly chew.

MAE: Hey, I chewed a lady's ear off once.

FRED: You did?

MAE: Well, almost. See this? *(She shows him her missing tooth).* I accomplished this on Beth Phoenix. I got her ear, she got my tooth. Hah huh!

FRED: That must have hurt!

MAE: In wrestling, when you lose a tooth, you just finish the fight, go to the locker room and rinse with piss and vinegar. Yup.

FRED: Wow.

MAE: What's wrong with you?

FRED: Ahh… well, I sort of got mugged. I couldn't fight back. It was two guys. They were big.

MAE: Two?

FRED: Yes.

MAE: I got a great move for that!

FRED: You do?

MAE: Double Bum! *(FRED stares blankly)* You never heard of that one?

FRED: Ah, no?

MAE: You don't watch wrestling?!

FRED: Well, my mom and I used to watch sometimes. She wanted me to be tougher. I got beat up a lot when I was a kid.

MAE: So did I, but that didn't stop me. No siree. Listen, you just need some moves. You need the Mae Young "Double Bum".

FRED: I do?

MAE: Actually, if you live here in the city, it's a necessity. I'll show you. Come on. Stand up.

FRED: Ah, I don't think—

MAE: —I'm not going to hurt you. I promise.

FRED: Really?

MAE: Come on. *(FRED stands. MAE wants him to visualize.)* Now think of it. The assholes. Those "two guys", they're coming at ya. Right?

FRED: Yeah?

MAE: They look like they're gonna take you and you think you're gonna go down but, what you have to do is, "go with it".

FRED: Go with it.

MAE: That's right. *(FRED seems bewildered)* Now, stay with me Fred.

FRED: Okay.

MAE: First you gotta have the correct wrestling stance.

FRED: Stance.

MAE: Yes. Like this. Bend at the knees and the waist. See? *(MAE demonstrates, and FRED tries to follow)* Hands almost touching the ground. Head up. Keep your eye on the enemy! Elbows in. Move side to side. *(FRED puts one leg behind other)* No, don't cross your feet. You'll trip yourself. Legs apart!

FRED: Like this?

MAE: Good. Now, Fred, it's time for Mae's Double-Sweep-Leg-Take Down. *(war cry)* AHHHHHH!

> *(MAE barrels toward FRED.)*

FRED: NO!

> *(MAE stops short.)*

MAE: Fred! Don't panic! That's rule number 2. Don't panic. Here, I'll just grab around your knee.

FRED: OH! *(he protects his privates)*

MAE: Okay, *(trying to be patient)* you do it on me. Grab around my leg. *(He does)* Good. Squeeze. Harder. You can be stronger. *(He is)* Good! Now pull me toward you and *(she buckles to ground)* there, I'm down. See? Nice work. Nice! Way to go!

FRED: I did it!

MAE: Yes, you did. Easy right?

FRED: Sort of.

MAE: Now with two people comin at ya, you just use both arms. Wrap around one guy's right leg and the other guy's left. Bam. That's what you do. Once they're down, well, in your case you might just wanna run away but… anyway, that's it and, as you see, the "Leg Take Down" is a substantial part of Mae Young's "Double Bum"!

FRED: Thanks!

MAE: You're welcome. You try that one out in the wild kingdom of this city and you'll get results.

FRED: I'm grateful. *(short pause. FRED picks up clipboard.)* Did you fill out the form?

MAE: Huh?

FRED: The dental form?

MAE: I've filled that out several times, okay.

FRED: You've been here before?

MAE: I'm not afraid of him.

FRED: Dr. Glassman?

MAE: Whatever.

FRED: He's a very good dentist.

MAE: He is?

FRED: Haven't you met him?

MAE: I'm the toughest person I know.

FRED: I bet.

MAE: People are afraid of me.

FRED: Yes. *(touching his face)* Oh, geez, I need some aspirin.

> *(At the ready, MAE immediately offers FRED pill from her shirt pocket.)*

MAE: Take this. Don't tell anyone where you got it.

> *(MAE offers water bottle).*

FRED: You come prepared.

MAE: Yup. *(winces)* Ah.

DENTAL ASST V.O.: Ms. Young? You're next.

FRED: Good luck.

> *(we hear a buzzing drill sound – NORMAL volume)*

MAE: What?

FRED: The dentist? They called your name.

> *(Buzzing Drill sound increases in VOLUME)*

MAE: Ah.

FRED: I guess you're before me.

MAE: You were here first. You go. I don't mind.

> *(BUZZING DRILL sound - LOUD)*

I CAN'T!

FRED: What?

MAE: No, my teeth are fine.

FRED: I thought you…

MAE: My teeth are fine, okay?!

> *(MAE gathers up her things.)*

FRED: Doesn't it hurt? Shouldn't you see the doctor?

MAE: I'm fine.

FRED: You're the champion.

MAE: So?

FRED: Champs must get their teeth repaired once in a while.

MAE: NO. No, they don't.

FRED: The dentist freezes your gums.

MAE: They do?

FRED: Yes mam. I mean… Ms. Young.

MAE: Just call me Mae.

FRED: Okay. Mae. Dr. Glassman uses Novocain, so you don't feel anything. It doesn't hurt.

MAE: Right.

FRED: He does. And later, you'll feel a lot better. Your mouth won't hurt anymore.

MAE: Good luck with the moves Fred. You can do it.

> *(MAE shakes FRED's hand, he holds it trying to keep her there)*

FRED: You created the Double Bum, Mae.

MAE: Yeah?

FRED: You're in the Hall of Fame.

MAE: See ya Fred.

> *(MAE breaks away from FRED's grip and turns to exit)*

FRED: Really? That's your finish?!

MAE: What?

FRED: You're going to stay down on the mat? Mae Young down? Don't do that, please. Listen to me Mae! Listen: 1, 2… 3 *(On "3" Mae abruptly turns back toward Fred.)*

FRED: Yes!

> *(Sound track of CROWD CHEERING)*
>
> *BLACK OUT*

THE END

PLAYING WITH FIRED
STEVEN HAYET

BEST 10 MINUTE PLAYS 2019

THE PLAY:

Playing With Fired

THE PLAYWRIGHT:

Steven Hayet

SYNOPSIS:

In order to get the job of her dreams, a young ambitious candidate has to fire the man who currently holds the position.

ABOUT THE PLAYWRIGHT:

Steven Hayet is a New Jersey playwright whose work has been performed from Los Angeles to London and New York to New Zealand. His short plays include *Talking Points* (City Theatre Winter Shorts), *George Orwell's 1989: A "Swift" 10 Minute Adaptation* (Week 1 People's Choice Winner, Short+Sweet Hollywood), *Everlasting Chocolate Therapy* (Audience Choice Runner Up, The Oakville Players TOP 10 Festival), and Stage Mom. He also co-wrote the short film *Frame of Reference* (Bronze Remi Award for Best Romantic Comedy, Worldfest Houston). He is a graduate of the College of William & Mary and Rutgers University.

CONTACT:

stevenhayet@gmail.com

WEBSITE:

stevenhayet.com

THE THEATRE:

Tipping Point Theatre
361 E. Cady St., Northville, MI 48167

MISSION:

To create personal experiences through affordable, professional theatre.

ABOUT:

Tipping Point Theatre is a professional, nonprofit theatre located in Downtown Northville that operates year round. Founded in 2006, we believe that the theatre we create has the power to inspire tipping points for the individual patron as well as the community as a whole. Offering six full scale productions, jazz concerts, classes, and the Sandbox Play Festival, there's something for everyone at the point!

The Sandbox Play Festival is a 10 minute play writing competition that highlights Michigan artists who may not have an outlet for their work otherwise. Originally featured during Northville's Arts and Acts Festival, selected scripts are now fully produced for a weekend at the theatre. Audiences vote on their favorite of the festival while a judge along with the Producing Artistic Director decide on first and second place winners.

CONTACT:

James Kuhl
James@TippingPointTheatre.com
248-347-0003

WEBSITE:

TippingPointTheatre.com

PRESENTING THE PLAY:

Playing With Fired

CHARACTERS:

JOHN- male, 40's, the Senior VP of J.C. Toys, Inc.

SAM- female, 20's

RONALD- male, mid/late 40's

SETTING:

A corporate office at J.C. Toys, Inc. in present day. JOHN O'Brien is seated behind his desk hard at work. On his desk are several files, a phone, and an odd assortment of toys.

(SAM enters.)

SAM: Hello, Mr. O'Brien?

JOHN: Do I know you?

SAM: Not yet, but you will. My name's Samantha Dansby and I'm going to be your new Senior Assistant Director of Product Distribution.

JOHN: I'm sorry, but we're not looking for anyone right now-

SAM: - that's great! My mother always says you find the best things when you're not looking. So I was-

JOHN: How'd you get in here?

SAM: That's not important. Now about-

JOHN: No, it's very important. I'm the Senior VP of the 3rd largest Toy Manufacturer in the world. I keep a busy schedule with appointments & meetings all day long. I have 2 secretaries and they each have 2 secretaries to make sure I don't have to deal with distractions, such as people walking into my office unannounced. So, one more time, how did you get into my office?

SAM: It's really not that interesting.

JOHN: Indulge me.

SAM: I just walked in with 2 Starbucks gift cards, told them it was for Administrative Professional's Appreciation Day- which I guess is still a thing?- and told them I was a temp you hired so that they could take the next 30 minutes to grab a latte on you. They say "Thank You" by the way. Anyways, boring, right? Can we get back to talking about the job?

JOHN: There is no job.

SAM: Of course there is. Now I can start right away-

JOHN: Let me re-phrase. We aren't hiring for that job. The position was filled two weeks ago.

SAM: But I need that job.

JOHN: If you give me your resume and leave in the next 15 seconds, I'll be sure to let you know if the position ever opens up.

SAM: Now when I say I need the job, I don't mean I "need it" need it, like I need the money or the benefits or the pension plan and all that fluff. I mean it's nice- don't get me wrong- but I can get that from anywhere since I'm smart and determined and pretty much any suit with half a brain would be lucky to have me. But I meant "I need this job" as in "I neeeeed it." I've always dreamed of working at J.C. Toys. It is what I've always set my sights on. Even as a little kid, I knew I wanted this job.

JOHN: Senior Assistant Director of Product Distribution?

SAM: *(Incredibly serious.)* Mr. O'Brien, overseeing toy distribution. Sending toys to children all over the world. That's the closest you can get to being Santa Claus.

JOHN: I never thought of it that way.

SAM: So how do you want to begin this interview? Would you like me just to tell you about myself or do you have some question you like to open with?

JOHN: We're not having an interview. There is no job. Now get out of my office before I have to call security.

SAM: Mr. O'Brien, I have two words for you.

JOHN: *(Hoping.)* Good bye?

SAM: *(Beat.)* Lieutenant Liberty

JOHN: Okay?

SAM: Lieutenant. Liberty.

JOHN: You can keep saying it -

SAM: Lieutenant Liberty, an action figure produced by J.C. Toys popular in the mid to late 1990s.

JOHN: I'm very well aware.

SAM: Then you know his slogan: "Don't Take No for An Answer."

> *(Pause.)*

Don't take no for an answer.

> *(Beat.)*

Now I may seem like a girl who played with Party Ponies or

Slender Sally dolls, but I'm a fighter, like Lieutenant Liberty.

JOHN: I've noticed.

SAM: When Christmas of 1998 came around, I wanted a Lieutenant Liberty. I asked my parents every day for two months. They would say no. They would say "Samantha, honey, wouldn't you be happier with a Party Pony?" I stayed strong. I would not settle for a Party Pony. I refused to take no for an answer then and I refuse to take it now.

JOHN: "Don't Take No for an Answer" was a marketing campaign I designed to make children annoy their parents into buying them Christmas presents.

SAM: Well, it also created a movement.

JOHN: Of one?

SAM: All movements start with one.

JOHN: It created a monster. That's what it did.

> *(Takes a breath.)*

Very well. You want this job?

SAM: Of course I do.

JOHN: I mean, do you really want this job?

SAM: Yes. I'd do anything.

JOHN: Glad to hear it.

> *(Into his intercom.)*

Erica, can you get Ronald and tell him I'd like to see him in my office? Thank you.

> *(Back to SAM.)*

Ronald is the current Senior Assistant Director of Product Distribution. You have to fire him.

SAM: Excuse me, sir?

JOHN: You want the job? You have to take it. I want you to look him in the eyes and tell him he's not going to work here anymore. Are you able to do that?

SAM: I-

JOHN: If you're not, that's fine. The door's that way.

SAM: No.

> *(Beat.)*

No, I can do this.

JOHN: Excellent.

> *(RONALD appears in the doorway.)*

RONALD: You wanted to see me, sir?

JOHN: Ahh, yes. Have a seat. Ronald, this is Samantha from HR.

> *(JOHN gives SAM the "go-ahead" look.)*

SAM: Ronald. It's nice to meet you.

RONALD: Likewise.

SAM: *(Awkwardly.)* Work. Am I right? Yuck. Now you can be honest with me. You don't really like this job, do you?

RONALD: No, I don't.

SAM: *(Relieved.)* Really?

RONALD: I love it.

SAM*: (Defeated.)* Oh.

RONALD: It has been absolutely incredible experience.

SAM: But the long hours, right? I'm sure they must be starting to take a toll.

RONALD: I don't mind it at all. To be honest, it beats coming home to an empty house.

JOHN: Empty house?

RONALD: Yes, sir. My wife passed away a little over 3 years ago.

JOHN: I'm so sorry to hear that-

> *(Glancing at SAM.)*

-again.

RONALD: I appreciate that, sir. It's been rough, but working here,

I think has been the best thing for me. Everyone here is just so friendly. It was my birthday on Tuesday and they all got me a cake that said "Ron" on it! "Ron!" Can you believe it? I've always wanted a nickname.

(Catching himself.)

I'm sorry for rambling and taking up your time. What did you want to see me about?

JOHN: Samantha?

SAM: Okay, I don't know how else to say this but Ronald,

(Beat.)

Ron.

(Beat.)

We're going to have to let you go.

RONALD: *(Like a sledgehammer hit him in the face.)* I-I don't understand. What did I do wrong?

SAM: Nothing. I wish we...I could tell you why, but please understand, it has nothing to do with you personally.

RONALD: *(Still processing.)* So I'm fired? Just like that?

SAM: I'm so sorry. It's just-

(Beat.)

- sometimes for the greater good of a company, it has to make sacrifices. If it isn't a good person you are letting go, it's not a sacrifice.

RONALD: When I got this job, I was so excited I called every relative, every friend, everyone I knew to say "Hey, look at me. I'm going to be working at J.C. Toys: Number 31 on Fortune Magazine's Best 100 Companies to Work For. I had reached the top third of the mountain!" And now, after two weeks of me busting my rump- arriving early, staying late, working through lunch- you are going to give me some cock and bull story about "greater good" and "Ron isn't a cool nickname." Let me tell you this: you may view me as just an easily replaceable cog in a machine, but I loved being a cog. I loved knowing that this machine ran because of something I did- even if the overall impact of my job was...

SAM: Ron, I-

RONALD: Please don't call me, Ron. My new friends called me Ron.

> *(Beat.)*

I mean, I get it. I'm only the Senior Assistant Director of Product Distribution at a toy manufacturer. It's not like I'm Santa Claus, but I was okay with that. As a kid on Christmas, I always would think of the elves. Children leave out cookies for Santa and carrots for the reindeer, yet the elves behind the scenes never get thanks. No kid opens a present and says, "Oh thank you, Elves!" but without elves, there is no Christmas. I'm sorry I wasn't a good enough elf.

> *(RONALD starts to walk off.)*

SAM: *(to JOHN)* Jonathan, you were 150% right. This man is an asset to the company. I didn't believe you until I saw this for myself. He's just what J.C. Toys needs as its Senior Assistant Director of Product Distribution.

> *(to RONALD)*

Thank you for indulging us in this exercise, Ronald. You may go back to work.

RONALD: But-but- I don't understand. So I'm not fired?

JOHN: Apparently not.

SAM: Someone would have to be an absolute idiot to think there was a better person for this job than you.

RONALD: Thank you. That means quite a lot.

JOHN: There you go.

> *(Beat.)*

Now you go back to work and keep up the good effort.

RONALD: Yes, sir. Thank you, sir.

> *(RONALD exits. As he does, SAM is gathering her things and starts to follow.)*

JOHN: Where are you going?

SAM: I'm sorry for wasting your time. I don't have what it takes. I'm not a Lieutenant Liberty- just a stupid Party Pony.

JOHN: *(Into his intercom.)* Erica, can you get Brian and tell him I'd like to see him in my office? Thank you.

SAM: - Sir, I can't. I'm just not cut out for-

JOHN: Brian will show you to your office. You said you could start immediately and I'm going to hold you to it.

SAM: I don't understand.

JOHN: Do you remember the original slogan for Party Ponies?

SAM: *(A little confused by where this is going.)* Yes. It was "Even after the cows come home, these Ponies keep partying."

JOHN: I hated that slogan. Thought it was incredibly irritating, but it made our company of ton of money. Like it or not, you are a Party Pony. And you said it yourself; any suit with half a brain would be lucky to have you.

SAM: Thank you. You won't be disappointed. So where am I working?

JOHN: I already told you. In HR. You said you wanted to be Santa Claus?

    (SAM nods.)

Then go manage your elves.

    (Blackout.)

IN BETWEEN THE DROPS
ELAYNE HEILVEIL

BEST 10 MINUTE PLAYS 2019

THE PLAY:

In Between The Drops

THE PLAYWRIGHT:

Elayne Heilveil

SYNOPSIS:

Ms. Shafer, an aspiring actress, is in the midst of reporting a secret crime that happened months before. She has come forth because she's heard reports of missing girls who may be victims of her perpetrator. But while telling her story Officer Grey becomes suspicious of her motives.

ABOUT THE PLAYWRIGHT:

Elayne Heilveil is an actress, journalist, director and award-winning playwright. As an actress she has starred in numerous television, film and theatre productions. As a playwright her many competition-winning short plays have been produced throughout the country. She is published by Dramatic Publishing Company, Smith and Kraus and Applause Cinema & Theatre Books. Publications in some recent anthologies include; Best Contemporary Monologues (Age 7-15; 2015); More 10-Minute Plays for Teens (2015); Best Ten-Minute Plays (2016; Smith & Kraus); Best Ten-Minute Plays (2016); Best Ten-Minute Plays (2017); Best Women's Stage Monologues (2017); Best Ten-Minute Plays (2018). Her most recent short play was produced in Australia and recorded for radio. She is a graduate of New York's High School for The Performing Arts and Carnegie Mellon University.

CONTACT:

elaynerh@aol.com
310-471-0778

THE THEATRE:

PlayGround-LA

MISSION:

The mission of PlayGround-LA is to support the development of significant new local voices for the theatre.

ABOUT:

PlayGround-LA is the first regional expansion of the celebrated Bay Area playwright incubator and theatre community hub, Playground. Playground was launched in San Francisco in 1994 by co-founders Jim Kleinmann, Brighde Mullins and Denise Shama.

In 1996, Kleinmann became Playground's first Artistic Director. Since its founding, PlayGround has developed and staged over 850 original ten-minute plays by 250 Bay Area and Los Angeles early-career writers and has commissioned/developed more than 77 full-length plays. In the process of staging those works, Playground has helped to identify some of the leading emerging writers and, at the same time, has engendered the creation of a true community of theatre artists, bringing together hundreds of local actors, directors and playwrights.

Each month, Oct-Mar, PlayGround-LA announces a topic to the thirty-six writers of the PlayGround-LA Writers Pool. Writers have four-and-a-half days to generate their original short plays and the top six are cast with leading local professionals and rehearsed for just 1.5 hours before being presented as script-in-hand staged readings on the second Monday of the month. At the end of each season, six of the thirty-six works developed in the Monday night series are selected for a one-night celebration, the Best of PlayGround Gala. "In Between the Drops" went on to be presented at CulturalDC's Source Festival in Washington, DC and subsequently performed at the Group Rep Lonny Chapman Theatre in Los Angeles in association with PlayGround-LA.

CONTACT:

Jim Kleinmann, Artisitic Direcor
jim@playground-la.org, 323-992-6766

WEBSITE:

playground-la.org

PRESENTING THE PLAY:

In Between The Drops

CHARACTERS:

Officer GREY: Male. Any age. Possibly African American. A no-nonsense, been around, somewhat cynical cop.

Ms. SHAFER: Female. 20's-30's. Caucasian. Attractive. Sensitive and expressive.

SETTING:

Int. Police Detective's Office.

AT RISE:

Officer Grey is seated at his desk with a phone and a stack of papers. He is pouring a glass of water into a paper cup. Ms. Shafer is seated opposite him. She pauses, watches him pour. It sparks a memory, as she continues, in the midst of her story.

SHAFER: Water. It was a glass of water.

(He looks up. Offers her the paper cup. She shakes her head, 'no'. He takes a sip.)

GREY: Kidney stones. I gotta' drink. Lots and lots. So, you said you had the glass.

SHAFER: On the floor. Yes. I don't remember exactly how it got there. On the floor I mean. I don't even remember if he took a sip.

GREY: You don't remember if he touched the glass.

SHAFER: It was two, three months ago. A hot August day. I was coming home from work.

GREY: And where was that?

SHAFER: At a studio. Universal Studios. I had worked in the morning. And I had a few hours off. So I decided to come home for lunch.

GREY: Uh huh. And what kind of work?

SHAFER: *(Mumbles)* I act.

GREY: *(Looks up)* Excuse me?

SHAFER: I'm an actor. I was working on a show that week.

GREY: No kidding. Is it something I mighta' seen?

SHAFER: I don't know…what you watch.

GREY: I mean have I seen you in anything? Or do you just stand in the background, kind of, you know, in the crowd, waiting for the big break?

SHAFER: *(Offput)* I'm sorry. I don't see how…*(Starts to get up)* This was probably a mistake. My mistake.

GREY: No, no. Please. Ms… *(Looks at his notes)* Shafer. We get a lot of stories. A lot of cranks. Seems like everyone in this town wants their two minutes of fame. Please, sit down.

(She sits back down, slowly)

So… you came home in the afternoon, twelve, one-o'clock? And when you got home the street…?

SHAFER: …was empty. Yes.

GREY: *(Checks notes)* Beechwood Place.

SHAFER: It's just a little street. In the hills. But no one else was out. In the middle of the afternoon, no one else was there.

GREY: Okay…

SHAFER: Except…this man.

GREY: The one you recognized from the sketch on TV?

SHAFER: Yes. But I don't know. I mean, I can't be sure. But I just thought… when I saw the girls…the missing girls. I…I thought they could be…

GREY: …dead?

SHAFER: …me. And it could be him. And if it was…maybe I could help.

GREY: Anything, Ms. Shafer. Any detail. Big. Small. That could connect the dots. Please….

(He indicates 'continue' and pours himself another cup of water. She stares at it.)

SHAFER: The water. How he asked for the water. I was coming home and I saw him on the street. And he looked…out of place. Like he didn't fit…in the neighborhood, you know? He was standing there… sort of looking around. And he just didn't look…he looked…

GREY: …suspicious?

SHAFER: Yes. It was just a feeling. You get these feelings some-times… but, well, you don't like to categorize someone by, well, the way they look. If you know what I mean.

(Grey 'gets' she means African American.)

GREY: Never judge a book by it's cover? Well, sometimes we're right, Ms. Shafer. Sometimes…not. So, he's on the street…

SHAFER: Yes, and as I got to my apartment, it's a two story Spanish kind of place with neighbors upstairs and next door and apartments all around, this, this...person, this man, stopped me by my door. "Excuse me," he said, "can I have a glass of water?" And I looked at him... and he had...sweat, beads of sweat on his face. And, and it was hot. And I thought, just because he looks... I mean because he didn't look...

GREY: ...like he belonged in that kind of neighborhood...?

SHAFER: I didn't want to... you know. So I said, "Okay. Why don't you wait here and I'll bring you out a glass." I just figured I could bring the water out. To be safe. So I went into my apartment and shut the door and walked into the kitchen, filled a glass of water and started to walk back out. And when I got into the living room, he was there. Inside. My house.

GREY: He had entered your residence at...*(Checks notes)* 15410 Beechwood Place.

SHAFER: I had closed the door. I...I guess it wasn't locked.

GREY: Uh huh.

SHAFER: And then... I can't remember if I had the glass, or if he took the glass... I just remember seeing the knife.

GREY: He had a knife.

SHAFER: It was sort of small with a wooden handle and looked sharp. It was in his hand. So...I can't remember if he took the glass or not. But he was standing there, in the middle of the room with the knife and just said, "Go into the room." It was the bedroom. The door was open and the covers on the bed were undone. I... I was in a hurry in the morning and left the bed... And... and he must have...

GREY: *(Checks phone)* Excuse me, *(Into phone)* Uh huh. Could you check on the burger and fries, Claire? Yeah, and skip the onion. Right. *(Hangs up; smiles to Shafer)* Sorry, blood sugar thing. So, you were saying...?

SHAFER: I'm sorry... I think this was a mistake. Nothing happened. I mean, really. It probably isn't him. *(Gets up, pauses)* It's just that I don't sleep very much. And I have these dreams and....

GREY: ...and he had a knife, Ms. Shafer?

SHAFER: A knife? Yes. *(She clutches her bag. Sits back down, slowly)* At my neck. And his eyes. Like fire, they burst into flames when I screamed. In the middle of the afternoon, I screamed. And no one came?

GREY: *(Writes down notes)* So, there was no one else to witness this event...at 154..?

SHAFER: I could feel his breath, at my throat, and suddenly there was this weird kind of silence, and all I could hear was this... PLOP...PLOP.

(He looks up from writing; watches her)

It must have been the faucet. When I got the water? I must have not closed it tight and all I heard was this huge sound in the middle of this silence...*(Elongates the sound; remembering)* PLOP. PLOP.

GREY: *(Stares at her)* You heard...a leaky faucet. Okay.

SHAFER: It was just like in the movies. You know, a scary movie and in the silence you hear a little creak, like a door that opens slowly only this was just a drop... of water. A tiny drop... like... an atom bomb, and then, nothing, like the whole world froze, and just waited... waited to hear another...

(He sits back and stops writing. Suspicious; sizing her up.)

GREY: ...Plop? *(Beat)* You're quite...expressive, Ms. Shafer. Just getting it all down.

SHAFER: I don't know how else to say it. But something happened...in that time, in that space between the drops when anything could happen...when everything was full and empty, dead, alive, and everything you ever knew or felt or was, could end... just like that? *(Beat)* Have you ever listened to a drop? Or tried to walk between the raindrops and never get wet?

GREY: *(Watching her)* I prefer umbrellas, Ms. Shafer.

SHAFER: I used to do that when I was young. Practice. Between the raindrops. My mother used to tell me that if I knew how to walk between the drops I would never get wet. If I knew how to listen…what to do, how to be in that space… in the silence between… I would hear. I would know. How to be… safe.

GREY: And what did you... hear, Ms. Shafer. In this…space?

SHAFER: I heard, 'No. No! You will not go in that room. You will not rape me and then kill me and you will not be the last person I will ever see, the last thing I will ever feel before I am dead!' *(Beat)* Then something got calm in me. And I just looked him in the eyes, those crazy black, brown, wild eyes, and I went underneath the fire and the rage and just *said (Simply; honestly. With deep intent)* "Why?" I didn't scream, I didn't plead, I didn't beg. I just wanted to know. You. To me. *(Laser connection as if back in the moment. Really asking)* "Why… Are…You…Doing…This?"

GREY: What did he do?

SHAFER: His whole body… changed. Like everything… let go. And he stopped. His eyes got soft, sad, I don't know. What, why. Maybe he was coming down, from drugs? Or my voice, calm, or maybe no one ever asked him before. Or cared enough to know? And then he told me. About his mother, how she raised him by herself. How they lived. The other kids on the street, how it was all he ever knew. And I told him, he didn't need to do it this way. He had a choice. And that, if he didn't, I wouldn't tell a soul. I promised. Do you understand? I promised him, I wouldn't tell a soul.

GREY: So, you promised this man, this man with black, brown, wild eyes, who had this knife, who…

SHAFER: … let me live! He gave me back my life! He trusted me. Not to tell. And I felt…grateful. To him. He gave me back my life.

GREY: I see. And the girls? Did they get theirs back?

(Beat. She gets up. Paces.)

SHAFER: After he told me, he looked tired. Drained. Coming down, I guess. And he asked if I knew a place he could stay. And I thought, Sure, I'll call up my friends and ask if this guy with a knife can crash on their couch. I said, 'No.' And then he asked if I could drop him off down the street to get a bus.

GREY: You do know that when you're in a car...

SHAFER: I drove him there...

GREY: ... that that is the most dangerous time.

SHAFER: And he got out. And that was it.

GREY: I see. *(Beat)* So, there's no one to corroborate, no marks, no...

SHAFER: I thought I should tell someone when I got back. My boyfriend was working at the time, I never bother him at work, never call, but I had his number on this piece of paper, and I took it out and sat down on the floor. I looked around the empty space, then stared down at the number and saw this...blotch. The ink was blurred. And then... another...

GREY: ...Plop?

> *(He starts to gather his papers.)*

SHAFER: It was a tear. I must have been crying but I didn't feel it. There was a wetness on my cheek but I didn't feel a thing. I just saw this...

GREY: You should talk to someone, Ms. Shafer.

SHAFER: I'm talking to you!

GREY: There were no witnesses, no...

SHAFER: Sometimes, I curl up on the bathroom floor and turn on the shower... and just listen...to...to the...

GREY: ...no marks, or...

SHAFER: ...or I sleep by the door. Every night. In case he comes back.

GREY: Just give us a call...

SHAFER: He trusted me. And he left... He left...

GREY: I'm sorry. *(checks watch)* Blood sugar. We're animals, Ms. Shafer. And we need to eat. And sleep. Get some rest.

> *(He EXITS. She sits there, alone. After a moment she reaches*

in her purse and takes out a plastic bag. Inside the bag is the knife.)

SHAFER: *(to herself)* …the knife. He… left… the knife.

(She stares at the knife as memories start flooding back. And as the LIGHTS begin to FADE we may hear the sound of the drops… PLOP. PLOP.)

END OF PLAY

STAMINA
DONNA KAZ

BEST 10 MINUTE PLAYS 2019

THE PLAY:

Stamina

THE PLAYWRIGHT:

Donna Kaz

SYNOPSIS:

Two octogenarians attempt to become the oldest women to summit Mount Everest.

ABOUT THE PLAYWRIGHT:

Donna Kaz is a multi-genre writer and the author of "UN/MASKED, Memoirs of a Guerrilla Girl On Tour," named best non-fiction prose of 2017 by the Devils Kitchen Literary Festival. Her plays and musicals have been produced around the world at Harlem Stage, New York Musical Theatre Festival, Trinity College/Dublin, The Spit Lit Festival/London, International Women's Arts Festival/UK, Women Playwrights International Conference/Sweden, City of Women Festival/Slovenia, Kultury w Poznaniu/Poland, Lincoln Center and the Edinburgh Festival Fringe. She has received the Venus Theatre Lifetime Achievement Award, the Yoko Ono Courage Award for the Arts and the Jerry Kaufman Award for excellence in playwriting. donnakaz.com @donnakaz

CONTACT:

kaz@donnakaz.com

WEBSITE:

donnakaz.com
ggontour.com

THE THEATRE:

American Renaissance Theatre Company
P.O. Box 255, Times Square Station, New York, NY 10108

MISSION:

Since 1976 the American Renaissance Theater Company (ARTC) has been dedicated to the development and production of new works by a multi-generational company of professional playwrights, actors and directors.

ABOUT:

The American Renaissance Theater was formed in 1975 by actors Robert Elston and Elizabeth Perry. Since its inception, ARTC has been a home to nearly five hundred professional actors, writers, directors, composers and musicians—theatre artists from a diversity of backgrounds who have found a congenial, stimulating environment in which to expand their resources and creativity. Plays developed through ARTC's workshop process have moved on to subsequent productions on Broadway, Off Broadway, and in America's leading regional theaters. ARTC is devoted to the development of new American plays and performance pieces and to the further growth of American actors, directors, playwrights and composers.

CONTACT:

Kathleen Swan, Producing Artistic Director
artcorg@gmail.com

WEBSITE:

americanrenaissancetheater.com

Presenting the Play:

Stamina

CHARACTERS:

CLARA, 81

SIMONE, 81

SETTING:

MOUNT EVEREST. The Hillary Step.

THE PRESENT.

AT RISE: MOUNT EVEREST. The Hillary Step. Dawn. Two Women - CLARA, and SIMONE, both 81 years old, are clipped to ropes on a sharp ridge of ice and snow. SIMONE removes her face mask.

SIMONE: Almost... *(inhales, exhales, inhales)* there!

(Suddenly the snow gives way under CLARA'S boot and she slides a few feet down the mountain)

CLARA: Oh! Oh no! *(takes off oxygen mask)*

SIMONE: Clara!?

CLARA: Falling!

SIMONE: Belay on!

CLARA: Wait! I'm fine. All clear! *(inhales, exhales, inhales)* My crampon slipped.

SIMONE: I can breathe.

CLARA: What?

SIMONE: I said I can breathe without my oxygen mask. Maybe we can summit without O's.

CLARA: Don't push it, Simone.

SIMONE: Climbing is pushing it, Clara.

CLARA: I thought there was supposed to be a bottleneck here.

SIMONE: We left before anyone else.

CLARA: Damn. I think my boot is stuck in a crevice.

SIMONE: That's not good.

CLARA: Thanks for you assessment.

SIMONE: Wiggle your foot back and forth.

CLARA: You think I haven't tried that?

SIMONE: This is the worst possible place to get yourself stuck.

CLARA: I didn't do it on purpose.

SIMONE: I really can't think of another place where this would be as bad. Here on the Hillary Step, the closest we can possibly get to reaching outer space without a rocket. Not a good place at all.

CLARA: Oh shut up, Simone!

SIMONE: I'm afraid that will be on the video.

CLARA: What?

SIMONE: My GoPro Helmet Cam. I'm recording our achievement, remember?

(CLARA gives SIMONE the finger)

CLARA: There. Did you get that?

SIMONE: I did and I will edit it out.

CLARA: If we survive.

SIMONE: Don't say that.

CLARA: If we survive.

SIMONE: Stop it! Try moving your heel up and down and side to side. Up and down and side to side. Up and down and side to ...

CLARA: My foot is out, Simone.

SIMONE: Good. Climb on.

CLARA: No.

SIMONE: Clara, one does not pause while summiting Everest. You will turn into a snow cone statue that way and remain here for the rest of your life. Well not life, of course. If you freeze you are dead.

CLARA: I can't do it.

SIMONE: Can't do what?

CLARA: Climb, Simone. Climb! What else would I be talking about? Not being able to drive my car any more or touch my toes?

SIMONE: According to my calculations we are just thirty minutes from becoming the oldest women to summit Mount Everest.

CLARA: Well, this old woman has to bail.

SIMONE: But we trained for months!

CLARA: Is that all that matters to you?

SIMONE: No.

CLARA: Then shut up and listen to me. I've been thinking about something ever since we entered the death zone.

SIMONE: What?

CLARA: That anyone close to death should not go near a place called the "death zone".

SIMONE: But we are here. We are fine!

CLARA: Not me. I cannot go on.

SIMONE: Why not?

CLARA: Because I just remembered I left the iron on. What do you think why?

SIMONE: You can do it, Clara.

CLARA: No, Simone, no I cannot. This was a stupid idea. And now it's over.

SIMONE: It is not over!

CLARA: You don't listen. Anyone ever tell you that?

SIMONE: You are experiencing altitude sickness.

CLARA: I need to lie down.

SIMONE: You cannot lie down, Clara. No one lies down on Mount Everest and ever gets back up!

CLARA: Sounds good to me.

SIMONE: You're not thinking straight. Put your mask back on. Drink some hot liquid.

CLARA: If I don't make it please play this back for my children. Goodbye Jeremy and Miranda! The key to the safe is in the small box on top of the, of the...oh, I can't remember. Good luck finding it.

SIMONE: Get up, Clara. Get up this instant. Our window of opportunity is closing.

CLARA: Where did that expression come from? Window of opportunity. It's lovely.

SIMONE: I said get up, Clara!

CLARA: I would like to know that you made it, Simone.

SIMONE: You are really scaring me now, Clara.

CLARA: When you pass me on the way down, if I'm still alive, just give me a nudge and I'll know.

SIMONE: You are not making any sense!

CLARA: I am going to un-clip myself from the rope now and step off to the side. Belay off.

SIMONE: NO! Put your belay back on right now!

CLARA: Forget about me, Simone.

SIMONE: I will not! I will tell everyone, for the rest of my life that you gave up. I will make sure that you are forever remembered as the one who proved women have no stamina!

CLARA: Well, we don't, so you're welcome everyone.

(PAUSE. SIMONE begins to cry)

CLARA: Are you crying?

SIMONE: Yes.

CLARA: Your eyes will freeze shut.

SIMONE: You are my oldest and dearest friend.

CLARA: Hmmmm....

SIMONE: Clara, listen to me. I would have let you go up first. You could have been the oldest woman ever to reach the top of Everest.

CLARA: Since you are older than I am, Simone, you would have broken my record the minute you summited.

SIMONE: I'm younger than you are, Clara.

CLARA: You are older by five days.

SIMONE: Not so.

CLARA: Your birthday is September 13th.

SIMONE: My birthday is September 18th.

CLARA: That's my birthday!

SIMONE: It is mine as well. I always wanted to be older than you, so I've been lying about my date of birth.

CLARA: That's ridiculous.

SIMONE: In high school, you were dating Harold and I was going with Peter and I wanted Peter to think he was dating someone more mature.

CLARA: By five days?!

SIMONE: Men love older women.

CLARA: By five days?

SIMONE: It mattered that I was older than you.

CLARA: By five fucking days!?

SIMONE: Yes! I was born on September 18th at 2:27 in the afternoon.

CLARA: I was born on September 18th at 9:07 in the morning.

SIMONE: You are five hours and twenty minutes my senior.

CLARA: And you've kept that from me for sixty five years?

SIMONE: Sixty six.

CLARA: Why?

SIMONE: It mattered to me back then. It doesn't matter now. The truth would have come out only if we both reached the summit. Only one of us could have claimed the title: oldest woman on top of the world.

CLARA: Then I'm glad you'll get your chance.

(PAUSE)

CLARA: *(CON'T)* You better leave now if you want to get there.

SIMONE: I believe I have been standing in one place for too long. My leg is frozen.

CLARA: You are lying! And I don't believe your birthday story either! You just made it up because ever since we met you've been ordering me around, trying to make me do what you want me to do.

SIMONE: I have never in my life ordered you to do anything! GET UP! GET UP! GET THE HELL UP RIGHT NOW CLARA!

CLARA: Ha. Ha. Ha. Ha, ha, ha, ha, ha....

SIMONE: Alright, Fine! Lay down and die. Turn yourself into a lump of ice-covered shit for all I care. Buy into the story they have shoved up your ass since you were born.

CLARA: What story?

SIMONE: Women aren't good enough.

CLARA: Baloney!

SIMONE: Why I ever chose you to accompany me, I'll never know.

CLARA: Cause I'm the only one who would go with you?

SIMONE: No. It's because when we are together, there is nothing we can't do. I picked you because you have always believed in me.

CLARA: I have.

SIMONE: I'm stronger when I am with you, Clara, and that's the truth. I'm sorry if I pushed you into this.

CLARA: You never pushed me into anything, Simone. That's the truth.

(PAUSE)

SIMONE: Clara, look! Do you see that? Right down there.

CLARA: You mean those lights?

SIMONE: I bet those are the head lamps of those assholes from Altitude Expeditions. They are moving up fast.

CLARA: Are those the ones who nicknamed us the old hags of the Himalayas?

SIMONE: The very ones.

CLARA: I hate those guys.

SIMONE: This place is going to be a bottle neck in about ten minutes. We could beat them to the top. Who will be the old hags then!?

CLARA: We will, damn it.

SIMONE: Right. Fine. Who cares?

CLARA: Why do we have to prove anything?

SIMONE: I don't know. We just do.

CLARA: Sometimes it seems I have spent my entire life looking uphill. *(PAUSE)* Alright. Let's go.

SIMONE: What?

CLARA: Belay on. *(getting up)* I am getting a second wind.

SIMONE: Oh, Clara. I am so happy. I promise I will never, ever again tell you...

CLARA: Don't push it, Simone. Let's just do this.

SIMONE: Right. Belay on. Climb on, Clara.

CLARA: Climb on, Simone.

(CLARA and SIMONE put their oxygen masks back on)

THE END

OY VEY MARIA
MARK HARVEY LEVINE

BEST 10 MINUTE PLAYS 2019

THE PLAY:

Oy Vey Maria

THE PLAYWRIGHT:

Mark Harvey Levine

SYNOPSIS:

It was a silent night. A holy night. Everything was going fine in the manger until Mary's Jewish mother showed up.

ABOUT THE PLAYWRIGHT:

Mark Harvey Levine has had over 1600 productions of his plays everywhere from Bangalore to Bucharest and from Lima to London. His work has been produced at such theaters as the Actors Theatre of Louisville and City Theatre of Miami. His plays have won over 35 awards and been produced in ten languages. He has had 14 plays published in volumes of "The Best Ten Minute Plays" over the years and 4 monologues also published in Smith & Kraus Anthologies.

Full evenings of his plays, such as "Cabfare For The Common Man", "Didn't See That Coming" and "A Very Special Holiday Special" have been shown in New York, Amsterdam, Edinburgh Fringe Festival, Sao Paulo, Sydney, Seoul, Mexico City, and across the US. A Spanish-language movie version of his play "The Kiss" ("El Beso") premiered at Cannes, showed at the Tribeca film festival, and subsequently aired on HBO and DTV (Japan).

CONTACT:

markle96@hotmail.com

WEBSITE:

markharveylevine.com

THE THEATRE:

City Theatre
444 Brickell Avenue Suite 229 Miami FL 33131

MISSION:

City Theatre's three-part mission is to: develop and produce new work, specifically in the short play and musicals genre; leverage our theatrical expertise to engage and educate our community and artists; and provide thought leadership to the wider theatrical industry.

City Theatre's long-range goal is for its performances and programming to be among the nation's premier forums for the development of new work; to be an organization that nurtures, supports, partners and collaborates with a dynamic creative and professional ensemble; and to create fresh and imaginative cultural and educational experiences that will enlighten, inspire and entertain audiences of all ages.

ABOUT:

Miami's City Theatre is an award-winning not for profit professional theatre company founded in 1996 by a trio of first-time producers (Susan Westfall, Stephanie Norman & Elena Wohl). They imagined a new kind of theatre festival comprised of original ten-minute plays that would entertain the often over-looked summer theatre lover, visitors and tourists. The festival, dubbed Summer Shorts, was instantly a critical and popular hit that sold out its original and extended run, and encouraged its producers to envision an annual festival with a future. Now entering its 24th Anniversary in 2018, City Theatre has evolved into a leading regional professional theatre with a growing national reputation for its unique niche and innovative programming. As the only theatre in the nation dedicated to the solicitation, development and production of the short play and short musicals genre, City Theatre has received thousands of submissions as part of the annual City Theatre National Award for Short Playwriting Contest, including scripts written by award-winning and emerging playwrights, composers and lyricists from South Florida and the country. It has produced and presented over 400 plays in an array of year round programming including: the annual Summer

Shorts Festivals; the annual LGBTQ focused Shorts Gone Wild productions; Short Cuts in-school, community center and camp tours; the City Shorts Winter Tour; the traveling "City Reads" series of free public readings; the national CityWrights Weekend for playwrights, theatre industry professionals, students and educators; the two-year Knight Foundation initiative, NextGen, which identifies, trains and mentors talented South Florida high school students as our next generation of playwrights, and now Winter Shorts, a collection of holiday themed plays to round out our year round programming.

Since 1996, thousands of audiences have enjoyed Summer Shorts at the Ring Theatre on the University of Miami campus (from 1996-2006), and the Adrienne Arsht Center for the Performing Arts where the Festival performs on the Susan Westfall Playwrights Stage of the Carnival Studio Theatre (from 2007 to the present). Summer Shorts; "America's Short Play Festival", is a theatrical event unlike anything else produced in South Florida, and is considered "the official kick-off of the summer theatre season". Every season yields a fresh and exciting collection of new short plays and musicals, and an award winning acting ensemble, creating a high-quality, enjoyable summer theatre experience.

CONTACT:

Susan Westfall
susan@citytheatre.com
305-755-9401

WEBSITE:

citytheatre.com

PRESENTING THE PLAY:

Oy Vey Maria

(The classic manger scene. Mary, Joseph, baby Jesus, scattered animals. The Three Kings are there, gift boxes in hand.)

KING 1: We have come seeking the one who—

(Suddenly, Ann enters. She is Mary's mother. She wears a babushka and carries a large tin foil pan of food with cellophane on it.)

ANN: Oy gevalt! What is this? A manger? You gave birth to my grandson in a manger?

MARY: Mom! What are you doing here?

ANN: What, you couldn't find a trench to have the baby in? A manger, yet.

MARY: Mom—

ANN: What's wrong with a hospital? Who delivered the baby, a cow?

MARY: Mom—

ANN: So where is he? Where is this darling grandson of mine?

She sees the baby and screeches with joy.

ANN: *(CONT'D)* Oh my God look at him he's so CUTE! I could eat him up! I will eat him up.

MARY: Mother.

ANN: I'm going to eat you up! Yes I am! Come here so I can eat you up! Um num num num.

MARY: Where's Dad?

ANN: He's still circling the block. They've got opposite side of the desert parking here.

She hands Joseph the pan.

ANN: Here. Make yourself useful. Go find an oven or something and heat this up.

Joseph leaves.

MARY: What are you DOING here?

ANN: You think I wouldn't be here when my own baby gives birth? I'm your MOTHER. Of course I'm here. Where else would I be? You'll understand when you become a mother. Oh wait, you just did. Not that I was invited.

MARY: Mom...

ANN: Was there not enough room in the manger? Move a few chickens over, I would have been fine.

MARY: Mom. This isn't a good time. We have company.

KING 2: Greetings! We have come to--

ANN: COMPANY? Your own mother you don't want here, but now you're entertaining?

MARY: Mom.

ANN: Me, you throw out. Them, you're putting out hors d'oeuvres?

(Joachim enters.)

JOACHIM: You wouldn't believe the traffic out there. Must be the holidays. *(hugs Mary)* Hello, darling. How are you feeling?

MARY: I'm fine, Dad. It's good to see you.

ANN: Don't take your coat off, we have to leave!

JOACHIM: Leave? We just got here. I haven't even seen the baby yet.

ANN: He's the one in the trough. There, you've seen him.

JOACHIM: Oh there you are! Hello, cutie! What did you name him?

MARY: Jesus.

JOACHIM: Hello, Jesus.

ANN: Jesus? I thought we agreed on Myron?

MARY: Ma, you agreed on Myron. We went with Jesus.

ANN: It doesn't even sound Jewish! Nobody's going to know he's a Jew. They'll have to remind each other when he leaves the room — "Did you know Jesus was Jewish?" "Oh, that's right."

MARY: We're not naming him Myron!

JOACHIM: Can I hold him?

ANN: No, they want him there. They left him out for the company.

It makes a better picture. Personally, I'd move that sheep over a little.

MARY: Ma.

KING 3: Um...is this a good time to give the gifts?

ANN: It's fine! We'll leave. We don't want to be in the way. We just shlepped three hours by camel, that's all.

MARY: You don't have to—

JOACHIM: We were gonna stay nearby but there was no room at the inn.

ANN: Can you believe it?

JOACHIM: Not one room.

ANN: And we flashed our Triple-A card.

JOACHIM: Nothing.

MARY: Look, Mom, we're just a little busy right now...

ANN: Oh, that's right, you have GUESTS. Well, if you don't want us here, you don't want us here. I understand. Promise me one day you'll describe me to the boy.

MARY: Mom, please.

ANN: Say that you turned me away, and I went home and died.

MARY: Mom, stay.

ANN: "They think it was her heart. It gave out from grief."

MARY: Stop it, Mother! Just stop! You're embarrassing me! You embarrass me all the time! You embarrass me in front of friends. You embarrass me in front of strangers. You embarrassed me in front of John the Baptist!

ANN: "John The Baptist"! I knew him when he was "John, The Kid Who Almost Drowned His Hamsters".

MARY: And now you're embarrassing me in front of my guests!

JOACHIM: Could YOU get a room at the Inn?

KING 2: We called ahead.

JOACHIM: There weren't any when we got there, that's for sure.

MARY: Dad.

JOACHIM: No rooms.

ANN: Not one.

JOACHIM: Not for love or money.

MARY: Dad! They're three Wise Men. They've come to--

JOACHIM: The Three Weismanns? I know them. They're in carpeting. They got a store in Galilee.

MARY: No, dad, they're Wise Men. Wise Men.

KING 3: We've come to adore the child.

ANN: Well, I've come to adore the child, and I brought a brisket! *(To Mary)* Pay attention, you have to know this now. This is what Jewish mothers do. We bring food. When someone is born, when someone dies, or gets sick, or gets married. We bring food. I brought a brisket. Mrs. Bergstein is sending over a tray. *(looking around)* Who sent the loaves and fishes?

MARY: I don't know, Mom, they just showed up.

JOACHIM: *(looking at Jesus)* It's a shame his birthday is right around Hanukkah, he's gonna get robbed on his presents.

ANN: So this is your company? Three wise guys?

MARY: They're also Kings. They're three Kings.

ANN: One Jewish mother beats three Kings! Believe you me, little missy. You should know, you're one too, now.

MARY: I'm not going to be like you.

ANN: Oh ho, so smart now.

KING 1: Um, we've brought gold, frankincense and myrrh.

MARY: No! I'm not! I'm not going to drey him around all the time.

ANN: Yes you will. It happens to all of us. All Jewish mothers. It's in the blood.

MARY: No, no, that's your mishegus, mom. I'm going to be different!

KING 2: We'll just put them over here. *(They set down their gifts.)*

MARY: I've sworn to myself that I'm not going to turn into you.

ANN: That's nice. That's a nice thing to say to your own mother.

(The Kings begin slowly edging out.)

KING 3: *(whispering)* Thank you. We had a lovely time.

MARY: You drive me crazy, Mother! You drive me completely insane! You always have!

KING 1: We'll see ourselves out.

(The Kings quickly exit.)

ANN: And you didn't? You were no bowl of olives growing up, either. I don't know how we got you through high school.

MARY: I'm not going to be laying guilt on him all the time!

ANN: Guilt is good! Believe me, this world could use a little more guilt. You read the daily scrolls, what do you see? Robbery, murder, gladiator games! If people felt a little more guilty about these things, maybe they wouldn't DO them. If everyone had a Jewish mother—

MARY: And I'm not going to nag at him all the time. I hear your voice in my head even when you're not around!

ANN: Did you hear it when you got the idea "Hey, let's have the baby in a stable"?.

MARY: There was no room at the Inn, Mother!

JOACHIM: We couldn't get a room either. And we tried!

ANN: Wait a second, wait a second — do you hear what I hear?

MARY: What?

The Little Drummer Boy enters, energetically playing his drum. Ann grabs the sticks from his hands and smacks him over the head.

LITTLE DRUMMER BOY: Ow.

ANN: Are you out of your MIND? There's a baby here!

LITTLE DRUMMER BOY: Come, they told me--

ANN: I don't care who sent you! Tell them to send a basket of fruit next time! Get out of here!

(The Little Drummer Boy runs off.)

ANN: *(CONT'D)* What's next, a mariachi band? Vey is meer.

MARY: I just wanted to have a nice night. A silent night. A holy night.

ANN: When I gave birth to you, we didn't have percussionists dropping in. Everything was nice, quiet, clean. Immaculate, really.

MARY: I don't know why these things are happening! I don't know why Kings and Shepherds and small boys with snare drums are showing up! I just know that I have a little baby. And we're going to love him! We're going to love him like crazy! We're going to worship him, in fact! We're going to treat him like he's God!!!

(Pause.)

ANN: NOW you're a Jewish Mother! Was that so hard?

More Jewish mothers show up, all with babushkas, all with food. They put a blue babushka on Mary.

ANN: *(CONT'D)* Welcome to the club!

The Jewish mothers all begin to talk at once, giving instructions on how to heat up the food, rearranging the manger, screaming with joy over the baby, etc., as...

LIGHTS FADE

ONE IS THE ROAD
MARK LOEWENSTERN

BEST 10 MINUTE PLAYS 2019

THE PLAY:

One is the Road

THE PLAYWRIGHT:

Mark Loewenstern

SYNOPSIS:

The Driver tells us what he is thinking and doing, moment by moment, as he drives home from a vacation with his wife, whom he has put on a pedestal.

ABOUT THE PLAYWRIGHT:

Mark Loewenstern is a winner of the Samuel French Off-Off Broadway Short Play Festival, among others. Plays: Carnality (published by Smith & Kraus), A Doctor's Visit (published by Samuel French), The Nastiest Drink in the World (published by Samuel French), Near Nellie Bly (O'Neill semi-finalist), Parish Dunkeld, The Bloomingdale Road, The Slightly Exaggerated True Story of "Civic Virtue," Grandmother's House, One is the Road. Films: 6 Love Stories (with Alicia Witt), Holiday Rumble, 26 Months After Katrina. Currently working on a commissioned play for California Stage Company about real-life 59-year old female serial killer Dorothea Puente. Dramatists Guild member #516.

CONTACT:

goodyarn@hotmail.com

WEBSITE:

markloewenstern.com

The Theatre:

Lucky Penny Productions
Lucky Penny Productions, 1357 Foster Road, Napa, CA 94558

Mission:

As Napa Valley's premier theatre company, Lucky Penny Productions creates, develops and presents professional quality theatre, and fosters educational opportunities for youth and adults in our community.

About:

Lucky Penny Productions was founded in 2009 in Napa, California by Taylor Bartolucci and Barry Martin. Our first production had a budget of under $1,000, and was so well received we just kept going, achieving 501c3 non-profit status in 2012 and increasing the size and scope of our productions. After five years as a gypsy company we opened the Lucky Penny Community Arts Center in January 2015. Now in our 10th season, we have an annual budget over $300,000 and produce eight to ten fully staged plays and musicals each season in our 97-seat black box theatre. We operate under the Actors' Equity MBAT Tier 2 agreement. Our artistic growth has led to multiple awards from Theatre Bay Area and the San Francisco Bay Area Theatre Critics Circle.

Lucky Penny Productions has produced five 10 minute play festivals, from 2012-2018. These events welcomed scripts from all over the country, and these entries were winnowed down to eight selections in a blind reading process. Our "8 x 10" festival is currently on hiatus but we continue to look for opportunities to present new works on our stage.

Contact:

Barry Martin
info@luckypennynapa.com
707.266.6305

Website:

luckypennynapa.com

PRESENTING THE PLAY:

One Is The Road

CAST:

THE DRIVER - 35-65, college grad, tries to be decent.

PLACE:

The road

TIME:

Now

THE DRIVER: One is the road, the sight of asphalt and vehicles stretching away for miles.

Two is the sound of the car radio. David Lee Roth is singing "Just a Gigolo."

Three is the feel of the leather steering wheel in my hands. It's sticky from hours of driving.

Four is a memory from five minutes ago, when I looked at the dashboard and saw that we were down to a quarter of a tank.

Five is the smell of Valerie's cigarette.

Six is the sound of Valerie's voice. It's high and sweet, even though she's annoyed.

Seven is the sense of what Valerie is saying. She asks, "Are you listening to me?"

One is the road. I see a sign up ahead.

Two is David Lee Roth getting to the good part of the song.

Three is an image I always get when I hear this song: an image of Roth's disembodied head looking down and realizing "I-I-I-I ain't got no body! No body!"

Four is a piece of trivia that pops into my mind for no reason. Maybe Roth's head summoned it. It's something I learned years ago in Psych class: the human brain can do up to seven different things at once. It can experience seven sensations. Or contemplate seven thoughts. Or send seven commands to the body. Or any combination of those things, all at the same moment.

Five is me answering Valerie that yes, I am indeed listening to her.

Six is Valerie saying, "No you're not. You're worrying about the gas tank."

Seven is me worrying about the gas tank.

One is the road. We pass the sign.

Two is what the sign says. It says nothing about a gas station.

Three is Valerie in the corner of my eye. She's beautiful although she's no longer so young.

Four is a memory that Valerie has always looked beautiful. And not just to me.

Five is silence from Valerie. She's waiting for me to prove I was listening.

Six is her cigarette.

Seven is the music.

One is repeating back what Valerie said before. She said that the three star hotel where we just spent our vacation was a big disappointment.

Two is Valerie. Her face doesn't change.

Three is the road.

Four is her cigarette.

Five is the gas tank.

Six is a memory. Ten minutes ago I asked Valerie to help me look for a gas station. She just sighed.

Seven is David Lee Roth singing, "I'm so sad and lonely. Sad and lonely."

One is me turning off the radio.

Two is Valerie crossing her legs.

Three is Valerie saying, "The room service was atrocious, don't you think?"

Four is knowing what Valerie is really saying. She's really saying I was in charge of booking the hotel. So it's my fault if it wasn't nice enough.

Five is the road.

Six is the cigarette.

Seven is the gas tank.

One is the silence of the radio.

Two is Valerie, now saying, "And the bellboy was so rude. I couldn't hear what it was he said to me, but I'm sure it was rude. Promise me that you'll call tomorrow and get our money back, okay? Okay?"

Three is a sign. It says exit now for gas.

Four is knowing that I can't exit now. I'm in the middle lane.

Five is the road.

Six is the cigarette.

Seven is the gas tank.

One is my face. It feels hot.

Two is the gas tank.

Three is me turning to look at Valerie.

Four is Valerie.

Five is me shouting at Valerie that she's made me miss the gas station.

Six is the cigarette.

Seven is the road in the corner of my eye.

One is my face. Still hot.

Two is me asking Valerie why she couldn't have watched for the sign, why she couldn't have done that one thing?

Three is the gas tank.

Four is Valerie's face, still beautiful.

Five is Valerie shouting back, "All you can think about is the gas tank!"

Six is the cigarette.

Seven is my conscience, telling me it's really not Valerie's fault. It's mine. Even though I asked Valerie to help, even though I must think about the driving, and the listening, and the answering. Still, I should have been taking care of things. That's my job. I should have been paying more attention.

One is Valerie. She's not looking at me. She's looking through the windshield at something else.

Two is Valerie's voice. It is loud, high, urgent.

Three is a premonition. Something terrible is about to happen.

Four is the sound of wheels screeching.

Five is my heart, giving one painfully hard pump.

Six is my conscience, still talking, still telling me that it's not fair to blame Valerie, because I knew when I married her that she had many, many needs. And by marrying her, I had promised to fulfill those needs. All of them. Because that's the sort of man she deserved. A man who could keep track of everything for her. Like the hotel. And the gas tank. And the road.

(Blackout. End of play.)

A DEPARTURE
GRANT MACDERMOTT

BEST 10 MINUTE PLAYS 2019

THE PLAY:

A Departure

THE PLAYWRIGHT:

Grant MacDermott

SYNOPSIS:

Connie and Conrad have been married for many years. When Connie has to go on a trip for business (the longest she's ever been gone) she asks her husband what he will do with his time alone. When he won't come out with it, she tells him she knows exactly what he is going to do and details it.

ABOUT THE PLAYWRIGHT:

Some select pieces include Kings Richard (Boston Theater Marathon); Sit Down, Daisy (Nylon Fusion Theater, Abberant Theater); What Men Do Alone on Islands (Heart & Dagger Come As You Are Festival); 10 Reasons Why Hamlet is Totally Gay (Edinburgh Fringe Festival), and Dinner now published by Indie Theater Now after being developed and performed by Project Y Theater in New York City.

He has been a member of the Interim Writer's Writing Accomplice in Boston, the Project Y Playwrights' Collective in New York City, and a 2018 Athena Writing Fellow in New York City. His play, An Independent of Race and the Brain, was a semi-finalist at the 2014 Eugene O'Neill Playwrights' conference and the 2015 Play-Penn Conference and his play without you but also with you too as well was a semi-finalist for PlayPenn in 2017. His Play Jasper was the 2018 TRU New Voices Official Selection.

CONTACT:

grant.macdermott@gmail.com

WEBSITE:

grantmacdermott.com

The Theatre:

Athena Theatre

Mission:

Athena Theatre Company has dedicated itself to developing and producing contemporary, off-beat and irreverent psychological dramas and dark comedies that challenge traditional stereotypes. Athena is committed to introducing future classics: theatrical works that not only entertain, but also inform, enlighten and deepen audience awareness of issues without sacrificing universality for the sake of the topical. We actively and responsibly invest in new voices for the stage by nurturing playwrights and promoting original works without regard to gender, politics, race or religion.

About:

Athena Theatre was founded in 2002 in Los Angeles in order to develop new work in an intimate, Off-Broadway-style environment. After producing 14 shows in LA, garnering 16 Critics Picks from local papers and audience praise and support, Athena moved to New York City in 2009. Athena Theatre is dedicated to developing and producing contemporary new plays that challenge traditional stereotypes, work that is thoughtful and complex, and stories born out of philosophical conversations, particularly the challenges and issues surrounding modern living and communication between diverse people and perspectives. Our Core Programming includes: Athena Reads, a monthly play reading series that develops new works that fit Athena Theatre's mission; Athena Writes, a playwriting fellowship that expands on Athena Reads and deepens our relationship with emerging New York City playwrights and Athena Theatre produces Full Productions selected from our Athena Reads and Athena Writes programs.

Athena Theatre's new playwright group, Athena Writes, selected eleven playwrights assembled for a one-year exploration of the theme: "Falling Forward," and centered on Athena Theatre's commitment to supporting new work which pushes at the boundaries of live theatre.

CONTACT:

> Veronique Ory
> Veronique@AthenaTheatre.com
> 818-642-6294

WEBSITE:

> AthenaTheatre.com

PRESENTING THE PLAY:

A Departure

(A living room to an elegant home. CONRAD, a man of 70 [but barely looks it] sits and reads the paper. His wife, CON-NIE, is offstage, upstairs, packing.)

CONNIE: Have you seen my scarf?

CONRAD: Hm?

CONNIE: The Hermes.

CONRAD: Which one?

CONNIE: The one you got my for my birthday?

CONRAD: Which one?

CONNIE: The last one.

> *CONRAD is about to say the number of the birthday to get a cute flirty rise out of her but she cuts him off.*

CONNIE: Say the number and I'll poison you.

CONRAD: Wouldn't dream of it.

CONNIE: Scarf?

CONRAD: I don't know, check your closet.

(She doesn't respond. A moment. Then she comes on with an elegant rolling suitcase, and she is elegantly dressed. It's effortless and lovely. An older woman who knows how to put herself together for her age without being at all frumpy or dowdy.)

CONNIE: Alright.

CONRAD: Found it?

CONNIE: No. But I wore this one instead. You like it?

CONRAD: Very much.

CONNIE: What are you reading?

CONRAD: The news.

CONNIE: And what's in the news today?

CONRAD: Death, destruction, misery, scientific marvels, lying politicians, scandal, cheating celebrities, young people I no longer recognize with more money than I can ever hope to have, and the funnies.

CONNIE: And you're reading?

CONRAD: The funnies.

CONNIE: Good choice.

CONRAD: I thought so.

CONNIE: No crossword today?

CONRAD: Stuck.

CONNIE: On?

CONRAD: 17 across, a 9-letter word that means a new word undefined.

CONNIE: Neologism.

CONRAD: I knew there was a reason I married you.

CONNIE: Miss me?

CONRAD: I will tomorrow when I inevitably am confounded by this demon puzzle.

CONNIE: Two weeks is a long time. I've never been away from you that long. Makes me nervous. Isn't that silly?

CONRAD: Why nervous?

CONNIE: *(withholding something ever so briefly, but then she says)* Lots more puzzles to confound.

CONRAD: Not that long. For an old man like me that's nothing. I could nap through it.

CONNIE: And have.

CONRAD: That famous weekend.

CONNIE: You were so sick.

CONRAD: I was fairly proud of it.

CONNIE: Almost called the Guinness Book of records.

CONRAD: Smashing records even near death's door.

CONNIE: What do you think you'll do?

CONRAD: Oh I don't know.

CONNIE: I put your gym clothes in the hamper.

CONRAD: You didn't have—

CONNIE: Yet like a good domestic, I did.

CONRAD: Nevertheless she persisted?

CONNIE: *(a wry smile, then)* Don't just sit around and be old.

CONRAD: I like sitting around and being old. I'm very good at it.

CONNIE: You're good at one of those things.

CONRAD: I don't know. The gym. Perhaps a movie. Or three. They come so fast at awards season and I never manage to see them all even though I don't have much to do otherwise.

CONNIE: I put your phone on the charger upstairs.

CONRAD: Thank you.

CONNIE: Think you'll see any friends?

CONRAD: I don't mind being alone.

CONNIE: I don't want you being all alone. I don't like thinking of you by yourself.

CONRAD: I'll have my thoughts of you.

CONNIE: I might vomit.

CONRAD: Shall I fetch you a towel?

CONNIE: No I'll just do it on you.

CONRAD: Kinky.

CONNIE: Your phone was buzzing every four seconds.

CONRAD: Was it?

CONNIE: Sure was.

CONRAD: I'll answer later.

CONNIE: You sure? I can bring it to you now.

CONRAD: That's fine. I'll answer later. Not in the mood.

CONNIE: Maybe it's someone asking you to dinner.

CONRAD: Why do you say that?

CONNIE: Because that's what phones were designed for, dear. To ask people to dinner with more ease. Instead of riding those pesky carriages four miles to drop off your calling card in hopes that the lady of the house would be home.

CONRAD: You're better than the funnies.

CONNIE: Except I don't need writers although I'm very animated and have been known to strip.

CONRAD: When?

CONNIE: You have a birthday coming up too. You'll find out.

(Looking at all her stuff.)

CONNIE: Looks like I have everything. Do I have everything?

CONRAD: Everything plus my heart.

CONNIE: The cardiologist called.

CONRAD: Funny.

CONNIE: No he really did. I forgot to tell you.

CONRAD: Oh.

CONNIE: It's nothing. It was just to reschedule your appointment. I did it for Monday. Is that alright? I won't be back but—

CONRAD: Oh. Yes.

CONNIE: You had plans?

CONRAD: Just a maybe something. That's fine. I can reschedule.

CONNIE: If it was something important I'm sure they won't mind. It's just a follow up. We know you're fine.

CONRAD: Well I can call them if I need.

CONNIE: With your phone. Which is upstairs.

CONRAD: Why'd they call you?

CONNIE: Probably because you never answer your phone and I'm the second number because I'm your wife.

CONRAD: That's who you are, right. I knew you looked familiar. I was sure my wife was some old woman, you know she turned—

(She puts her hand over his mouth.)

CONNIE: You are asking for it, old man.

(She kisses him. He looks at his watch.)

CONRAD: You're going to be late.

CONNIE: *(looking at her watch)* Ah! I am. Alright. Off I go. Love you.

CONRAD: You too. You're sure you want to take a cab?

CONNIE: And have you drive forty-five minutes each way for no reason? Cabs are designed expressly for this. Plus it will eat up your whole evening and I think you should go out.

CONRAD: I heard you the first four times.

CONNIE: Oh! I forgot. There are some meals I made in the fridge.

CONRAD laughs.

CONNIE: What?

CONRAD: Nothing.

CONNIE: What?

CONRAD: Meals. It just struck me as an odd word to say.

CONNIE: Food then.

CONRAD: Word doesn't matter. Thought that counts.

(Putting on her coat.)

CONNIE: Well we all know what happens when you get in the kitchen.

CONRAD: Applejack omelets are good and I'll stand by that until the day I die.

CONNIE: Serve them again and that day will come sooner rather than later.

CONRAD: Bon voyage.

CONNIE: Love you.

(She goes to the door. He air kisses at her, two kisses.)

CONRAD: *(with a small sudden urgency)* Before you go!

CONNIE: Yes?

CONRAD: 6 down: 9 letter word for how a hejira begins? I don't even know what that is, a hejira. . . these clues are so--where's my phone. . . ?

CONNIE: *(with knowledge)* A departure.

> *(That was it. He gives her a wink of thanks and writes it in. She watches him just a bit. Then back to her rushed and buoyant self while getting on her coat.)*

CONNIE: Go out. Do something. Belch in your underwear. Man things. Are you sure I can't get you your phone?

CONRAD: I don't know if I want to belch up two hundred dollar scotch, and no, thank you.

CONNIE: Perhaps it'll be half as expensive coming up.

CONRAD: I'll fill my time. I always do.

> *(She has her suitcase, is in her coat, her purse on her shoulder, she is about to leave then she stops and turns. An almost imperceptible shift in lights after her first sentence.)*

CONNIE: Will you be with men? Will you. . . ? As I know you've done countless times? Will you touch them? Will you look at them the way I deserve to be looked at but never have been? Not by you, not by anyone. But do I even deserve it? Who says we deserve looks of passion and complete admiration? I suppose we've been taught we will all be loved like that. It feels like it's on the Bill of Rights. This, that, and then to be looked at with an understanding that sates a restless soul.

Will it be in some desperate corner of the gym you go to and yet your clothes are never sweaty, in his bed, in his sad car, so he can drive the evidence away from his wife? Or do you bring them here? To our home. To our bed.

Will you? Do you top or do you bottom? I looked up the lingo online after I found a condom in your gym bag and thank you for using those that's very responsible it makes it possible for me to think you care for me still. Which you do. I see it. Your eyes. Care, yes, but is it still love? I'm not sure. Do you love them? Do you find yourself thinking of any of them when you're driving or at a store? Oh, Chip would like that. Peter does have a sweet tooth. What if I. . . —will you? Will you talk to them after? Do you talk? You're always so quiet with me. I wonder if you prefer quiet men too. Something maybe we have in common. Something, that if things were different we could giggle about, about how the same we really are. Do you lie to yourself? You lie to me, that's to be expected, we're married, but to yourself? Do you tell yourself you're a heterosexual man? Or do you admit to your desires? To the touching and penetration. And kissing. But does it go past that ever? Do you find your mind finding them when they aren't around the way that our union has allowed you to forget me. Should be added to the vows: do you promise to forget them little by little no matter how much you love them? I do.

Would it frighten you to know that it doesn't hurt me as much as you think it might? Would it hurt you to know that once I move past the pain I actually wouldn't mind having a peek? Would it frighten you to know I've touched myself thinking of you kissing our neighbor Glenn, the one you've caught me looking at, the one I've caught looking at you. The one whom when I allow myself to think about it is tender then rough. . . looking into your eyes.

Would it shatter you to know I know your secret? Do you need it to be one in order to do it? Would it destroy you to know that the only reason I feel I love you is because you keep this from me and if you told me the truth I'd leave not because of what you're doing but because I love your secret because it is the very definition of you and without it you'd undefine yourself, unravel, a word without a definition.

(The lights shift.)

Well then, don't stay up too late and eat too much ice cream.

CONRAD: You know I will.

CONNIE: I do. I do.

(She's leaving.)

CONNIE: Bye, my love.

CONRAD: Bye.

(She's gone. He watches her go. He goes back to his paper. Black.)

SHARPIES
DAVID NARTER

BEST 10 MINUTE PLAYS 2019

THE PLAY:

Sharpies

THE PLAYWRIGHT:

David Narter

SYNOPSIS:

Christina and Brett, desperate to see their child admitted to an exclusive preschool view his "audition" play date through an observation room window. Unfortunately, things go wrong. Horribly wrong!

ABOUT THE PLAYWRIGHT:

David Narter is a teacher and writer, and the host of the Chicago education salon, "Detention Hall." He is the author of the parody books, *The Worst Baby Name Book* and *Don't Name Your Baby*, which have been featured on CNN, ABC and WLS-Chicago. His essays have appeared in *English Journal* and *The Book Group Book*, and he is a frequent contributor to *The Heckler*.

CONTACT:

dnarter@mac.com
847-691-7672

THE THEATRE:

The Unknown Artists

MISSION:

The Unknown Artists' mission is to provide opportunities for talented, unknown individuals to thrive on a stage, enabling them to show off their gifts of music, acting, dance, comedy, film, and all categories of art. The Unknown Artists search far and wide for an explosive amount of talent that is of a specific, unheard of, untraveled artistry. Our goal: to make Unknown Artists KNOWN.

ABOUT:

The Unknown Artists was founded in 2007 in New York City by Emily Clark and Pamela Eberhardt. Our first NYC production was in 2007, and in 2010, the Unknown Artists moved to Los Angeles.

CONTACT:

Emily Clark
iamanunknownartist@gmail.com

PRESENTING THE PLAY:

Sharpies

CHARACTERS:

CHRISTINA: A willfully successful, business professional. Aggressive and addicted to her phone. Early 30's.

MR. GLENN: Derives a sense of authority and beneficence as the admissions officer of an exclusive daycare.

BRETT: A stay-at-home dad who is happy to let Christina take charge, as long as he doesn't have to. Early 30's.

SETTING:

The conference room of an upscale daycare.

TIME:

Morning.

(BRETT and CHRISTINA are in a waiting room in which there is a single chair upon which is a scattering of brochures and forms. CHRISTINA is pacing. Frequently, they look toward the audience - the window of the playroom.)

CHRISTINA: Oh, God. This is so nerve-wracking.

BRETT: No. Tyler's fine. He'll do fine.

(Long pause)

CHRISTINA: Did you talk with him last night?

BRETT: Excuse me?

CHRISTINA: When you two were out for ice cream, you were supposed to talk to him about this.

BRETT: About what? What am I supposed to tell him? Be smart?

CHRISTINA: So you didn't talk to him? Brett, you were supposed to let him know the situation and what was expected of him.

BRETT: Oh, Christina. C'mon. Does it really matter what I say to him? He's going to be doing arts and crafts and listening to storytime.

CHRISTINA: Yes, it matters! *(her phone rings)* Some of these kids are going to cry as soon as they get here and some kids are going to be comfortable in the situation and doing what they're supposed to do – maybe going beyond what's expected, Brett. Are you familiar with that expression, Brett? Beyond what's expected?

BRETT: Christina, I'll be happy if he doesn't eat the paste. *(ring)* Seriously, how does watching him play tell them anything about him.

CHRISTINA: It doesn't, Brett. It tells them about us.

BRETT: What?

CHRISTINA: How we parent. *(ring)* That's what they want to know.

BRETT: So this is about us. Don't you think that's a little self-centered?

CHRISTINA: *(ring)* Ugh!

(She rips the phone out of her purse and turns it off)

So did you tell Tyler anything at all, Brett?

BRETT: Well actually, I told him... *(in an announcer voice)* "kill the competition!"

CHRISTINA: What are you talking about?

BRETT: It's an ad. It was an ad for Home Depot or something. He was a little freaked out, and I told him it was a figure of speech about competition and doing your best. I told him...confidence. *(reconsiders and then comes back to it)* Confidence.

CHRISTINA: Oh. Oh. Well, good.

BRETT: Yeah. You know, I wasn't really talking about this at all though. It was actually – to be honest, I think he was kind of freaked out about the slogan. So, I just kind of generalized.

CHRISTINA: Well, sure. You tell a toddler to "kill the..."

BRETT: Right. Listen, Christina, I said that there's lots of people and you have to do your best if you want to get noticed. That's all.

CHRISTINA: Right. Well good. That's good. That's good. So why didn't you just tell me that when I asked?

BRETT: Because I wasn't really talking about this. I mean I think he really thought about it, but I don't remember if I really said anything specific about today.

CHRISTINA: Hmm. Well, that's fine. I did.

BRETT: Yeah? When?

CHRISTINA: When we were driving in.

BRETT: What'd you say?

CHRISTINA: Same as you.

BRETT: Yeah?

CHRISTINA: Yeah, I told him that there are a lot of other kids who he'll see in his life and a lot in the room today and there are winners and there are losers. I told him it's best to think of himself as the sun and always make sure the teacher can see him shining bright.And that it is his job to be sure no one got in the way of his sunshine.

(Long pause)

BRETT: Oh.

CHRISTINA: I just reminded him that it's a big world. And one little person can get crowded out by a lot of the mediocrity around him if he doesn't make sure he gets himself in the front of the line. Just like you – kill the competition.

BRETT: Just like me? I told him to be confident! I didn't tell him to "kill the competition"!

CHRISTINA: Well, neither did I.

BRETT: Are you kidding????

CHRISTINA: *(realizing this is getting out of hand)* Brett. Brett. Listen. Listen. You said it before. This isn't about Tyler. It's about us.

BRETT: I didn't say that. You did.

CHRISTINA: Anyway. We don't want to be arguing when they're watching him. Tyler is going to be Tyler and he's a part of us both. And I'm sure they'll see the best of us when they see him.

Okay? Okay?

BRETT: Yeah, you're - right. *(looks to audience: a glass through which they can see Tyler play)*

Hey, there he is!

CHRISTINA: Hey, baby. Who's my little handsome man?

(MR. GLENN enters)

MR. GLENN: Oh, he can't see you. That's a one-way window – or mirror. I suppose it all depends on which side you're on.

BRETT: Well, that's a little creepy.

MR. GLENN: Oh, for the most part it's pretty benign. We use it to evaluate staff members usually. But of course, assuming Tyler is accepted into the program, you're always welcome to watch him play without affecting the…the chemistry of the classroom environment.

CHRISTINA: Oh. That's nice. What a little fella. He's gonna do a little painting.

MR. GLENN: He's an interesting young man.

CHRISTINA: Really?!

MR. GLENN: Absolutely. We had a good conversation before we went in. He told me he got ice cream last night.

BRETT: Yes he did.

MR. GLENN: He also said something about the radio scaring him. It seems he was a little anxious about it.

CHRISTINA: Really?

BRETT: Yeah. There was some ad - really freaked him out. I changed the station.

CHRISTINA: Yeah. Tyler's a very quiet – well - thoughtful boy. He thinks a lot.

(long pause)

MR. GLENN: Well, that's good.

BRETT: Oh, look at that. He's got himself a girlfriend.

CHRISTINA: No, no. Tyler's teaching her how to paint.

BRETT: Yeah, how bout that? They're painting together.

CHRISTINA: No. He's teaching her.

MR. GLENN: Really?

CHRISTINA: He's teaching her how to paint. See he's helping her hold the brush. No. No. Take turns, now. Hmm.

BRETT: Whoa, yeah that's not a lesson. That's a fight.

CHRISTINA: Nonsense, he's helping her, but she's not paying attention.

BRETT: Hmm. Nope they're fighting over that brush. Yeah, that's a fight.

CHRISTINA: Well, of course it's not a fight. Tyler is twice her size. He's helping her.

BRETT: I don't know. Okay, that's a shove.

CHRISTINA: Hey, now! That really was a shove. That little girl just pushed Tyler down. Mr. Glenn, shouldn't the teacher be interceding at some point?

MR. GLENN: I'm not sure that she's seen it yet. Oh!

(All of them gasp in horror)

BRETT: Oh, my God. That's just right in her eye!

CHRISTINA: No, of course it isn't.

BRETT: Oh, it's in there.

MR. GLENN: Oh dear. *(calling to be heard through the window)* Mrs. Schiff!

CHRISTINA: That's not his fault.

BRETT: Christina.

CHRISTINA: It's not his fault. That girl was pulling and he just let go. He was letting her have the brush. He was being generous!

MR. GLENN: Finally, she's noticed.

BRETT: Whoa that was quick!

MR. GLENN: We do have a nurse on sight. And if that button is pushed…well, as you can see, she's there in an instant.

BRETT: Jeez, I am so sorry…I don't know what happened there.

CHRISTINA: It was an accident.

MR. GLENN: Of course. Of course it was.

CHRISTINA: Tyler no, no. No, honey. There are other brushes, you don't need that one. Not that one!

(Horrified gasp from all three)

BRETT: Oh. That just popped right out.

CHRISTINA: What? Why is she yelling at Tyler? Oh, c'mon now. She's just upsetting him more.

BRETT: *(rushing offstage)* Okay, this is over. I'm going …

(offstage)

Mr. Glenn. Do you have a key?

MR. GLENN: No. I didn't even know there was a lock.

BRETT: *(offstage)* Well, there's something keeping this from opening!

MR. GLENN: Dear God. He's locked us in here.

CHRISTINA: That's ridiculous. Tyler could not have done that.

BRETT: *(offstage)* There's no way out!!!

CHRISTINA: Tyler, honey. This is mommy. It's okay. It's okay.

MR. GLENN: He's going for the scissors!

BRETT: *(reentering)* No, Tyler!

CHRISTINA: Tyler! Tyler! Use the roundies, honey. Not the sharpies, not the sharpies!

> *(Both men freeze and look at Christina in shock. Then, looking back at the window, they all gasp in terror)*

BRETT: There goes the nurse.

MR. GLENN: *(patting his pockets)* He's taken my cellphone!

BRETT: Christina. Your phone.

CHRISTINA: Don't be rude, Brett.

> *(Brett makes a dash for her purse and rifles through it till he gets the phone)*

CHRISTINA: No. No. Tyler. That's not nice. Gentle hands. Gentle hands.

BRETT: *(fumbling with the phone)* C'monC'mon!

CHRISTINA: Don't you run with those scissors.

MR. GLENN: Why is he climbing up there? *(Their eyes follow him up a jungle gym)*

CHRISTINA: He's playing king of the mountain! He's a little Moufasa! *(She does a tiny wave)* Look, Brett. They're all his little subjects!

> *(Their eyes follow him jumping from the jungle gym. Again, the men gasp in horror and Brett drops the phone.)*

BRETT: Oh, God.

CHRISTINA: Tyler. Mouths are for food. No biting! No!

MR. GLENN: Oh, that's the entire ear!

CHRISTINA: Tyler, no! People are not food! No!

(Suddenly they all exhale.)

MR. GLENN: Oh, dear God.

CHRISTINA: Oh, look who's tired. No. No. Find your own space. Let her sleep. No! *(As the men become even more shocked)* Hands to yourself, Tyler. That's your body! Hands to yourself!

MR. GLENN: How did he…? He knew exactly where the heart was.

BRETT: Well, that's something.

CHRISTINA: We have a few anatomy CD's. He's very advanced.

MR. GLENN: Dear God, he's walking to window.

BRETT: It's like he can see us.

MR. GLENN: He's looking right at us!

CHRISTINA: Hi, baby. *(In baby talk)* Who's got the messy red hands? Who's my messy boy? No. No.Wipe on a towel sweety. Not the window.

MR. GLENN: *(recoiling in terror)* He sees us! He sees us!

CHRISTINA: Don't be silly. He's writing letters. C – O –

MR. GLENN: They're backwards. Oh God! He can see us!

CHRISTINA: I know. He is very smart. Aren't you Tyler sweetie! Aren't you!

BRETT: N – F – I – D –

MR. GLENN: Confidence. He spelled confidence.

CHRISTINA: Oh, my little Moufasa is tired. Look at the little angel. He's just gonna lie down and have a"widdle nappie."

(She watches him lovingly while Mr. Glenn cowers in the corner, panting)

BRETT: Mr. Glenn. I'm so…well, I just don't know what to say.

MR. GLENN: There's nothing to say.

BRETT: Of course. Of course…I just…this is just…unbelievable.

MR. GLENN: Yes. Yes.

(He collects himself and organizes his notes. He then pulls two sheets from the stack.)

Well. You'll need to fill out these two forms. And I'll need a copy of Tyler's physical and a copy of your insurance card.

BLACKOUT

SHIMMERS
LINDSAY PARTAIN

THE PLAY:

Shimmers

THE PLAYWRIGHT:

Lindsay Partain

SYNOPSIS:

Amanda and Ryan take a walk through the forest on the darkest night of the year to find the spot where magic exists for those who are willing to see and give it.

ABOUT THE PLAYWRIGHT:

Lindsay Partain is an Oregon playwright, an editor for the online literary magazine Cascadia Rising Review, and a member of the Dramatists Guild. She received her B.A. in Theatre from Pacific University in Forest Grove, OR. Recently her work has been produced by the John DeSotelle Studio in New York ("Prayers in the Pines", "Shimmers" & "Dark Horse"), Five & Dime Drama Collective in Arkansas ("Until the Earth Breaks Open"), and was a finalist at the Midwest Dramatist Conference ("Last Dance with MJ"). Her collection of work is available on New Play Exchange.

CONTACT:

lgpartain@gmail.com
971-227-0483

WEBSITE:

lindsaypartain.com

PRESENTING THE PLAY:

Shimmers

THE CHARACTERS:

AMANDA...Late teens-early 20s. Female. Sweet; sincere; blind.

RYAN... Late teens-early 20s. Male. Young for his age; falling in love.

THE SETTING:

The middle of the forest on the darkest night of the year.

(AMANDA and RYAN, fast friends, take a very important walk through the forest on the darkest night of the year. AMANDA walks hesitantly but RYAN gently holds her linked arm and leads them both through the trees and the darkness.)

AMANDA: Ry- wait, just, hang on a minute.

RYAN: You okay? Did you trip?

AMANDA: No, I'm fine. I just- it's nothing.

Is it time yet? We've been walking awhile.

(RYAN looks up into the night sky)

RYAN: Almost. Are you cold? You're shivering.

AMANDA: Hm? Oh, no. I'm alright.

RYAN: You can have my jacket if you like?

AMANDA: N-no. No thanks. Really, I'm not cold.

You remembered to bring them didn't you?

RYAN: I remembered. I've got them right here. *(Touches his pocket)* You're sure you're alright?

AMANDA: I just, I really don't like the dark.

RYAN: But you're—

AMANDA: Don't mention it.

RYAN: But if you're scared—

AMANDA: -I never said I was scared—

RYAN: What I meant to say is that, if you don't like the dark, it— well it must be awful.

AMANDA: Is it time yet?

RYAN: Nearly.

AMANDA: Don't let go of my hand, kay?

RYAN: I won't.

AMANDA: I remember this. I can see it in my head perfectly.

RYAN: How's that? Watch your step, there's a fallen tree. Here, let me help.

AMANDA: I- thank you- I know it by the smell. The pine and the wet rock and the lemon balm. The feel of the moss on my palm. It must have just rained.

RYAN: It seems that way.

AMANDA: What can you see? Paint me a picture.

RYAN: Not much I'm afraid. It's very dark. The darkest night of the whole year I think.

AMANDA: Certainly seems that way.

RYAN: But you remember this place? It wasn't always like this? You didn't used to be-

AMANDA: No. I used to be able to-

RYAN: Did you get sick or something?

AMANDA: I gave it to someone.

RYAN: I don't understand. What do you mean you gave it?

AMANDA: I gave it to someone—it was a very special gift.

RYAN: But you're afra- you don't like the dark though?

AMANDA: It's not so bad. You kind of get used to it after a while.

RYAN: I guess you have to.

AMANDA: I don't have to do anything. I chose this.

RYAN: So, who did you give it to?

AMANDA: Her name is Amalia. Is it very nearly time?

RYAN: Soon. Did she ask for it?

AMANDA: No. No, how can you ask for something like that? I simply gave it to her.

RYAN: I don't understand.

AMANDA: Perhaps you aren't meant to. It was her wedding day. She was looking right into the beginning of her forever, if you believe that something like that can be a kind of forever. And the way he looked at her, with such- perfect joy. Swelling in his eyes, choking up his throat, making his fists tight around her little hand. He never looked at me like that.

It was a very special gift. She deserved to see how beautiful a thing she had. It was then, during the ceremony. He was looking at her, both of them holding the other so tight. She was crying and he- he reached up his hand *[she shows Ryan]* and, with his thumb, gently wiped away the tears from her eyes.

The last thing I saw was the look on his face when the clouds left her eyes for the first time. Afterwards I could hear their beating hearts, loud as drums. Sometimes when I dream I can still hear them.

RYAN: But why would you—

AMANDA: I forgot to bring a gift.

RYAN: But that doesn't mean that you—

AMANDA: It was mine to give to whoever I wanted. And I wanted to give it to Amalia.

RYAN: It's nearly time now.

AMANDA: Have you ever been in a position to give someone something of great importance? Something of great beauty? Something, greater than yourself?

RYAN: We're nearly there.

AMANDA: There are always doubts. You can be staring it right in the face. The most. Perfect person. Someone who deserves it so completely. And you'll want to keep it for yourself. Keep your gift. You start to wonder, do they really? Could they really? And most of the time, they do and they could, and there will come a moment where you will see your gift again. You always hope you will see it often enough to enjoy it. Pretend that it's still yours. So that you know perfectly well that you made the right choice. That you chose the right person. A worthy person.

RYAN: This is it. We're here. *(RYAN lets go of AMANDA and walks away.)* Just, close your eyes and stay right here.

(She covers her eyes with her hands. She's getting nervous.)

AMANDA: Ryan?

RYAN: I'll only be a moment.

(RYAN reaches into his pocket and pulls out hundreds of millions of little stars. He begins to walk around the clearing and throws them into the sky, lighting up in shades of pink, purple, and blue. Somewhere in the forest a slow and gentle hang drum plays--like bamboo wind chimes caught in the breeze.)

AMANDA: Ryan?

RYAN: Amanda?

AMANDA: Can I?

RYAN: Go ahead. *(Slowly AMANDA opens her eyes up to the sky, she can barely breathe.)* Can you-? Do you see them?

(She nods stiffly, not wanting to move her eyes for fear of losing sight. RYAN goes to her, takes both her hands, painting them the colors of the Northern Lights.)

AMANDA: *(Enamored)* Yea, I- I can-- I can-

(RYAN lifts her hand into the sky and paints the skies with green and violet. He's watching her face light up with the stars. Hands painted with stars, AMANDA watches the night sky, RYAN watches her.)

(Lights out. End of play.)

THE OFFER
BELLA POYNTON

BEST 10 MINUTE PLAYS 2019

THE PLAY:

The Offer

THE PLAYWRIGHT:

Bella Poynton

SYNOPSIS:

Grace was fired from NASA along with 30,000 other astrophysicists and engineers after the shuttle program was dismantled in 2009. Since then, she worked odd jobs until landing a gig at Virgin Enterprises. Grace's work at Virgin has been bold and innovative but is strictly theoretical. Today, she has been invited back to NASA for a meeting with her old boss.

ABOUT THE PLAYWRIGHT:

Bella Poynton is a playwright, director, and a PhD Candidate from Buffalo, NY. She is a Regional Playwriting Resident at Road Less Traveled Productions, and the Artistic Director of The Navigators Theatre Company, focusing on feminist science fiction. Recently, her artistic work has been produced and developed by Otherworld Theatre, Quantum Dragon Theatre, The Bechdel Group, The Alleyway Theatre Company, and MadLab Theatre, and Post-Industrial Productions. She has been a finalist for the Samuel French Off-Off Broadway Festival, the Heideman award, and the Bloomington Playwrights Project. Her research interests include representations of robots and AI in performance, object oriented ontology, and the history of playwriting. MFA: The Iowa Playwrights Workshop.

CONTACT: bdpoynton@gmail.com, 716-491-4744

WEBSITE: bellapoynton.com

THE THEATRE:

> The Samuel French Off Off Broadway Short Play Festival
> 235 Park Avenue South, Fifth Floor, New York, NY 10003

MISSION:

> The Samuel French Off Off Broadway Short Play Festival (OOB) is the nation's leading short play festival. Beyond playwrights, the Festival has given voice to many emerging directors, performers, and production companies. As part of our unique model that requires playwrights to partner with sponsoring producers, we've hosted prestigious theatre companies on our Festival stage such as The Royal Court, Circle-in-the-Square, Ensemble Studio Theatre, and The Yale School of Drama. It is an honor to provide a home for so many exceptional artists, and we're humbled when thinking back to the many great performances that have happened on our stage.

ABOUT:

> The Samuel French Off Off Broadway Short Play Festival offers a prize of publication and licensing for six short plays in the notable OFF OFF BROADWAY FESTIVAL PLAYS series. The application period for the Festival begins in late fall and lasts for four weeks. Playwrights may submit one unpublished play or musical that may be up to 15 pages in length and a max run time of 20 minutes (ideal run times are between 8-13 minutes). All submissions are read by the Festival's staff, and 30 semi-finalists are chosen to present their play during Festival week. Festival week starts with four nights of performance sessions that are presented in front of a judging panel comprised of professionals representing various parts of the theatre industry. At the end of each session, the judges deliberate, and one to three plays are selected to move on to the Festival Finals. During the Finals, the Festival staff will watch the final 10 to 12 plays and select six authors to be a published in the Off Off Broadway Short Play Festival series, which is published and licensed by Samuel French, Inc.

CONTACT: oobfestival@samuelfrench.com, 212-206-8990

WEBSITE: www.oobfestival.com

PRESENTING THE PLAY:

The Offer

CHARACTERS

ROGER –One of the Project Managers of NASA's Kepler Deep Space Telescope.

GRACE – An engineer and particle physicist. Used to work for NASA.

TIME:

The present

PLACE:

Roger Hunter's office at the Kepler Deep Space Telescope site in Mount View, California

NOTE:

In the script, both Grace and Roger refer to the year 2023 as "five years from now." Please change this year to whatever is five years from the current year of production.

(At rise, Roger Hunter, the program head of the Kepler deep space telescope, is sitting alone at his desk. The door opens slowly and a young woman, Grace, in dickies and maybe a polo shirt, walks in. She's in her early 30's. Roger immediately places his feet down on the floor again.)

GRACE: Your secretary said you were ready to see me now, sir?

ROGER: Yes, yes! I'm so sorry—Grace, come in. Sit down. I didn't mean to keep you waiting. Sorry about the um—

(Roger gestures to the mess on his desk.)

ROGER: Coffee? You want some coffee? I can get you—

GRACE: No. Thank you.

(Grace sits awkwardly in the empty chair on the opposite side of the desk.)

ROGER: Course not! You get called into the big office, no one ever wants coffee. Too nervous, right?

GRACE: I'm not nervous sir.

(An awkward pause.)

ROGER: No? Well, good. Jeez, I would be! I haven't seen you since—

GRACE: Since my last ISS briefing. Five years ago.

ROGER: Yes! Wow. Feels like five months, doesn't it?

GRACE: It feels like five years ago, sir.

(Pause.)

ROGER: ... Hey! So, I hear you've been doing some fantastic stuff over at Virgin. I've been following your work. Very nice. Very economical.

GRACE: Thank you, but NASA fired me, Mr. Hunter. So, I guess it wasn't nice enough.

(Pause.)

GRACE: ... I'm sorry. That was inappropriate.

ROGER: We had to fire a lot of people, Grace. You know that. I didn't make those decisions—I was just the person who had to—...Do you know why I called you in today?

GRACE: I know NASA recently started working with Apple on some micro-technologies, but I'm more of a large-scale person. So, I have no idea, really. I didn't even think I was on your radar anymore.

ROGER: Well, you're wrong. I've been speaking with Virgin about your work recently.

GRACE: I—had no idea Kepler was speaking with Virgin. Was there something I was supposed to prepare?

ROGER: All right, I get it. You can stop it with the formalities, Grace. Come on.

GRACE: Look, I'm sorry, but you did fire me, remember? With nowhere to go, and nothing to do. No back-up plan. Nothing.

ROGER: Do you think I wanted to fire you? Do you think I wanted to fire any of you? Do you think I like that the space program was completely shut down? I don't. But I didn't have a choice, just like I didn't have a choice when it came to you. You forget, I was an astronaut too, once. Until they tossed me here to be a professional paper pusher. I'm sorry. But hey, I heard you were working for Dell within a few months of leaving, and that's a lot better than most of the guys. Some of them are still unemployed.

GRACE: You shouldn't believe rumors. I'm an aeronautical engineer, not a computer geek. That Ph.D. in Theoretical Particle Physics doesn't do you much good trying to get rid of malware on PC's from 2005. Dell said I was over qualified, so I wound up working at Office Depot for a year. They didn't seem to care what kind of degrees I had, as long as I showed up and was nice to the customers. Which, believe me, was hard. Then I taught one class adjunct at Santa Clara. One. Class. Until Virgin called. At least I wasn't waitressing, right? So, are you going to give me my job back? I know you're not, but I still have to ask.

ROGER: How's the Mars project coming along?

GRACE: I'm not really sure if I'm allowed to discuss that with you. I signed a nondisclosure.

ROGER: Are you referring to this nondisclosure?

(Roger holds up the nondisclosure agreement.)

GRACE: How did you get that?

ROGER: Kepler's been working with Virgin for nearly two years. So, let's chat.

GRACE: Two years? Why am I just finding out about this now?

ROGER: There was no need for you to know before. Tell me how the project is going?

GRACE: You obviously know already. If you've been working with them that long.

ROGER: But I want to hear it from you. You're the one actually making the stuff. Does it work? In your opinion.

GRACE: Well, yes. As far as I can tell. But no one will really know until the stuff is actually up there being used, which won't happen in my lifetime. Honestly, I doubt anything like that will happen for at least 50 years. So, it's all just… fun and games for now. Lately, I've been working out some blueprints for the rover, and a self-sustaining pod living system. It's fun. I get to dream stuff up and try to make it as if it were real. It's like… extreme make-believe. But my work is only a tiny piece of the puzzle.

ROGER: They said the pod design was flawless. Nearly indestructible.

GRACE: Well, that was the assignment. But again, it's all theoretical.

ROGER: Is it? It didn't seem very theoretical when they tested it.

GRACE: How could they have tested it?

ROGER: The same way you test anything. You weren't told about it, of course. They didn't want to create any anxiety or disappointment if it failed. Morale is important. Specifically, yours.

GRACE: Wait—you're telling me my pods were tested? Where? When?

ROGER: A simulated Martian landscape in Nevada. About 5 months ago.

GRACE: Are you serious? What were the results? Who do I need to talk to? What do I need to fix?

ROGER: You don't need to fix anything.

(Pause)

ROGER: Which makes the mission much less theoretical than they've led you to believe.

That's why you're here today. There's really no easy way to tell you this, except to say that the work you've done in the past few years has pushed the reality of the Mars Mission up from 2040 to more like 2023. And they'd like you to go.

(Pause.)

GRACE: There must be some kind of mistake.

I'm not even a pilot, I have no—

ROGER: You wouldn't be flying the damn shuttle. You made the living system. The idea came out of your head, so they're going to need you there to fix the thing when shit goes wrong. And you know as well as I do that shit always goes wrong. You've been up to the ISS twice, what are you afraid of?

GRACE: Roger, 2023 is way too soon. It's only five years from now.

ROGER: Which is why training would start soon. I know, that probably seems like a lot more prep than is standard, but this is new territory. Literally.

GRACE: How big would the first party be?

ROGER: Small. Five or Six.

GRACE: Who else is going?

ROGER: I don't know the exact details, I just know that they're pretty avid about you being a part of the initial settlers.

(Grace is a bit dazed, staring off, overwhelmed.)

GRACE: In 2023, I'll be… I'll probably be the oldest person going.

ROGER: Probably. Of course, you're welcome to say no.

GRACE: Would you say no?

ROGER: This isn't about me.

GRACE: But would you?

ROGER: I don't know. I'd have to think about it. For a long time. It's a lot like—

GRACE: Dying.

ROGER: That's not what I was going to say.

GRACE: But it is. Like dying. That's part of the deal with Mars. You don't come back. No one ever comes back.

ROGER: I'm familiar with the parameters of the program—

GRACE: You go. And you stay—

ROGER: Again, if you're not interested, that's absolutely understandable—

GRACE: And you die there.

(Pause)

ROGER: That is true. You would die there. But not right away. The truth is, you'll probably live a long damn time up there. The filtered air will be a lot cleaner than what you're breathing here, and they won't let you eat the crap we pump into ourselves on Earth. So, really, you would probably be the first human being to live, die, and be buried there. And I'd say that's pretty momentous, wouldn't you? Your name in the history books. Little kids will do their school reports on you. For the rest of forever.

GRACE: What do I care about school reports? I'll be long gone.

ROGER: We'll all be long gone pretty soon. That's how time works. It passes whether we want it to or not. They taught you about time while you were doing your fancy PhD, didn't they?

(Pause)

ROGER: Listen, you can stay here and teach Physics 101 if you like—Make your little drawings of rovers and life pods and go see movies about space explorers at the damn cinema. There's no shame in that. That's probably what I would do if I were you. But I'm not you. You're a lot braver than I am. And you can go with them. Will it be lonely? Sure, maybe a little. But so is life here most of the time.

(A pause. After a moment, when Grace does not respond, Roger sighs and throws his hands up in the air.)

219

ROGER: All right. I understand. I'll give them a call and let them know you're not interested in the offer.

(Roger reaches for his phone, but at the last moment, Grace leans forward and places a hand on his to stop him.)

GRACE: I never said I wasn't interested.

(Blackout.)

End Of Play

HOW NICE OF YOU TO ASK
RICH RUBIN

BEST 10 MINUTE PLAYS 2019

THE PLAY:

How Nice of You to Ask

THE PLAYWRIGHT:

Rich Rubin

SYNOPSIS:

Alan makes his living by asking some very personal questions. Between sips of tea, Mavis responds with even more personal answers. What could possibly go wrong?

ABOUT THE PLAYWRIGHT:

Rich Rubin's plays have been produced throughout the U.S. and internationally in Europe, Asia, Australia, New Zealand, Canada and Mexico. His full-length plays include Swimming Upstream (winner, Todd McNerney Playwright Award; finalist, Reva Shiner Comedy Award), Caesar's Blood (finalist, Oregon Book Award; finalist, Ashland New Play Festival), Left Hook (finalist, Woodward-Newman Drama Award), September Twelfth (finalist, Playwrights First Award), Cottonwood in the Flood (winner, Fratti-Newman Political Play Award), Marilyn/MISFITS/Miller (finalist, Julie Harris Playwright Award), Assisted Living (winner, Neil Simon Festival New Play Competition), and Shakespeare's Skull (winner, Portland Civic Theatre Guild New Play Award). Rich is a proud member of the Dramatists Guild and Portland's Nameless Playwrights and LineStorm Playwrights. www.richrubinplaywright.com

CONTACT:

rhjarubin@aol.com

WEBSITE:

richrubinplaywright.com

THE THEATRE:

The Parish Players
Eclipse Grange Theater,
193 Academy Road, Thetford, VT 05074

VISION:

Over the past fifty-two years, the Parish Players Theater Company – located in the historic Eclipse Grange Hall in Thetford, Vermont – has embodied the concept of community engagement in the performing arts. As an organization created and continued by volunteers, the Parish Players Theater Company seeks to provide an infrastructure of talent and physical space that attracts all members of the community, from novice to professional, to participate in the living stage as an impetus for artistic achievement. The Parish Players hopes that such artistic achievement will continue and increase as a valued feature of our community.

ABOUT:

The Parish Players celebrated its 50th birthday in 2016, and is still going strong. The theater's players have produced more than 360 productions created through the tireless efforts of volunteers united by a shared enthusiasm for stories, community, and the power of theater to reach people's hearts and motivate change. The community benefit is immeasurable, as is the exact number of performers and audiences who have participated in Parish Players productions.

Always an audience favorite, and a cornerstone of our annual performance offerings, the TENS festival showcases eight 10-minute plays from authors around the globe. In 2018 over 400 short plays were submitted for consideration, and we're delighted that How Nice of You To Ask was one of the plays selected for production.

CONTACT:

ToniEgger81@gmail.com
802-785-4344

WEBSITE:

parishplayers.org

PRESENTING THE PLAY:

How Nice Of You To Ask

(Lights up on ALAN, a somewhat nerdy man in his late twenties, seated on one of two chairs at a small dining room table. Alan is neatly dressed in khaki pants and a white or blue button-down shirt open at the collar. A pencil and a several-page questionnaire are positioned directly in front of him. The scene begins with Alan calling out to the off-stage MAVIS, a woman in her seventies.)

ALAN: *(calling off-stage)* I hope you don't mind, Mrs. Steinloaf. There are quite a few questions.

MAVIS: *(off-stage)* Please call me Mavis.

ALAN: *(calling off-stage)* OK, I will. And please call me Alan.

MAVIS pokes her head in from stage-left. Mavis is a petite woman wearing minimal makeup, her hair conservatively coiffed. Her clothes are similarly conservative and age-appropriate.

MAVIS: Alan. What a nice name. I have a great-nephew named Alan … Or maybe it's Alex … Would you like a cup of tea, dear?

ALAN: A cup of tea would be very nice, thank you.

Mavis exits. She calls out to Alan from off-stage.

MAVIS: *(off-stage)* I only have Lipton. I hope that's alright.

ALAN: *(calling off-stage)* Whatever you have is fine.

MAVIS: *(off-stage)* Some people my age, they keep all sorts of tea on the shelf. Jasmine, lemon, ginger, mint … you name it, they've got it.

Mavis returns, carrying a tray with two cups of tea as well as a sugar bowl and creamer. She lays the tray on the table and repositions its contents.

MAVIS: To me, all that variety, it's crazy. I mean, why make it complicated when you can just keep it simple? Makes no sense. Does it make any sense to you?

ALAN: I guess I never really thought about it.

Mavis hands Alan a cup of tea.

ALAN: Thank you.

MAVIS: So what were you just saying about questions?

ALAN: This survey, Mavis, it has quite a few questions. I hope that's OK.

MAVIS: Oh, sure it's OK ... Just remind me. What kind of survey did you say this was?

ALAN: It's what I mentioned on the phone.

MAVIS: On the phone?

ALAN: When I called yesterday, remember?

MAVIS: Of course I remember. You're the nice man who called about my freezer, right?

ALAN: No, that must've been some other nice man.

MAVIS: That wasn't you? You mean you didn't come over to talk about refrigerators?

ALAN: No, sorry. Not refrigerators.

MAVIS: Oh. That's too bad. 'Cause the stories I could tell you about mine, you wouldn't believe half of them. Once it got so cold in there my tangerines ...

ALAN: Sorry to interrupt, but my survey, it's about something else.

MAVIS: It's not about my old Amana?

ALAN: No. It's about ... sex.

MAVIS: Sex?

ALAN: That's right. It's a sex survey. It's a survey that asks questions about sex.

MAVIS: Oh my. A survey about sex. What'll they think of next? So tell me: You make a nice living doing this?

ALAN: I don't. Not really. But Professor Carney does. Sort of. But he's been doing this a long time. Me, I'm just starting out. I joined the team just a month ago.

MAVIS: The team?

ALAN: You know, the research team.

MAVIS: These days you can do research on sex?

ALAN: Of course.

MAVIS: And they don't arrest you?

ALAN: No, no … it's perfectly legal. I'm interviewing lots of people. Lots of your neighbors. Right here in this very building. This very floor.

MAVIS: Really? And what did they tell you?

ALAN: Well, actually …

MAVIS: Whatever the men told you I would divide in two. And whatever the women told you I would double. That would be my advice.

ALAN: Thank you. That's very helpful. Is it OK if we start?

MAVIS: Certainly. Ask anything you'd like. Just ask away.

Mavis pours some whitish granules into her tea.

ALAN: What's that?

MAVIS: Metamucil. Would you like some?

ALAN: No, not right now. Maybe later. Hopefully much later … So here's the first question: Are you currently engaging in any kind of sexual activity?

MAVIS: Am I currently engaging in any kind of sexual activity.

ALAN: Yes.

MAVIS: *(pause)* You mean this minute?

ALAN: No. Not this minute. Say in the past month.

MAVIS: In the past month. Any sex in the past month … Why? Did someone in the building tell you I had sex in the past month?

ALAN: No, but that's not a question I asked them.

MAVIS: Good … Did anyone in the building tell you they had sex in the past month?

ALAN: I'm sorry, I can't answer that. All the responses are confidential.

MAVIS: If Mrs. Goldfarb said "no", don't believe her. You should see the way she looks at that poor Mr. Fineberg in the elevator.

ALAN: Is it OK if we go to the next question?

MAVIS: Sure. Why not?

ALAN: OK. Here goes: Do you prefer having sex with men, women or both?

MAVIS: Did you just say "both"?

ALAN: Yes. Men, women or both.

MAVIS: By both, you mean at the same time?

ALAN: No, that's not …

MAVIS: 'Cause there was this one night in Poughkeepsie back in '68 when …

ALAN: That's fine. I'm just gonna write down "men", OK?

MAVIS: Sure, why not? Keep it simple, right?

ALAN: The next question is a little more personal.

MAVIS: More personal? How much more personal can it get?

ALAN: Well, maybe just a little. Here's the question: If you had to estimate, what would you say is the total number of sexual partners you've had?

MAVIS: The total number of sexual partners I've had. You said an estimate?

ALAN: That's right. Just an estimate. You know … only one, two to five, six to ten, etcetera.

MAVIS: You mean just in the past month?

ALAN: No. Lifetime.

MAVIS: OK, now I understand. You want a lifetime estimate.

ALAN: Yes.

MAVIS: Alright. Let me see … But understand this is only a rough guess.

ALAN: That's all I need.

MAVIS: Two hundred forty-six.

ALAN: What?

MAVIS: Or two forty-seven. Depending on how you count the night in Poughkeepsie.

ALAN: Two forty-six.

MAVIS: Or seven.

ALAN: Two forty-seven.

MAVIS: You sound surprised.

ALAN: No … no, I …

MAVIS: Tell me the truth: You thought it'd be less or more?

ALAN: It's not my place to venture a …

MAVIS: Oh, come on … Don't you always make a little bet with yourself beforehand? I know I would.

ALAN: No, that's not the way it works.

MAVIS: No?

ALAN: No. I'm a professional.

MAVIS: I see. You're a professional. What kind of professional? A sex professional?

ALAN: No … Yes … No, I mean …

MAVIS: Admit it. You are a sex professional.

ALAN: Except that's not the terminology we usually …

MAVIS: You ask other people what they like to do in the bedroom, right?

ALAN: Well, yes …

MAVIS: And you get paid for what you do, right?

ALAN: Well, of course …

MAVIS: And you even get, you know, a little extra professional zing from your work sometime, right?

ALAN: Well, I wouldn't exactly call it …

MAVIS: So face it: You're a sex professional.

ALAN: That's not the way …

MAVIS: Look: When you do your income tax in April and they ask you what you do for a living, what are you gonna write down?

ALAN: Well, I hadn't really thought about …

MAVIS: Trust me: The one thing you should never do is lie to the government. Just tell 'em the truth and write down sex professional.

ALAN: No, I don't think I'm going to …

MAVIS: Why? You think it's something to be ashamed of?

ALAN: No, it's not that, it's …

MAVIS: You know who else was a sex professional? I don't mean recently, of course, but years ago, before approaching maturity?

ALAN: No, who?

MAVIS: Me, that's who. Penthouse at the Plaza. Nice view of the park. Cadillac clientele.

ALAN: You were a sex professional?

MAVIS: What? You thought I'm the sort of person who'd have sex with hundreds of men and not get paid for it? Just what kind of a girl do you think I am?

ALAN: Well, I …

MAVIS: Except what I told you before, it wasn't exactly true.

ALAN: It wasn't?

MAVIS: No. I didn't have sex with two hundred forty-six men.

ALAN: You didn't?

MAVIS: No. It wasn't two forty-six. It was five forty-six.

ALAN: Five forty-six?

MAVIS: That's right. Five forty-six. If we're talking only men.

ALAN: But why …?

MAVIS: 'Cause I didn't want you to get the wrong impression of me, that's why. But let me tell you something: Those five hundred and forty-six men? I can still remember the names of each and every one of 'em.

ALAN: You can?

MAVIS: Tell you the truth, it's not all that hard. Most of them were named "John."

ALAN: But gosh … I guess I'm still a little surprised.

MAVIS: Why? Can't you remember the names of all the people you've had sex with?

ALAN: Well, yes. But that's only been four people.

MAVIS: So what are you saying? Because I'm approaching maturity, I can't remember the names of five hundred forty-six men? Plus that lady in Poughkeepsie?

ALAN: No, that's not what …

MAVIS: You sure it's only been four, Alan?

ALAN: Well, yes, but …

MAVIS: What's the matter? You don't get out much?

ALAN: No, I …

MAVIS: Tell me the truth: What's your favorite position?

ALAN: Huh?

MAVIS: You ever try the inverted goldfish?

ALAN: What?

MAVIS: If you'd like, I could take you through it … but you'd probably have to do some stretching first.

ALAN: No, I … *(looks at his watch)* You know something? I think my time's just about up.

Alan starts to gather his papers.

MAVIS: That's it? That was only a couple of questions. What kind of survey was that?

ALAN: Sometimes we just do the abbreviated version.

MAVIS: The abbreviated version. That doesn't sound very professional. When people came to me, I never gave them the abbreviated version.

Alan stands up, papers in hand, and starts walking toward the exit.

ALAN: Thank you, Mrs. Steinloaf …

MAVIS: Mavis.

ALAN: Right. Mavis. Thank you. But I think I need to go and interview some other people in the building.

Alan exits. Mavis calls out to him from her dining room.

MAVIS: *(calling after him)* Alright. But just remember: When it comes to Mrs. Goldfarb, don't believe a word she says. The woman's a total slut!

Mavis daintily lifts her cup to her lips and takes a sip.

MAVIS: *(to herself)* I wonder if he would've stayed longer if I offered him coffee.

Lights down. End of play.

TESTIMONIAL
JACK RUSHEN

THE PLAY:

Testimonial

THE PLAYWRIGHT:

Jack Rushen

SYNOPSIS:

On a quiet summer night, a discouraged professor in the early stages of Alzheimer's and being discharged from the college faculty, meets a former student while taking a break from his testimonial dinner. During their conversation, he finds strength and his elusive self-worth through her kind words and actions.

ABOUT THE PLAYWRIGHT:

Jack is a two-time first place winner of the Julie Harris Playwriting Award, and a three-time semi-finalist for the O'Neill Conference in Waterford, CT. His first award-winning play, IMAGE, has been mentored in development at top theatres across the country, Including Emerging Artists in New York City, Theatre 40 in Los Angeles, Wordsmyth in Houston, Artemesia in Chicago, Centre Stage in South Carolina, and Penguin Rep in Westchester-- -just to name a few. TAMING THE LION was featured recently at the Berkshire Theatre Festival, and won a generous grant from the Arch and Bruce Brown Foundation, along with first place in the Julie Harris Playwriting Competition sponsored byt the Beverly Hills Theatre Guild. He has written 5 full length plays, over 30 one- acts, 2 screenplays, and several television pilots.

CONTACT:

jack58rushen@gmail.com
203-253-2232
jack58rushen

WEBSITE:

www.jackrushen.net

THE THEATRE:

Eastbound Theater/Milford Arts Center
40 Railroad Ave, Milford, CT 06460

MISSION:

To provide audiences, students, and artists with opportunities and experiences in the arts that enlighten, enrich, and entertain Milford, CT and beyond. Our vision is to see creativity happening everywhere, making Milford a thriving destination community of culture.

ABOUT:

The Eastbound Theater/MAC's main venue and home to staff is at 40 Railroad Avenue South in downtown Milford, residing inside an historic Civil War-era train station. The MAC offers a beautiful theatre with superior acoustics, intimate seating for up to 110 in theater or cabaret-style configuration, a projection theater system with a 10X20' drop screen, exhibition area, classroom, offices, kitchenette and a Speakeasy Lounge for concessions.

Since 2001, Eastbound Theatre has presented a series of one-act plays in July as part of the New England Arts and Crafts Festival. This year, as that festival shifts its calendar dates, Eastbound Summer opens a new chapter as a four-day theatrical festival, featuring six original one-acts and two readings. As with previous seasons, audience members can vote for their favorite show, with the Summer Audience Award going to the winner.

CONTACT:

Thomas Rushen
zenripple@yahoo.com
203-814-7132

WEBSITE:

milfordarts.org

PRESENTING THE PLAY:

Testimonial

(Night. On a moonlit hillside sits PROFESSOR JAMES HILLIARD. He is in his mid 70's, and the very picture of a scholarly gentleman. He is dressed in a suit with a colorful bow tie. He sits very still, lost in thought.

After a long moment, a young woman, ALLISON HEALY walks on.)

ALLISON: The party is that way, Professor Hilliard.

(Looking up.)

HILLIARD: Hm? I'm sorry?

ALLISON: All those people milling about with drinks in their hands? They are waiting for you.

HILLIARD: Oh yes, yes I know. Yes. I'm just taking a short break for some air. I'm sure they understand.

Beat. He looks around up at the sky, trees, etc.

HILLIARD: *(CONT'D)* The fall is so nice once it gets cooler. And nothing can beat those purple and gold leaves, am I right?

ALLISON: You are being a poet again, professor.

He laughs. She joins in for a bit.

ALLISON: *(CONT'D)* Beautiful party. Nice tribute to you. You should be very proud that people think so much of you.

HILLIARD: Very flattering. Yes. But I must say there is something very unsettling about walking into a dark room, though, seeing a rush of light, and having 200 people yell "Surprise."

(They laugh.)

HILLIARD: *(CONT'D)* Do you know what happened to a friend of mine? Had heart problems, went to the hospital and was in intensive care for two weeks. When he came home, they gave him a surprise party. The lesson is---Never give a heart patient a surprise party.

(Laughter once again.)

ALLISON: It's not really funny—

HILLIARD: I'll take my laughter any way I can get it, darling. It's good for the soul.

ALLISON: I remember you telling us that.

(He looks at her quizzically)

ALLISON: *(CONT'D)* Yes, I was one of your students.

HILLIARD: Really? Very nice. Did you hear about this?

ALLISON: Wouldn't miss it.

HILLIARD: I'm very pleased. Did I leave you with anything?

ALLISON: I remember the very first advice you gave about writing.

HILLIARD: I don't. Tell me.

ALLISON: I remember you saying that "there is a reason to be good, it shows hard work. There is a reason to be bad, because you can learn. But there is no reason to be mediocre because it serves no purpose. Never, never be mediocre."

HILLIARD: You remember that? I'll be damned. When did you graduate?

ALLISON: Seems like forever. You know how time passes.

HILLIARD: I certainly do. What is your name?

ALLISON: Allison.

HILLIARD: Allison. One "L" or two.

ALLISON: Two.

HILLIARD: I've seen it both ways.

ALLISON: You taught us quite a bit for the short time in intro to lit. I still can't walk by a copy of 'Paradise Lost" at the library and not think of you.

HILLIARD: Well, that is nice. I appreciate that Miss...I'm sorry.... again?

ALLISON: Healy. Allison Healy.

HILLIARD: Were you a good student?

ALLISON: I worked really hard, but you never gave me an "A". No one I knew ever got an "A" from you.

HILLIARD: Why? Tell me why. Do you remember?

ALLISON: Because no one is perfect.

HILLIARD: We start to focus on perfection, we lose sight of the structure.

(He taps his pipe on the bench, cleans it out, and refills it with fresh tobacco.)

HILLIARD: *(CONT'D)* Do you know how many students I've had over fifty years? Figure it out. Fifty years times one hundred students a year on the average. Including lectures.

ALLISON: Five thousand students.

HILLIARD: Give or take.

ALLISON: That is incredible. I bet the only thing you went through more of were bow ties.

HILLIARD: Well, slightly more students.

ALLISON: I'd say bravo.

HILLIARD: For my bow ties? Or my students?

ALLISON: Both.

Laughter. Transition.

ALLISON: *(CONT'D)* Professor?

HILLIARD: Hm?

ALLISON: Are you okay?

HILLIARD: Sure. I have the mind of an artist. Sometimes it floats away and I have to catch it. It's better than sitting here and rambling like an idiot. I do that too sometimes. I'm old.

(Beat. He puffs his pipe)

HILLIARD: *(CONT'D)* The mind is a funny thing. I was in the Stop and Shop the other day and I saw this kid with a name tag. Nice fellow...big smile. Worked behind the deli counter. Said Kevin Arnett. Then my mind flashed back to a time in the mid- seventies...maybe it was the sixties, I don't know...anyway, Kevin Arnett was this difficult student I had in Intro to literature. Didn't give a goddamn about getting to class on time, had no ambition, and he always had a pack of yodels, I remember. He'd crinkle the paper and eat them during class. He always came in late. God, did I hate that. The whole thing came back to me as long as I saw that name tag. So I started to wonder what ever happened to the other Kevin Arnett. Did he make something of himself? Where did he go? Would he remember me if he saw me? Would I remember him? Did I help him at all? Faces of students are starting to just...appear. I close my eyes and see them, but I can't remember their names. There was this girl... what was her name? Barbara? No. Andrea, I think. She used to come to class with a big smile on her face, so eager to learn. God, her face lit up with the anticipation of knowledge. She sat right up in front, took furious notes, and you know what? Every time class was over, she made a point of walking up to me, taking my hand, looking straight into my eyes and saying, "Thank you, Professor Hilliard. I appreciate everything I learned from you." She thanked me. Every class. Can you imagine? What year was that? Jesus, it has to be twenty years ago now. Time pulls the rug right under you. When she graduated, she wrote me a poem. Still have it in my desk. Never moved from my top right hand drawer. She signed the bottom of the card. Why can't I think of it now? Jesus, nevermind. What was I talking about? Yes. The poem. It was a masterpiece. I told her she should have it published, but she didn't want to. She wrote it for me, so I respected her wishes. A week after graduation, her mother sent me a note and told me she was in a terrible car accident. She passed away at twenty-two years old. God in heaven, all that potential.

(Beat. For a moment, he is distant again.)

HILLIARD: *(CONT'D)* Do you know the other day they gave me a string of numbers to remember?

ALLISON: Numbers? Why?

HILLIARD: As a test.

ALLISON: Who did?

HILLIARD: Some people who think they know everything. Doctors. They wanted to see if I could remember sequences. I got so frustrated, I walked out and slammed the door. Why the hell should I deal with numbers? I'm not a mathematician. I love words! Give me words, my dear. Let me be a wordsmith.

(Pause. Hilliard puts his head down for a second, lost in thought.)

HILLIARD: *(CONT'D)* I'm sorry. I'm silly. I'm a silly man. I get just sometimes sentimental. You're going to think I'm such a... spam. I'm such a spam sometimes.

ALLISON: Spam?

HILLIARD: No, what's the word. Comes out of trees. They make syrup out of it.

ALLISON: Sap.

HILLIARD: That's it. I'm a sap.

(Pause. A few puffs on his pipe)

HILLIARD: *(CONT'D)* I think they didn't want me here anymore, you know what I mean? They ease you out. You can tell by the change in the way they greet you. They don't make eye contact with you like they used to. Communication? Sometimes the spoken word is the last clue that people don't feel the same way.

(He stares off for a moment, then begins to recite a poem.)

HILLIARD: *(CONT'D)* "What majesty of brow hath he...what softness in the eyes was there..." Oh, Jesus, what is the next line? I don't know what the next line is...God, I'm useless. I can't remember things, the faces of my students melt like putty when I try and think what they looked like. Useless.

(Long pause.)

ALLISON: Do you know what you did for so many people?

HILLIARD: What?

ALLISON: You shaped their lives.

HILLIARD: I don't know about that. There is a certain percentage of kids out there who don't want to learn a goddamn thing. Dammit, what was her name? Why can't I remember her name?

(Pause. He thinks a bit, the starts to recite the poem.)

HILLIARD: *(CONT'D)* "What majesty of brow hath he, what softness in the eyes was there..."

ALLISON: "Can you imagine a lesser man behind those eyebrows,
head, and hair..."

HILLIARD: This man of earth, so young at heart...

ALLISON: For all the world, he did his part...

HILLIARD: "He'd reach out to that blue, blue sky ..."

ALLISON: "A rush of words and one sweet sigh."

(Pause. Hilliard stares at her)

HILLIARD: How did you know that poem?

(She is silent.)

HILLIARD: *(CONT'D)* Really. How did you know that poem? I
never showed it to anyone. How did you know it? Tell me. It's
been locked up in my desk for years.

(Beat.)

HILLIARD: Tell me how you can know about that poem. YOU
CAN'T KNOW.

ALLISON: I do know.

HILLIARD: THEN TELL ME!! TELL ME HOW YOU KNOW!

(Beat.)

ALLISON: I wrote it.

(Long pause)

ALLISON: *(CONT'D)* Just for you. No one else has ever read it but
the two of us. Did you ever show it to anyone?

HILLIARD: Not a soul. I never shared it.

ALLISON: Then how could I know?

HILLIARD: You couldn't have written that poem.

ALLISON: Why?

HILLIARD: It was written by that student I was telling you about.
She died very—

(He stops abruptly.)

ALLISON: Yes.

HILLIARD: You knew the poem.

ALLISON: I did. Why would I know that poem, Professor? You're a logical man. Tell me what the only answer may be.

HILLIARD: That is impossible! How could you—? Please don't do this to me. You are confusing me. If you're in my mind, you're confusing me. I don't need this.

ALLISON: I don't want to confuse you. I want to congratulate you. For a lifetime of unselfish guidance. That is why I'm here.

HILLIARD: I don't think you're here. Really. I don't think you really can be.

ALLISON: You hear my voice. You see my face.

HILLIARD: I don't know what is real. It happens every day. It's getting worse. I don't know what to believe.

ALLISON: It doesn't matter if you hear my voice or if you see my face. What matters is that you realize what you have done for people. Lots of people. And I'm here to remind you. How did I know so much about you? I wrote it on a purple sunburst card which faded into gold at the top. Who else could have known that? Am I right? Ask yourself. Are those the colors? How would I know? I signed it Allie Healy.

HILLIARD: Allie—Healy.

ALLISON: Two "L's"

HILLIARD: My God. My God in heaven.

   Pause.

ALLISON: I am here to wish you the best, Professor Hilliard. Nothing but the best. Nothing, or no one in your life was wasted.

HILLIARD: So young. Twenty-two.

ALLISON: But I appreciated everything I ever experienced. While I was here. In part, thanks to you. Words, pictures, stunning visuals, and gentle poetry. Is the world beautiful after all, Professor? Is it?

HILLIARD: There are many, many beautiful gifts in this life, Allison. Those trees, that sky. Your smile. Yes, I do appreciate life, Allison. But there is one thing I absolutely detest.

ALLISON: What? That it isn't fair? I'm very surprised that such an erudite man would lean back on such an old cliche.

(He smiles.)

HILLIARD: I guess we all do that from time to time.

(Hilliard tries to think of a response. He is silent for a moment. She gets up and starts to move away.)

HILLIARD: *(CONT'D)* Sit with me for a while. You don't have to leave.

ALLISON: You have people who are waiting for you. I suggest you get back to them, being the guest of honor.

HILLIARD: You are so full of wisdom. Don't we have anything else to say? Can you say something to me I can remember for these times that will come? When I'll most need it?

(She reaches down and takes his hand, taking a moment to look deep into his eyes.)

ALLISON: Professor Hilliard. Thank you. I appreciate everything I've ever learned from you.

(She smiles at him and slowly walks away. He sits for a moment. He puts his pipe in his mouth, lights it, and smiles.)

HILLIARD: *(reciting poem)* "What majesty of brow hath he, what softness in the eyes was there...can you imagine a lesser man beneath those eyebrows, head, and hair?

(Hilliard sits still, staring off, smiling.)

Lights fade.

TWO PEOPLE
MARK SAUNDERS

BEST 10 MINUTE PLAYS 2019

THE PLAY:

Two People

THE PLAYWRIGHT:

Mark Saunders

SYNOPSIS:

In the Afterlife, a married couple find they are not "parted" and remain together. Over lunch, they try to understand what went wrong with their marriage. Eternity is two people and a ham, according to the old quip.

ABOUT THE PLAYWRIGHT:

Mark Saunders prefers to write short, humorous pieces befitting his height and attention span. He is a former winner of the Walden Fellowship, awarded to three Oregon writers or artists annually. In addition to three feature film scripts and two short scripts optioned, Saunders has had more than 70 productions or staged readings of his short plays in North America; back in his cartooning days, 500 of his drawings were published nationally. He once owned a Yugo (please don't ask about the car).

CONTACT:

msaunderswriter@yahoo. com

WEBSITE:

msaunderswriter. com

THE THEATRE:

> Stray Kats Theatre Company
> Newtown, Connecticut

MISSION:

The company, founded in 2003, is a not-for-profit professional theatre company with a mission of presenting contemporary classics, radio shows from the golden age of radio and new works.

ABOUT:

Since 2006, Stray Kats Theatre Company of Newtown, CT has presented new works and contemporary classics that are of interest to a mature audience. We seek topical, insightful works, whether comic or dramatic, and are thrilled when audience members walk out talking about what they've seen. Our staged readings and full productions have included originals from such playwrights as Frederick Stroppel (Small World) and Christopher Demos Brown (Our Lady of Allapattah) whose American Son is currently playing on Broadway, to the contemporary classics of Edward Albee, Arthur Miller, Frank Gilroy and more. "Still Crazy After All These Years" festival is an annual event featuring short plays pertaining to the lives of today's Senior Citizens: active, engaged, vibrant.

CONTACT:

> Kate Katcher, Artistic Director
> info@straykatstheatrecompany. org
> 203-514-2221

WEBSITE:

> straykatstheatrecompany. org

Presenting the Play:

Two People

Characters:

WIFE (Female, 60-70s)

HUSBAND (Male, 60-70s)

Setting:

A dining room in the Afterlife. The table may or may not have a table cloth. On the table should be plates, silverware, two glasses of water, and a large covered food tray (bubble shaped or rectangular).

Time:

Lunch time, although time itself is irrelevant.

(AT RISE: A married couple sit at a dining table, set for two. They have a glass of water in front of them. A large covered serving dish is on the table.)

HUSBAND: What's for breakfast?

WIFE: We just had breakfast. We're waiting for lunch. The bell should ring any minute now and then we can start eating.

HUSBAND: I can't believe how time just seems to whiz by. What's for lunch?

(She peers under the covered plate.)

WIFE: Ham.

HUSBAND: I assumed it was ham. But how is it prepared? Is it chowder? Quiche? Croquettes? Pizza? I loved the ham risotto. Maybe they'll serve that again. I keep thinking about it.

WIFE: That was a long time ago.

HUSBAND: Yes, which means it could be time for it again. Assuming they rotate their menu items. I didn't realize how much I liked risotto until I got here.

(Husband stands, crosses right, and shouts to someone O. S. Wife looks in the same direction.)

HUSBAND: Hey, could we get some risotto for lunch for a change? Anybody? Hello?

(No response. He walks down center stage and looks up at the ceiling.)

HUSBAND: Would it kill you to serve risotto?

(Beat. No answer. Husband returns to the table and sits.)

WIFE: You could have ordered risotto in restaurants when we dined out. Nobody stopped you.

HUSBAND: If I had known what it tasted like, I would have. How come you never made it?

WIFE: Risotto is tricky. You can't cook it like rice. You need to stir it constantly, pour in broth, stir, more broth. You don't want it to get too gummy. It's a fine line.

HUSBAND: Go ahead and take another peek. What kind of ham are we getting for lunch?

(She peers under the covered plate a second time.)

WIFE: Deviled.

(Husband GROANS. He stands and paces, throwing his arms in the air in frustration.)

HUSBAND: Are you kidding me? They served us deviled ham this morning. And yesterday.

WIFE: And the day before.

HUSBAND: And the day before that and that and that and that. The days all run together. I can't tell one day from another. I can't even tell what hour of day it is. No clocks. No calendars. No sunrises or sunsets.

WIFE: I think that's the point. Please sit down. You're making a scene. You seem edgy today.

(Husband looks around the room one more time and then sits. He takes a sip of water.)

HUSBAND: Point or no point, at the very least they could put ice cubes in our water. … You know, I used to love ham. It was my favorite meal. That's why on Thanksgiving we always had both ham and turkey.

WIFE: I know. I made both, every Thanksgiving. I did all the cooking.

HUSBAND: I helped.

WIFE: *(Scoffs)* When did you ever help in the kitchen? No, you watched football.

HUSBAND: Maybe I did the dishes. I recall doing dishes. I'm trying to remember.

WIFE: Nope. You sat on your ass and ate dessert. Usually two servings.

(Wife stands and strikes a yoga pose, Warrior or Tree. Holds it for a beat, then sits.)

HUSBAND: I'll never understand how some people consider that exercise. You realize all you're doing is standing still.

WIFE: And I'll never understand how I died first. You should have gone before me. I watched my diet and walked everywhere. You played golf and poker. Two activities not exactly known for improving one's cardiovascular system.

HUSBAND: You were hit by a bus while jogging.

WIFE: Oh, right. Forgot about that. . . . Well, I was distracted.

HUSBAND: That's because you were texting. Distracted jogging, the police called it. *(Beat.)*

HUSBAND: Truth be told, I didn't expect to outlive you. If I thought there was a chance of that, I might have learned how to cook.

WIFE: All you had to do was ask. I would have been glad to teach you the basics of cooking. But, that would have interfered with your other hobbies. Face it, your hobbies were an excuse to get away from me and the kids. *(She sips water.)*

WIFE: So, how'd you do?

HUSBAND: Do what?

WIFE: Cooking for yourself.

HUSBAND: Much easier than I thought. I just microwaved everything. What I didn't microwave, I barbecued. What I didn't barbecue, I put between two slices of bread. I don't think I ever opened the oven door. Keeping the house clean--now that was the hard part. Stripping the bed, doing laundry, making the bed. You have to walk around the bed. Once my knees gave out, just making the bed took all morning. I sure missed you.

WIFE: You missed having a cook and a maid, not a partner. You assumed you had married a domestic worker. I had dreams, too. I was also supposed to be your best friend, not to mention lover. At least I thought that was the plan. You know, on our wedding day when we exchanged vows.

HUSBAND: Yes, let's talk about our vows. I thought those vows were supposed to last till death do us part. We are now dead.

WIFE: Dead as a doornail, as Dickens would say. You know, I saw him dining here before you arrived.

HUSBAND: Charles Dickens the writer was here?

WIFE: No, Charles Dickens the yoga instructor. Yes, the writer. Why do you always question what I say?

(Husband stands and looks off-stage.)

HUSBAND: What's taking so long. Why won't they ring the bell?

WIFE: They'll ring the bell when they ring the bell. You have a more pressing engagement?

HUSBAND: No. This is pretty much all I have to look forward to.

(He sits.)

WIFE: Till death do us part. Five simple words.

HUSBAND: And yet here we are dining together. We remain, in a word, unparted.

WIFE: Do you want to be parted?

HUSBAND: Why? What would be the point now? It's not as if speed dating is an option.

(Awkward silence, as they both sip water. Beat.)

WIFE: Maybe our situation is like that favorite movie of yours.

HUSBAND: "Turner and Hooch"?

WIFE: No. The one where every day is the same.

HUSBAND: Oh, you mean "Groundhog Day". I love that movie. I could watch it over and over.

WIFE: That's good, because I think you're in it now. Over and over.

HUSBAND: Really?

WIFE: Think about it. Every day is the same. We're stuck in the dining hall of what looks like a low-end assisted living facility and all they serve us is ham. Breakfast, lunch, and dinner. Ham. Even for happy hour and late-night snacks. All ham, all the time.

HUSBAND: So, instead of experiencing the same day every day, we're eating ham.

WIFE: Again, I think that's the point.

HUSBAND: If it is, I really don't get it. I mean I sort of get it but I don't get the end-game. What comes after ham?

WIFE: How'd that movie end?

HUSBAND: The main character, the TV weather guy, had to change. He started out as a jerk and had to become a better person in order to break the spell.

WIFE: There it is.

HUSBAND: There what is?

WIFE: Our way out of hamville. We have to learn to be nicer to each other.

HUSBAND: Want to give it a try?

WIFE: Sure. What do we have to lose?

HUSBAND: I'll go first.

> *(They play the next sequence with over-the-top, ahem "hammy," enthusiasm, not meaning what they say.)*

HUSBAND: My dear, you look simply ravishing today. Whatever did you do with your hair? It's perfect. I've never seen your hair looking better.

WIFE: How kind of you to notice.

HUSBAND: And those shoes. Are they new?

WIFE: Yes, they're Manolo Blahnik's. From Nordstrom. I bought them at their half-yearly sale.

HUSBAND: I don't care where they're from or how much they cost, as long as they're on your feet.

WIFE: How sweet of you to say. And how was your golf game this morning, my precious?

HUSBAND: Splendid. Pars, birdies, and a hole-in-one.

WIFE: Bravo, my love. I must admit, you don't look a day over 50. *(Husband indicates lower.)*

WIFE: Over 40. *(Again, he indicates lower).*

WIFE: Over 30.

> *(He indicates lower still; she shakes her head No. He shrugs.)*

HUSBAND: What's for lunch? I'm famished.

(They both look at each other, hopeful. Beat. She looks under the meal cover and frowns.)

WIFE: *(Disappointed)* Ham. Deviled ham. No change.

HUSBAND: *(Sighs)* Maybe they could tell we weren't sincere.

WIFE: Why can't we be honest with each other? We were in love once. Very much in love. What happened?

(Beat. They play the next sequence with sincerity).

HUSBAND: I don't know. I guess things kept coming between us.

WIFE: You're right. That's what happened. Our jobs.

HUSBAND: Those long commutes.

WIFE: All the kids' activities. If I see another soccer ball, I'm going to scream.

HUSBAND: Buying and selling houses.

WIFE: All that packing and unpacking.

HUSBAND: Mowing lawns.

WIFE: I thought you liked mowing?

HUSBAND: Are you kidding me? You mow the lawn, it grows back. Mow it again, grows back again. I hated lawn. It's like your house has a beard that never stops growing.

WIFE: College for the kids.

HUSBAND: Then the grand kids came. . . . I guess life got in the way.

WIFE: Life's not the problem now. We're both dead.

HUSBAND: Dead as a doornail, as you already said. . . . You're right, you know.

WIFE: How so?

HUSBAND: For much of my life, I was a better friend to my friends than I was to my wife. Believe me, if I had it to do over again, I'd put you first. Always.

(They reach over the table and clasp each other's hands, affectionately.)

WIFE: And I'd do the same for you.

HUSBAND: I wouldn't wait until I lost you to miss you.

WIFE: I look at you and I still see that same handsome young man I danced with at our wedding. I remember thinking what a miracle it was that two people, two very different people, could become one so easily. We were so close, I could feel your heart beating.

HUSBAND: And I see the same beautiful, amazing woman I twirled around the church hall to great applause. We were quite the couple.

WIFE: Quite the couple. I miss that couple.

(O. S. the meal bell RINGS. They drop their hands.)

(She opens the covered dish fully and it's a cooked fish.)

WIFE/HUSBAND: *(Together)* Salmon!

WIFE: With creamy dill sauce.

HUSBAND: Just like they served at our wedding reception.

(They stand, high-five or fist bump each other with excitement, then click their water glasses in a toast. They sip.)

HUSBAND: Before we eat, I would be honored if you would dance with me again, my lovely wife.

WIFE: The honor would be all mine, my dear husband.

(They begin to dance. As they dance, the end of the song "Two Sleepy People" plays softly in the b. g., the Fats Waller version, if possible; otherwise, any romantic background music will do.)

WELL, HERE WE ARE JUST ABOVE THE SEINE FOGGY LITTLE FELLA, DROWSY LITTLE DAME TWO SLEEPY PEOPLE BY DAWN'S EARLY LIGHT AND TOO MUCH IN LOVE TO SAY GOODNIGHT BON SOIR, BON NUIT.

(Lights slowly down.)

END OF PLAY

I HAVE A SECRET
MARSHA LEE SHEINESS

BEST 10 MINUTE PLAYS 2019

The Play:

I Have a Secret

The Playwright:

Marsha Lee Sheiness

Synopsis:

Mother and daughter express intimacy and love during a mid-day visit at an assisted-living facility. Even though Sylvia doesn't recognize her daughter, Rachel, their relationship reveals that a parent and child can become best friends.

About the playwright:

Marsha Lee Sheiness' plays have been produced Off-Broadway, Off-Off Broadway, on Television, at Regional, Community, University, and High Schools, also in Japan, Canada, England, and New Zealand. Awards: National Endowment for the Arts for Playwriting, and the Exxon Award for her PBS production of MONKEY, MONKEY, BOTTLE OF BEER, HOW MANY MONKEYS HAVE WE HERE? presented by Theater in America. She is also an Actress, Director, and Playwriting teacher. Memberships: Dramatist Guild, WGE, AEA, SAG. Publishers: Dramatic Publishing, Samuel French, Inc., ArtAge, and Blue Moon Plays.

Contact:

Msheiness@gmail.com
212-924-9256

Agent:

Leo Bookman
Leobookman@yahoo.com
(212) 472-8976

Website:

Marshasheiness.com

THE THEATRE:

City Circle Theatre Company
1301 5th St, Coralville, IA 52241

MISSION:

To present professional caliber theatrical productions and events that provide education, enrichment, and enlightenment to the public.

ABOUT:

City Circle Theatre Company was formed in the summer of 1997 as City Circle Acting Company and incorporated as a non-profit organization on January 5th, 1998. In March of 1998, City Circle was formally adopted by the Coralville City Council as Coralville's community theatre. In 2011 City Circle became the resident theatre company of the new Coralville Center for the Performing Arts (CCPA). In 2014, City Circle merged with the City of Coralville and became a program committee of the CCPA. In 2018 the name was changed to City Circle Theatre Company. A Board of Directors conducts and manages the affairs of City Circle and is advised by and works closely with CCPA staff and the Coralville Arts Commission. Tax deductible contributions can be made to City Circle through the Community Fund of Johnson County.

CONTACT:

Elizabeth Tracey
etracey@coralville.org
319-248-9369

WEBSITE:

citycircle.org

Presenting the Play:

I Have A Secret

Cast:

SYLVIA: 75-80

RACHEL (SYLVIA'S Daughter): 50-60

Scene:

(Early spring. SYLVIA sits alone on the porch of an Assisted Living facility. Her eyes closed as SHE quietly enjoys the mild spring breeze. An open book, a romance novel, sits on her lap. A pair of reading glasses hangs around her neck like a necklace. Sound of a television is coming from the open window behind her. Occasionally we hear laughter and an isolated word or two coming from inside.

RACHEL enters. SHE casually walks toward an empty chair next to SYLVIA and sits. SHE places a bag under a small table that is between the two chairs and closes her eyes. Sandwiches, coffee and desert are inside the bag. The two of them sit quietly for about 15 seconds. SYLVIA slowly opens her eyes, puts her glasses on and resumes reading her romance novel.)

RACHEL: *(with closed eyes)* Beautiful day, isn't it?

(SYLVIA glances in RACHEL'S direction, and then continues to read)

SYLVIA: Yes – beautiful.

RACHEL: I think spring is my favorite season.

SYLVIA: Spring is for lovers.

RACHEL: Yes, it is.

(pause)

What are you reading?

SYLVIA: Something about spring.

RACHEL: That's a nice title.

SYLVIA: Yes. – But she's not happy.

RACHEL: Maybe she's not happy now, but when you finish the book she will be – won't she?

SYLVIA: Sometimes yes, sometimes no. It's the journey.

RACHEL: You're so right. It's about the journey.

SYLVIA: I never got there. I wanted to, but I never did. He didn't like to travel.

RACHEL: Where – was it – you wanted to go.

SYLVIA: To Israel – but I never got there. I wanted to, but I never did. He didn't like to travel.

RACHEL: I know.

SYLVIA: Except on business.

RACHEL: I know – he didn't like to travel?

SYLVIA: I think so – maybe – I'm not sure.

RACHEL: But you never went.

SYLVIA: Where?

RACHEL: To Israel.

SYLVIA: I planted trees – I sent money.

RACHEL: So you're there in spirit.

SYLVIA: I guess I am. Yes.

RACHEL: You definitely are.

SYLVIA: *(referring to book)* Where did this come from?

RACHEL: It's yours. You're reading about spring.

SYLVIA: I am? How wonderful. — I wish I could remember —

RACHEL: Would you like some coffee?

SYLVIA: Coffee! Yes, I would.

> *(RACHEL reaches into the bag, takes out the coffee and takes the top off of both paper cups)*

RACHEL: You like it black, right.

SYLVIA: That's exactly how I like it.

RACHEL: Black – no sugar.

SYLVIA: That's right.

RACHEL: And not too strong.

> *(Carefully hands her the coffee)*

SYLVIA: Just like my momma did.

RACHEL: Really? Grandma liked it black, too?

SYLVIA: Who?

RACHEL: You said your momma liked it black, too.

SYLVIA: I did?

RACHEL: Um-hum.

SYLVIA: *(sipping the coffee)* This is the best cup of coffee I've ever had.

RACHEL: Wonderful.

> *(SYLVIA takes another sip of coffee)*

I'm so glad you like it.

SYLVIA: Do you work here?

RACHEL: No, I don't.

SYLVIA: You should work here — you're very nice.

RACHEL: Well, thank you very much.

SYLVIA: I don't work here either. — No, I don't work here either. I don't know what I do here, but I don't work.

RACHEL: Are you hungry?

SYLVIA: Hungry — maybe — I don't know.

RACHEL: I have an extra sandwich.

SYLVIA: I guess I could be hungry —

RACHEL: *(takes both sandwiches out of the bag)* I'm afraid you don't get a choice – they're both the same. Swiss cheese -- lettuce and tomato – with a little mayo.

SYLVIA: Where did this book come from?

RACHEL: It's yours. You're reading about spring.

SYLVIA: I am? How wonderful.

> *(RACHEL unwraps and hands her half a sandwich and a napkin)*

RACHEL: I hope you like Swiss cheese.

SYLVIA: I love Swiss cheese.

RACHEL: Then this is your lucky day.

> *(SYLVIA takes a bite of the sandwich)*

How do you like it?

SYLVIA: What's not to like? It's Swiss cheese.

RACHEL: You've got a point.

SYLVIA: You're very nice.

RACHEL: Thank you – so are you.

SYLVIA: I have a secret.

RACHEL: You do?

SYLVIA: Yes.

    (pause)

RACHEL: Are you going to tell me?

SYLVIA: What?

RACHEL: Your secret –

SYLVIA: Why would I do that? It's a secret.

RACHEL: *(confused)* I'm sorry – I just thought –

SYLVIA: I have a secret.

RACHEL: I know.

SYLVIA: You do?

RACHEL: You told me.

SYLVIA: So — what is your secret?

RACHEL: You mean your secret.

SYLVIA: I don't remember.

RACHEL: That's okay.

SYLVIA: Good. Because that's the way it is.

RACHEL: I have a secret too.

SYLVIA: You do?

RACHEL: Want to know what it is?

SYLVIA: If you want to tell me.

RACHEL: Promise you won't tell anyone?

SYLVIA: I promise.

RACHEL: I love you Mom. I love you very much.

SYLVIA: You do? How nice. Thank you for telling me.

RACHEL: You are so welcome.

SYLVIA: I love you too.

(RACHEL keeps herself from crying)

RACHEL: — So — what sandwich shall I bring you tomorrow? More Swiss cheese?

SYLVIA: How about something different?

RACHEL: I know. I'll surprise you.

SYLVIA: I love surprises.

RACHEL: I know.

(pause)

SYLVIA: I like you.

RACHEL: I like you, too.

SYLVIA: I hope you'll come to see me again.

RACHEL: How about tomorrow?

SYLVIA: Tomorrow sounds wonderful.

(closes her eyes)

Just wonderful.

RACHEL: Then tomorrow it is.

(kisses SYLVIA)

I love you Mom. See you tomorrow.

(exits slowly, trying not to cry)

END OF PLAY

ONE FINE ALL HALLOW'S EVE
JAMES EYCHANER

BEST 10 MINUTE PLAYS 2019

THE PLAY:

One Final All Hallows Eve

THE PLAYWRIGHT:

James Eychaner

SYNOPSIS:

A widower is confronted by a policewoman for being in a cemetery after closing on Halloween. The widower is keeping a promise to his late wife. The policewoman has a rare opportunity to show compassion.

ABOUT THE PLAYWRIGHT:

After a career in nonprofit management, state government, and other day jobs, James Eychaner became a new playwright when he was inspired by a class led by Bryan Willis. He likes to write about the challenges of aging. He loves to travel with his wife and writes travel blogs on www.mytripjournal.com. He is listed on New Play Exchange https://newplayexchange.org/users/21485/james-eychaner

James Eychaner lives in Olympia,

CONTACT: james.eychaner@gmail.com

One Fine All Hallows Eve was staged in cooperation with the Seattle Playwrights' Salon on October 13, 2017. http://seattleplaywrightssalon.com/past-shows/#/spooky-shorts-october-13-2017/ :

PRESENTING THE PLAY:

Cast of Characters

WIDOWER: An old man

POLICEWOMAN: 30s

Setting : An urban cemetery after dark.

Time: Halloween, present era

At rise, THE WIDOWER is carrying a small bag or rucksack, going from headstone to headstone, carefully reading the inscriptions with a small flashlight.

WIDOWER: We have plenty of time. We'll get there soon. She's not far. I walk here every Tuesday. I know the way, even in the dark. But these folks – no one ever comes to see them. No one weeds the plots. No one leaves flowers or stones or gifts. Just plain forgotten. Is that tragic or just sad?

(POLICEWOMAN enters with flashlight. She observes the WIDOWERS as he examines a headstone.)

Oh, this one is so sad. Only a month old. Baby Heloise. That's a name you don't hear any more. Tragedy? Pathos? Just plain sad? Heart break for the mom and dad. And the grandparents. Heart break. Sad.

(POLICEWOMAN shines flashlight on WIDOWER.)

POLICEWOMAN: City police, sir, may I talk to you?

WIDOWER: Me? Can't see you with the light in my eyes.

POLICEWOMAN: May I talk to you, sir?

WIDOWER: No one wants to talk to an old man. I'd love it if you talked to me.

(WIDOWER starts to approach POLICEWOMAN.)

POLICEWOMAN: That's close enough, sir. Right there. I can see you now. Please turn off your flashlight and put it on the ground.

(Puzzled, the WIDOWER does as he is told. POLICEWOMAN lowers the light from the WIDOWER'S face.)

WIDOWER: Whatever you say. A fine evening to you, ma'am.

POLICEWOMAN: Do you know what time it is?

WIDOWER: Seven?

POLICEWOMAN: It's after hours here, sir.

WIDOWER: It's all right. They know me here.

POLICEWOMAN: How do they know you?

WIDOWER: I come here every week. Every Tuesday.

POLICEWOMAN: Did you check in with the office tonight?

WIDOWER: No. I don't need to. They know me here.

POLICEWOMAN: Do you know what day it is?

WIDOWER: Yes. It's Tuesday.

POLICEWOMAN: Anything special about this Tuesday?

WIDOWER: Yes. It's All Hallow's Eve.

POLICEWOMAN: Halloween, yes, sir.

WIDOWER: It's a fine one, too. Clear, mild. The stars are already out. You could even see Venus a bit earlier.

POLICEWOMAN: Sir, you are in a cemetery after hours on Halloween.

WIDOWER: It's all right. They know me. I come here every Tuesday.

POLICEWOMAN: Why do you come here?

WIDOWER: My wife is here.

POLICEWOMAN: A lot of people have loved ones here, but you're the only one here after hours.

WIDOWER: The groundskeeper knows I come here late. He knows I like to be alone.

POLICEWOMAN: But you didn't check in with anyone?

WIDOWER: I waved.

POLICEWOMAN: Waved?

WIDOWER: Yes, I waved to the groundskeeper. I like him. He's a nice man. He's very kind to me.

POLICEWOMAN: A neighbor called about a man in the cemetery after hours.

WIDOWER: That would be me.

POLICEWOMAN: Yes, it would, sir. What's in the bag, sir?

WIDOWER: My bag?

POLICEWOMAN: Yes, sir.

WIDOWER: Just a few small things.

POLICEWOMAN: May I see, sir?

WIDOWER: Why?

POLICEWOMAN: For your safety and my safety.

WIDOWER: I'm no harm to anyone.

POLICEWOMAN: Just checking things out.

> *(WIDOWER sets his bag on ground and opens it, starts to reach in.)*

POLICEWOMAN: Don't reach in, sir. I need to see your hands. Can you just turn it over and empty it out for me?

> *(WIDOWER does as he is directed. A garden trowel, stone, and stuffed black cat fall out. POLICEWOMAN shines her flashlight on them.)*

POLICEWOMAN: Night gardening with your friend?

WIDOWER: My friend?

POLICEWOMAN: The cat.

WIDOWER: That's Captain Kirk.

POLICEWOMAN: Captain Kirk?

WIDOWER: My wife was a Star Trek fan.

POLICEWOMAN: What's the tool for?

WIDOWER: I tend my wife's plot. To keep the weeds down.

POLICEWOMAN: This time of year?

WIDOWER: All year.

POLICEWOMAN: And the rock?

WIDOWER: It's for her headstone.

POLICEWOMAN: Headstone?

WIDOWER: The Jews do it. They leave a stone at a grave to show they remember, to show respect.

POLICEWOMAN: This is a Catholic cemetery.

WIDOWER: I just like the idea. I found the stone when I was in

Scotland last month. The color reminded me of my wife's hair, so I brought it home for her.

POLICEWOMAN: So, you're here alone in the dark in a cemetery after hours on Halloween to tend your wife's plot?

WIDOWER: Yes, ma'am.

POLICEWOMAN: Anything else?

WIDOWER: What do you mean?

POLICEWOMAN: Drug deal – hooking up – mischief.

WIDOWER: Oh, no, nothing like that, no mischief.

POLICEWOMAN: So there is something else?

WIDOWER: Well –

POLICEWOMAN: Tell me the truth, sir. For your own safety.

WIDOWER: Well–

(WIDOWER starts to reach for the toy cat.)

POLICEWOMAN: Leave everything there, sir.

WIDOWER: It's the cat. Captain Kirk.

POLICEWOMAN: Yes, sir?

WIDOWER: He's not the real Captain Kirk.

POLICEWOMAN: He isn't?

WIDOWER: When my wife was sick, the real Captain Kirk was sick, too.

POLICEWOMAN: You had a cat named Captain Kirk?

WIDOWER: Yes, ma'am. My wife made me promise – don't laugh –

POLICEWOMAN: I'll be respectful of your wife, sir.

WIDOWER: She made me promise I'd make sure Captain Kirk would be buried next to her when he died. I promised. Margaret, my wife, she died – Captain Kirk, the cat, he hung on. For a while. Then he disappeared.

POLICEWOMAN: Disappeared?

WIDOWER: Yes, ma'am. I hoped he'd come back, to die at home.

He didn't. And I'd made a promise. I keep my promises.

POLICEWOMAN: Sir, do you mean to bury the toy cat tonight?

WIDOWER: Yes, ma'am. I aim to keep my promise.

POLICEWOMAN: Sir, are you on any medications?

WIDOWER: Medications?

POLICEWOMAN: Antidepressants, that kind of thing.

WIDOWER: Well, I —

POLICEWOMAN: Did you forget to take your meds?

WIDOWER: I didn't forget. I just didn't take them.

POLICEWOMAN: Didn't take them?

WIDOWER: I don't like the way they make me feel. They make me n*ot feel.* I don't like it.

POLICEWOMAN: Sir, I should escort you home.

WIDOWER: Ma'am, I'm OK. My head is clear. I know what I'm doing.

POLICEWOMAN: Sir –

WIDOWER: Damn it, officer, I'm a lonely old man, not a crook. I'm just a lonely old man. I can't, I couldn't hurt anyone. Not even if I wanted to. Not even myself.

POLICEWOMAN: How much time do you need?

WIDOWER: Just a few minutes. The groundskeeper knows me. He said he'd dig a little hole for me. I just need to tidy up.

POLICEWOMAN: I'll wait. When you're done, I'll escort you out. Gather your stuff.

WIDOWER: Yes, ma'am.

(WIDOWER gathers up his items.)

WIDOWER: I know the way. I walk here every Tuesday, every week. Well, maybe not when I'm in Scotland. I won't be long.

(WIDOWER exits.)

POLICEWOMAN: *(To her radio)* It's Officer Ward. I'm at the cemetery. I have an elderly gentleman who wandered in. I'll make sure he gets home. Repeat that? Well, OK. A fine Halloween to you, too.

END OF PLAY

I LOVE LUCY

BARA SWAIN

BEST 10 MINUTE PLAYS 2019

ANOTHER PLAY from Bara Swain

THE PLAY:

I Love Lucy

THE PLAYWRIGHT:

Bara Swain

SYNOPSIS:

When Desiree and Ethel meet in the waiting room of an obstetrics office, they have different agendas. How far would a mother go for her child?

The Theatre:

Short+Sweet International (The World's Biggest Little Festival)
PO Box 462 Newtown NSW 2042 Australia

Mission:

Short+Sweet is a global festival brand, presenting highly successful Theatre, Dance, Cabaret, Comedy, Bollywood, Film and Song Festivals around the world, providing audiences with exciting and contemporary works that challenge and entertain. Short+Sweet's mission is to build theatre-going audiences around the world.

About:

Short+Sweet Canberra enjoys the support of Canberra Theatre Centre, where the festival is staged each year in The Courtyard Studio. Canberra Theatre Centre provides the city with the finest performing arts and the most diverse selection of entertainment from around the country as well as performance space for many local theatre companies and performers. (www.CanberraTheatreCenter. com.AU) As an open access festival, Short+Sweet Canberra brings together a broad range of artists. Plays are submitted from all over the world, and the festival director shortlists approximately half of the festival's content from local writers, and half from interstate and overseas.

The Short+Sweet family is committed to building a more creative world, 10 minutes at a time. The platform provides an accessible and enjoyable theatrical experience to individuals from all walks of life, and gives them the opportunity to connect with creatives from all over the world.

Contact:

Pete Malicki, Literary Manager
pete@shortandsweet.org

Website:

shortandsweet.org

PRESENTING THE PLAY:

I Love Lucy

CAST:

DESIREE: 28-35
ETHEL: 45-52

AUTHOR'S NOTE:

Ethel is 17 years older than Desiree.

TIME:

The present

PLACE:

A waiting area in Dr. Friedman's Ob/Gyn practice

(AT RISE: DESIREE (28), about 6 months pregnant, and ETHEL (45) are seated in an Ob/Gyn waiting area. THEY are both reading parenting magazines, holding the magazine close to their faces. Simultaneously, THEY lower their magazines, place them on their laps, then lick their right index fingers. Both women touch the corner of the right page, and turn. Simultaneously, THEY cross their right leg over their left leg, and lean forward in order to decipher the fine print. Silence. ETHEL's left heel starts moving up and down with a seemingly nervous energy. DESIREE notices it.)

DESIREE: Umm .. is this your first?

ETHEL: Oh, no. No. No. *(laughs nervously)* You thought I was —? That I had a bun in the oven? I'm flattered but, no. Really, it's sweet of you. *(patting stomach)* Maybe I'll do a few crunches later … Don't be. Don't be. *(Pause)*

DESIREE: I'm sorry. Geez, I didn't mean to … I just thought — Dr. Friedman specializes in high-risk, you know, pregnancies, and so I figured --Oh, I'm so embarrassed. You don't look pregnant at all. At all, I mean it.

DESIREE: I'm really sorry.

ETHEL: We all make mistakes. Some worse than others.

DESIREE: You can say that again.

(Pause. DESIREE starts bouncing her heel up and down, nervously. ETHEL watches.)

ETHEL: *(gently)* Not planned, huh?

DESIREE: Oh, I planned to have children. Just – not yet. I'm not ready … yet.

ETHEL: Nobody ever is.

DESIREE: Do you want to trade?

ETHEL: *(laughs)* Ohhh, no. Not me! I already pushed out two 7-pound bowling balls, thank-you-very-much! I broke the blood vessels in my eyes. Both times, both eyes.

DESIREE: (uneasily) I meant … trade magazines.

ETHEL: Of course you did! I'm so sorry, of course you did. That's so … insensitive of me.

(Sliding her magazine to DESIREE.)

Honestly, I didn't mean to upset you. It's the furthest thing from my mind.

DESIREE: It's nothing, it's nothing. You don't need to apologize. I'm just … overly sensitive.

(Sliding her magazine to ETHEL.)

I know you didn't mean anything by it. It's me. It's just me.

(Silence. THEY both pick up their magazines, but neither reads. THEY tuck locks of hair behind their ears several times. DESIREE breaks the silence.)

DESIREE: Can we start over?

ETHEL: I was hoping you'd say that.

(THEY smile bashfully at each other.)

TOGETHER: Is this your first time here?

(THEY laugh. Then they both answer simultaneously.)

TOGETHER: You first.

(THEY laugh again. ETHEL gestures to herself, and indicates that SHE will speak first.)

ETHEL: Uh, well, let's see. My oldest —

DESIREE: *(helpfully)* — bowling ball …

ETHEL: That's right, my first bowling ball was delivered by Dr. Friedman's father —

ETHEL: — Dr. Friedman. Right! He had a receptionist with red hair. She looked like she walked off the set of I Love Lucy with her checkered pencil skirt and poodle-do. Or those flared skirts and blouses and 3-inch heels. … Oh, I wish I had those shoes.

DESIREE: — Dr. Friedman. Hal Friedman! My grandmother was friends with his sister. The redhead was his sister. She and grandma idolized Lucille Ball. Oh, that skirt was from The Chocolate Factory. It was one of grandma's favorite episodes. … Oh, I wish she had lived longer.

DESIREE: *(wistfully)* Just a little longer. Long enough to meet her great-granddaughter.

ETHEL: You're having a girl?

DESIREE: *(nodding)* I'm naming her Melody.

ETHEL: It's a beautiful name. Just … perfect.

DESIREE: I think so. You think so? I think so.

> *(ETHEL nods amicably. Suddenly, DESIREE becomes animated.)*

> Season 2, episode 11. Lucy's pregnant, right? …

ETHEL: Sure, I remember. Sixty million viewers remember!

DESIREE: … And Lucy says to Ricky: "I want the names to be unique and euphonious." And Ricky says, "Okay …"

TOGETHER: "Unique if it's a boy, and Euphonious if it's a girl."

ETHEL: Gimme some skin.   DESIREE: High 5. High 5.
(SHE gives a High 5.)   *(SHE gives a High 5.)*

DESIREE: *(explaining)* "Euphonious." "Melodious." "Melody!" Get it? My grandmother will love it!

> *(After a moment, DESIREE corrects herself.)*

Would have loved it.

> *(ETHEL shakes her head 'yes.' DESIREE shakes her head 'no.')*

She passed away …

ETHEL: … I gathered that. I'm sorry.

DESIREE: … a little over a month ago. And I feel … so ashamed because --

ETHEL: *(gently)* It's all right.

DESIREE: It's not all right. It's not all right! *(struggling)* Because even though Grandma was in so much pain, you know? Even though she couldn't swallow ... and she – she had trouble with words and speaking and then — towards the end … this – she had this blank stare …

ETHEL: *(gently)* Parkinsons?

> *(DESIREE is slightly surprised. SHE nods.)*

I know. Too well.

DESIREE: But I still wanted her to stay – here, with me. And I know it's ... unreasonable, but I'm so angry at her for – I don't know — leaving me?

> *(after a moment)*

For leaving me.

ETHEL: That's ... rough.

DESIREE: "Fool me once, shame on you. Fool me twice, shame on me."

ETHEL: I'm sorry, I don't — follow ...

DESIREE: My mother left me, too.

ETHEL: *(confused)* She didn't ... die, did she?

DESIREE: Worse. She just left. And never came back. Not a card, not a call, not a word, not a ...

ETHEL: Nada.

DESIREE: Yeah, right.

ETHEL: I'm sure she had a good reason.

DESIREE: Grandma said it was for the best. "Babies having babies." I never met my mother... but I heard that she was wild and vain and self-destructive and ... well, 17.

ETHEL: The same age as my youngest daughter. My Lucy.

DESIREE: *(amazed)* You're kidding!

ETHEL: No, I'm not kidding	DESIREE: You're putting me on ...
... I didn't mean to ... It's	My mother's name is Ethel. ...
just a name. ... They're	Ethel and Lucy. It's ... uncan-
quite a pair. We're quite a	ny, right? I was raised on those
pair. Best friends, I'd say.	women from I Love Lucy.
... I mean, I love Lucy!	

> *(THEY both sigh and sit quietly in thought. ETHEL and DE-SIREE tuck their hair behind their ears. Silence.)*

DESIREE: I know it's … magical thinking but …

ETHEL: There's nothing wrong with magical thinking.

DESIREE: I thought maybe, just maybe, Ethel would show up at her own mother's funeral. I prepared myself, you know? — so I wouldn't be surprised. Pretty stupid, huh?

ETHEL: You're a smart girl.

DESIREE: *(pointing at belly)* Oh, yeah, I'm real smart.

ETHEL: But you don't like surprises.

DESIREE: No. *(speaking to belly)* Right, Melody? Isn't that right, sweet girl?

> *(ETHEL shifts uncomfortably, then rises. SHE crosses downstage, a short distance away from DESIREE. DESIREE looks up.)*

Is something wrong?

ETHEL: I'm here to surprise my daughter. She's expecting …

DESIREE: Congratulations!

ETHEL: … Just not me. We've never seen … well, eye-to-eye. Ever.

DESIREE: 'Ever' is a long time.

ETHEL: Mmm hmm.

> *(ETHEL is distracted. DESIREE tries to engage her.)*

DESIREE: Is this your first grandchild?

ETHEL: First grandchild and last resort to … you know, work things out with my older daughter.

DESIREE: *(optimistically)* Ninety percent of parenting is showing up! That's what my grandmother always said. And here you are. You showed up!

ETHEL: Surprise!

> *(DESIREE waits. ETHEL turns towards her, and holds DE-SIREE's gaze.)*

I said, surprise … Desiree.

> *(Silence. Finally, ETHEL moves towards her.)*

DESIREE: *(rising)* Oh, my God, DON'T!

> *(ETHEL stands still. Then SHE starts towards DESIREE again.)*

ETHEL: I'm sorry ...

DESIREE: DON'T! ... How dare you. How DARE you!

ETHEL: But you don't understand. I didn't have a choice.

DESIRE: I can't believe you just — just showed up here like this. Choice! Oh, don't talk to me about choices. You have no right to talk to me about anything!

ETHEL: I didn't come here to talk about the past. I can't change the past.

DESIREE: YOU HAVE NO RIGHT!

ETHEL: If there was anything else I could do ...

DESIREE: You can leave, that's what you can do. Just get out of here!

> *(ETHEL approaches her. DESIREE backs up.)*

Don't come near me. I mean it.

ETHEL: I was there. I was at the funeral, Desiree. ... Yes, you do. You will.

DESIREE: ... I don't want to hear it! Stop it. I'm not listening.

DESIREE: What do you want!

ETHEL: I want to ask you for something.

DESIREE: This is incredible. This is absolutely incredible. What do you want ... Ethel. What could you possibly want from me that is SO fucking important that you barge in here, into my life and --

ETHEL: I'm sorry ...

DESIREE: You want to be my best friend? My confidante? My mother!?

ETHEL: I'm a good mother.

DESIREE: RIGHT! AND I'M THE VIRGIN MARY!

> *(DESIREE paces. ETHEL watches her. Finally, DESIREE*

sits down again. SHE takes some long breaths until SHE is more in control of herself.)

ETHEL: Your grandmother –

DESIREE: — is dead.

ETHEL: *(evenly)* But there's still hope for / Lucy –

DESIREE: — A reconciliation? / Never.

ETHEL: I don't expect a reconciliation. I just need –

DESIREE: — My forgiveness? Well you can't have it.

ETHEL: I don't care! I don't want it!

DESIREE: You're pitiful, you know that? I feel sorry for you. I don't have anything you want. I gave everything to the only mother I ever knew. I have nothing left for you.

> *(Silence.)*

ETHEL: *(steadily)* Yes, you do. You can give me your cord blood.

DESIREE: My …what!?

ETHEL: Your umbilical cord blood. I need your stem cells, Desiree. For Lucy. *(desperately)* I have the money. I can take care of everything. Please. You just need to sign some papers.

DESIREE: You make me sick.

ETHEL: Then blame it on your grandmother.

DESIREE: Shut up.

ETHEL: Blame it on the saint who raised you, who made me leave my home and my friends and my baby!

DESIREE: You're crazy. You're lying. You have no right … no right to talk about her like that.

ETHEL: (fiercely) Do you know what's worse than watching a selfish old woman die of a … a horrible, debilitating, terrifying disease?

DESIREE: — I don't know! I don't care! --

ETHEL: — Watching your own little girl … your own baby fighting for some kind of — of normalcy! — between her hand tremors and her … losing her balance and … You can give Lucy

287

a chance. She deserves a chance.

DESIREE: Go to hell.

ETHEL: Stem cell research is promising, so promising, Desiree. And I can bank the blood for 15, maybe 20 years.

ETHEL: Maybe long enough to treat Lucy's symptoms before ...

DESIREE: If you're not leaving, then I'm leaving.

(ETHEL is overwhelmed)

DESIREE: Why did you have to come here today?

ETHEL: Because I love Lucy!

(DESIREE stares at ETHEL. Silence. DESIREE pivots on her heels. SHE calls out as SHE leaves.)

DESIREE: That's not my problem.

(DESIREE heads quickly toward the exit. ETHEL shouts after her.)

ETHEL: SHE'S YOUR SISTER!

(DESIREE stops short. Pause. Then SHE finishes her exit. Lights fade to black.)

End of play

TRADE SECRETS

P. DAVID TEMPLE

BEST 10 MINUTE PLAYS 2019

The Play:

Trade Secrets

The Playwright:

P. David Temple

Synopsis:

A chance encounter of two competitive bakers—a man renowned for his bread-making and a woman famous for her muffins—reignites a years-old longing. As each seeks to learn from the other, they discuss a risky plan to trade secrets and explore together the essential chemistry of baking.

About the playwright:

Trade Secrets was voted audience favorite at the San Miguel de Allende 2017 Diez Minutos Festival and received an encore performance on the main stage of the 2018 San Miguel International Writers Conference. David Temple's play, The Purple House on Page Street, was a finalist in the National Playwrights Festival. He has worked as a producer, commercial film director, cameraman, and lighting director (IATSE Locals 600 and 52). His short film, Eve's Rib, won the Bronze Star Award at the Sacramento Film Festival. He studied philosophy at the University of Michigan and playwriting at HB Studio in New York. Please visit his website (pdavidtemple.com) for publication news of his recently completed novel, Five Times Lucky.

Contact:

pdavidtemple@gmail.com
917-302-3182

THE THEATRE:

Players Workshop
San Miguel Playhouse, Avenida Independencia #82, 37700 San Miguel De Allende, Gto, 37700 Mexico

MISSION:

Dedicated to the quality production of theater in San Miguel de Allende, Mexico, since 1982.

ABOUT:

Dedicated to the production of quality theater for more than 30 years, Players Workshop has made a positive cultural impact on the community of San Miguel de Allende. We wish to thank all of those supporters, sponsors, volunteers and artists who've made Players Workshop the "go-to" theater company in SMA.

Diez Minutos, co-founded by Mark Saunders and Michael Hager, is an annual international festival of ten-minute plays in English held in San Miguel de Allende, Mexico. The festival receives approximately 200 entries from around the world, from which it gives full productions of eight plays to sold-out audiences. "Trade Secrets" won Audience Favorite.

CONTACT:

Clara Dunham, Director
claradunham@hotmail.com
207-217-9668

PRESENTING THE PLAY:

Trade Secrets

CAST:

GEOFF—is of a certain age, nearing the end of his successful career as a "Master Baker." He is proud of his accomplishments and recent fame. He comes across at first as a bit full of himself. Yet he is wistful for the other missed experiences in life (i.e. intimacy) that he set aside in pursuit of his profession.

KAREN—is of a certain age, perhaps a year or two younger than the Geoff. Successful in her own right as a "Muffin Maker," she has blazed her own career path after having been frozen out of the men's world of master baking. She is focused on chemistry.

(NOTE: The characters are sincere. Theirs is a conversation between two professional bakers about baking. They are oblivious to the sometimes overtly sexual double meaning of their dialogue.)

SETTING:

The indoor atrium of CHELSEA MARKET, a Manhattan landmark renowned for its glassed-in bakeries, as well as its proximity to the Food Network, upstairs.

—LIGHTS UP

(A mature man, GEOFF, sits on a bench across from Amy's Bread taking a break from work. A sign on an easel says: MASTER CLASS TODAY! He is dressed in a white baker's uniform topped with the tallest of baker's hats. KAREN enters. She is about his age and similarly dressed in baker's clothes, although she wears a (less ostentatious) pink cap. KAREN is pre-occupied with looking downstage (into the bakery). She sits. She doesn't see GEOFF until she is too close not to acknowledge him.)

KAREN: *(surprised to see him up close)* Oh!

(she musters the resolve to speak to him)

Oh! Hi!

(awkward)

You work here at Amy's Bread. I work down at the end, at Sarabeth's Bakery, so I go past here every day. No demo today?

GEOFF: I'm waiting for a producer from the Food Network. They were supposed to be videotaping a segment on me today.

KAREN: Wow, to play on TV? You're really getting famous.

GEOFF: *(reserved, but with a hint of self-importance)* I wouldn't go that far...

KAREN: On Monday, the crowd out here was so deep that I had to stand on my tip-toes to see your demo.

GEOFF: I think people are just naturally interested in what I do.

KAREN: I don't know how you stay so focused with all those people looking in——so confident and controlled. It's quite an exhibition! You've taken baking to a higher level.

GEOFF: I've been doing it a long time. Since I was thirteen.

KAREN: I don't think I could ever master that level of concentration. It's mesmerizing!

GEOFF: I do enjoy working with my hands.

(changing the subject)

You and I, we've met before. You applied for a job here when we opened.

KAREN: That was years ago. You probably thought that I was just trying to buck the system.

GEOFF: In those days everybody just assumed that dough was the domain of men.

KAREN: I was so inexperienced. My only "hands-on" was an adult education class at the 'Y'.

GEOFF: Perceptions are slow to change. But I am as much to blame. When I first started, I, too, assumed that only a man could be a master baker.

KAREN: I guess that's why I got into making muffins. My mother steered me away from the dough. She told me to put my faith in chemistry. Not that I don't enjoy my work, but for us, the truth was always in the mix, the melding of ingredients.

GEOFF: She might be right.

KAREN: I'm not saying that I'm not proud of what I do, but I do sometimes think that I have missed out on some higher calling—that I never mastered the dough.

GEOFF: A perfect dough is a joy to behold.

KAREN: For me baking bread was always one of the great mysteries of life. How, microscopically, the pushing and pulling of complex molecules unites them into elongated proteins, stretching the gluten in one direction and then allowing it to pull back, stretching out and pulling back. And on top of that, how the action of the yeast works to further knead the dough, forming millions of miniature air bubbles which themselves stretch the molecules into gluten. The science in itself is so exciting...but I am afraid I might be over-intellectualizing it.

GEOFF: It's easy to do. Kneading dough is just a straightforward physical act. The perfect dough is simply one that bounces back when you poke it.

KAREN: You're right, of course. But isn't kneading dough more than just a matter of touch? I mean... I'd like to think... Isn't kneading about bonding?

GEOFF: *(beat)* Most people forget that.

KAREN: I always thought that heat had a lot to do with it.

GEOFF: *(beat)* Well, yes, of course, heat. Kneading creates heat and heat stimulates the yeast. Cookbooks in America call for the dough to stand at 80 degrees. The French like to work colder, extending the process and yielding exquisite results. There's a bakery out on Fire Island, *(beat)* a place I have never been, where they add a little dry ice, a technique they call teasing the dough, which prolongs the rising process even further. It can make for some very fluffy crusts.

KAREN: People really like experimenting with it.

GEOFF: Yes. And then there are those who are only interested in speed. With a KitchenAid, you could be done in sixty seconds, although you risk overdoing it. The end result of over-kneading of course is the loss of elasticity. I don't have to tell you any of this, but that's why I do all my kneading by hand. It takes a little longer—I like to spend ten to fifteen minutes or more—but it would take a Herculean effort to overdo it by hand. Remember, the goal here is to have a dough you can be proud of, one that rises fully and stands with dignity when you slip it in the oven.

KAREN: You make it sound so… simple.

GEOFF: Straightforward.

>   *(sincere)*

>   I learn a lot about a person by the way they knead dough. By their rhythm, both hands working in concert, pushing the dough with the heel of the right hand into the cup of the left. You see right away whether they trust the dough to rise. In capable hands it begins to rise immediately.

>   *(getting lost in a memory)*

>   Your hands were slender, not at all like a man's. I watched your fingers as you lifted the dough in front of you and then began to work it. Your fingers were very long. You began to ease the dough into shape, folding it over, stretching it out with your

palm, wrapping your fingers together and rolling them over the top. Then you pulled the dough back, folding it in upon itself. Yours was a rhythm, like a wave, the surf rising onto the beach at high tide, surging, then pulling back, then surging again, strong and persistent, firm but understanding, practiced, yet nuanced with improvisation. All very much in control. It was a performance one does not soon forget.

(sighs)

I have long regretted not taking you on.

(recovers)

But now you are famous for your muffins.

KAREN: I have a reputation. Nothing like yours.

GEOFF: I saw you in the crowd out here yesterday, through the window.

KAREN: We made eye contact.

GEOFF: You were in your uniform.

KAREN: I came early to watch you bake.

GEOFF: Those flourishes were for you. I may have overdone it.

KAREN: There was a rousing ovation.

GEOFF: After work, instead of going home… I stopped by your store.

KAREN: *(knowing he was there)* At Sarabeth's Bakery. I might have seen you.

GEOFF: There were samples of muffins on the counter.

KAREN: Those would have been mine.

GEOFF: *(aroused by the memory)* They were still warm.

KAREN: *(feeling the chemistry)* Muffins are best when buttered fresh.

GEOFF: I would never have thought to sprinkle cherries into the mix. The results were quite… surprising to the tongue.

KAREN: *(guarded)* An acquired taste, I'm sure. Not for everyone.

GEOFF: It leaves me wanting more.

KAREN: *(breathless)* Oh! Well... If you were to stop by again...

> *(unsure of the depth of his interest)*

You would probably only have the appetite for a quick treat, something like my Coconut Kisses. They melt in your mouth.

> *(happy even if his is just a passing fancy)*

Or if you have the time and a taste for tarts, mine are filled with Ambrosia. I'm told that they're an experience one does not soon forget.

> *(hoping for more)*

Unless I've misjudged you, and you're in the mood for something more satisfying. My Cinnamon Buns. They're spicy, though. Not for the faint of heart.

GEOFF: If I were to "stop by," it would be for something... longer lasting.

KAREN: *(nervous, excited)* Whatever your heart desires. I'm sure I could whip something up.

GEOFF: I am just so taken with your muffins. They're so delectable. I was wondering whether, if there is any way, you might allow me to see how they are made?

KAREN: You want the recipe?

GEOFF: I was hoping for something hands-on.

KAREN: Oh. A demonstration. I guess that could be arranged. After work, after everyone else has gone home? But I would expect something in exchange.

GEOFF: Name it!

KAREN: Show me how you knead! It's not enough to watch you through the window.

GEOFF: You want to see it closer-up.

KAREN: It's not enough to watch. You are a renowned master baker. You entertain the world with your kneading of the dough, performing solo, but I feel there is something more you could show me.

GEOFF: Hands-on?

KAREN: More. If kneading is about bonding, and you agree with me that it is, then I would want you to show me how the molecules unite.

GEOFF: You're looking for chemistry.

KAREN: What woman isn't?

GEOFF: You're proposing we...

> *(ponders her offer)*

...trade secrets?

KAREN: You show me yours and in exchange, I will show you mine.

GEOFF: The kisses and the tarts...?

KAREN: ...The buns and the muffins.

GEOFF: And in kind...

KAREN: ...You teach me to master the dough.

GEOFF: There is a whole body of knowledge to explore.

KAREN: It consumes me.

GEOFF: Were you thinking... tonight?

KAREN: We close at seven.

GEOFF: You're sure it's not too late?

KAREN: No, it's not too late. Not at all.

> *(glancing off-stage)*
>
> *(afraid that this will preempt their deal)*

Here comes your television crew.

GEOFF: Oh! Hello!

> *(stands to greet them)*
>
> *(turns his attention back to her)*

So, we have a deal?

KAREN: Tonight at seven.

> *[He offers his hand in a business-like handshake. She shakes*

his hand, then pulls it toward her and holds the back of his hand to her cheek.]

BLACKOUT

GROWN-ASS LOUIS

BRUCE WALSH

THE PLAY:

Grown-Ass Louis

THE PLAYWRIGHT:

Bruce Walsh

SYNOPSIS:

When Louis was 10 years old, he wrote a note to his recently deceased father, tied it to a balloon and released it to the heavens. Now, even though he's a grown-ass man, he can't stop wondering if Dad ever got the message.

ABOUT THE PLAYWRIGHT:

Bruce Walsh's fascination with sacredness pervades all of his plays. But not in the ways people sometimes expect. His characters are bold, queer, angry, ridiculous, joyous, deeply sexual beings. Bruce writes most often about people he encountered in his many day jobs, working for companies like UPS, Trader Joe's, and a slew of downsizing newspapers. He is endlessly fascinated by those that seek the "courage to be" – a great meaning or purpose – even amidst a culture that is so often absurdly, even hilariously, out of touch with those needs.

In 2017, Bruce graduated from Indiana University with an MFA in playwriting. Since then his plays have been presented by Azuka Theatre, Outpost Repertory Theatre, Fat Turtle Theatre Company, Actors Theatre of Louisville, where he won the 2017 Heideman Award, and The Kennedy Center for the Performing Arts, where he won the Gary Garrison National Ten Minute Play Award. Before attending IU, he lived in Philadelphia for over a decade, working as an arts journalist, site-specific theater maker, and playwright.

CONTACT:

biwalsh@umail.iu.edu

THE THEATRE:

> Actors Theatre of Louisville
> 316 West Main St., Louisville, KY 40202

MISSION:

> Actors Theatre unlocks human potential, builds community, and enriches quality of life by engaging people in theatre that reflects the wonder and complexity of our time.

ABOUT:

> Now in its 55th Season, Actors Theatre of Louisville, the State Theatre of Kentucky, is the flagship arts organization in the Louisville community. Actors Theatre presents almost 350 performances annually and delivers a broad range of programming, including classics and contemporary work through the Brown-Forman Series, holiday plays, a series of theatrical events produced by the Professional Training Company, and the Humana Festival of New American Plays—the premier new play festival in the nation, which has introduced more than 450 plays into the American theatre repertoire over the past 42 years. In addition, Actors Theatre provides over 15,000 arts experiences each year to students across the region through its Education Department, and boasts one of the nation's most prestigious continuing pre-professional resident training companies, now in its 47th year.

WEBSITE:

> actorstheatre.org

PRESENTING THE PLAY:

Grown-Ass Louis

CHARACTERS:

LOUIS

MR. WYNEWSKI

MRS. HEINEMANN

WETSUIT GUY

MR. HEINEMANN

(LOUIS is a grown-ass man. But he's dressed like a little boy from the 90's, perhaps checkered Umbros and Bart Simpson shirt. He holds a balloon with a prominent manila tag at the end of the string. He does this with great purpose, hope, and trepidation.)

LOUIS: *(To us)* In my dream I'm still on the soccer field holding my balloon.

(MR. WYNEWSKI enters. He's a grown-ass man, too, an elementary school teacher. His tie has the pi symbol on it.)

MR. WYNEWSKI: You don't wanna let go or what?

(No response.)

Okay…

Time to let go. Don't you want your balloon to…

Like the other kids.

(Pause. MR. WYNEWSKI tries a new tactic.)

(Admiring the skyline:)

MR. WYNEWSKI: Look at 'em all…

Where do ya think the farthest one'll go? China? You think one'll get all the way to China?

(Pause, a glance at LOUIS.)

You're a smart kid, Louis. I'm not gonna play around with you.

I should say – from an empirical perspective – there's very little chance any of these balloons will travel more than three hundred miles.

I am a scientist, after all.

(Fingering his tie.)

Had one mailed back from Sweden, though. Can you believe that?

About five years ago.

But it turns out this lady found the tag in the parking lot at the airport and took it with her.

To Sweden.

But.

So.

Still, pretty cool, huh?

Sweden.

(Pause.)

MR. WYNEWSKI: Okay. Mrs. Copenhaffer's class is already headed in. I need you to line up, too.

(A beat.)

If you don't say anything, I can't help ya.

Okay, buddy, I'm gonna break it down like this:

Three options here:

One, you let go of the balloon, and line up with your classmates.

Two, you hang on to the balloon, and line up with your classmates.

Three, you tell me what is goin' on inside your head right now, and we figure somethin' out together.

(No response. WYNEWSKI goes nuclear:)

… Okay… okay… maybe there's four options….

I just thought of an additional possibility.

Option number four: I walk away… I just leave you here, and the next person you see is Dr. Putsavage.

You wanna talk to Dr. Putsavage 'bout the…

The… failure of communication you and I are experiencing right now?

(No response.)

Okay. Option four.

(MR. WYNEWSKI begins to exit.)

LOUIS: My dad is dead.

(A beat.)

MR. WYNEWSKI: ... I know. Buddy, I know.

Come on, talk to me. I can't help, unless you –

LOUIS: I wrote a message to him on the tag.

MR. WYNEWSKI: That's sweet. I think that's very sweet.

LOUIS: I asked God with all my heart to deliver this message.

MR. WYNEWSKI: ... What did he say?

LOUIS: I can't hear God, yet. My mom says I have to wait 'till after my bar mitzvah to hear God.

I don't know if I should let go.

I don't like thinking of my balloon drifting out there, and God ignoring it, just... floating...

Do you think God would ignore my balloon?

MR. WYNEWSKI: I'm a scientist, Louis. We're sort of trained not to think of things in that way.

(LOUIS looks sad.)

... Wait a minute...

(MR. WYNEWSKI looks at the manila tag.)

I think this penmanship is just too beautiful for God to ignore.

LOUIS: ... Penmanship...?

MR. WYNEWSKI: Sure, don't you know that God needs scribes up there in heaven? Haven't you seen the paintings of little angels writing with feathered pens?

LOUIS: Mr. Wynewski: Don't feed me a plate of bull crap and call it pizza.

(Pause. MR. WYNEWSKI gazes at the skyline.)

MR. WYNEWSKI: You didn't write that note so you could keep it at your desk.

You did it to let it go.

You need to let go. Now.

(A beat.)

… Let go.

Let go, Louis.

Let go.

(LOUIS closes his eyes, takes a deep breath, and lets go of the balloon.)

(MR. WYNEWSKI exits.)

(Someone puts a white robe on LOUIS.)

LOUIS: *(To us)* And then I wake up. But I don't actually wake up; I just wake up in the dream. And I'm wearing my father's robe.

(MRS. HEINEMANN enters in a matching robe.)

MRS. HEINEMANN: Louis, there's a man at the door for you.

LOUIS: Mom… why are we wearing matching robes?

MRS. HEINEMANN: I'm wearing a robe?

So I am, look at that.

And with my initials on it, too. Nice touch.

Hey…. Yours has Daddy's initials on it.

LOUIS: Why am I wearing a robe with Dad's initials on it?

MRS. HEINEMANN: I don't know. I thought I gave all your dad's clothes to Goodwill.

LOUIS: Yeah, I drove them over in the van.

MRS. HEINEMANN: Thanks for that, sweetie. I just couldn't keep walking around the house with his stuff everywhere.

All those corduroy blazers in the closet.

I needed a clean break.

Time to start over.

Now I make my coffee in a French press.

LOUIS: I never started over, mom.

MRS. HEINEMANN: It takes a bit longer, but tastes MUCH better.

LOUIS: You said I'd be able to hear God when I was a man. I got bar mitzvahed. I'm thirty-two years old. Why can't I hear God?

What am I doing wrong?

MRS. HEINEMANN: You ask too many questions.

You'll hurt your head, you ask so many questions.

Look at me: I walk into the room; I can't remember why I walked into this room.

You don't see me asking why. You don't see me complaining.

You say we're wearing robes. I say, lovely, a very comfortable way to get through your day. More people should try it.

It's like I wake up fifty times a day.

I'm watching Ryan Seacrest on *Morning Joe*. I'm thinking: Who let Ryan Seacrest interview the Attorney General? Ryan Seacrest is as dumb as my left ass cheek. But wait. Ryan Seacrest isn't on *Morning Joe*. Who is the guy on *Morning Joe*?

He has good hair. The hair on that Morning Joe guy. And his fiancé is a Democrat. They balance each other nicely.

And then there's a knock at the door. Somebody wants to see Louis. And I come in here, and you tell me I'm wearing my bathrobe.

I never know why or how anything happens to me.

It could be very disconcerting. But it's not.

Here's the secret: Do like me, just focus on the breath in your nose. Like this. Watch.

(Pause.)

LOUIS: ... Mom, I can't see you focus on your breath. Your focus is not a thing I can observe.

MRS. HEINEMANN: Oh, you're so smart, wise guy. You're so smart: Tell me why you're wearing your father's bathrobe, if you're so smart.

LOUIS: I DON'T KNOW.

MRS. HEINEMANN: You're getting worked up. What did I say? Focus on the breath...

In. Out. Let it happen. Make an effort. Try not to try. Just let go. Like me.

Eckhart Tolle says that taking conscious breaths is the way to invite God into your heart.

I'm gonna tell the man at the door you're in here.

He's very nice. He's from the National Oceanic and Atmospheric Administration.

LOUIS: ... um... ?

MRS. HEINEMANN: Oh, you're so smart. You don't know what the National Oceanic and Atmospheric Administration is?

It's a subsidiary of the U.S. Department of Commerce.

Silly.

(MRS. HEINEMANN exits.)

(A very wet grown-ass man wearing fins klop-plops into the room, carrying a dead dolphin.)

(Perhaps the man wears an air tank and a wetsuit as well. Maybe a snorkel. He's very official looking, like a Navy SEAL.)

(He plops the dolphin corpse down in front of LOUIS. Water splashes everywhere.)

(The man reaches toward the dolphin's mouth, where there is a crumpled manila tag, hanging from a string.)

WETSUIT GUY: Are you Louis Heinemann?

I'm with the National Oceanic and Atmospheric Administration. We're a subsidiary of the U.S. Department of Commerce. A lot of people don't realize that.

We found your balloon.

(Examining the tag.)

This is excellent penmanship.

LOUIS: Thank you.

WETSUIT GUY: A dolphin tried to ingest it and choked to death.

LOUIS: ... Oh.

WETSUIT GUY: We found it in the Yellow Sea.

LOUIS: Really? Where's that?

WETSUIT GUY: Off the coast of China.

LOUIS: *(Slightly uplifted)* Oh?

WETSUIT GUY: What are you so happy about?

LOUIS: Nothing. Sorry.

WETSUIT GUY: You should be sorry.

What were you kids thinking in the 90's?

LOUIS: I have no idea.

WETSUIT GUY: All of you dumbass kids releasing thousands of balloons into the atmosphere?

How did you not know that was going to cause a problem?

Where did you think all the balloons were going to go?

Did you think they would just magically disappear?

What were you thinking?

Tell me.

Tell me what you thought was going to happen.

LOUIS: I thought God was going to deliver it to my dad, in heaven.

WETSUIT GUY: … What?

LOUIS: Do you think he got it?

WETSUIT GUY: … ahh… No, dude, I think a dolphin ate it and choked to death.

LOUIS: You don't think Dad got the message?

WETSUIT GUY: … Buddy. You're a grown-ass man. It's time to respect science, like an adult. Accept the reality before you.

LOUIS: He didn't get it?

WETSUIT GUY: … You gotta let this go.

LOUIS: I can't.

WETSUIT GUY: Let go.

LOUIS: I'm trying.

(MR. WYNEWSKI enters.)

MR. WYNEWSKI: Let go, Louis.

(MRS. HEINEMANN enters.)

MRS. HEINEMANN: Let go.

(An alarm clock sounds in the distance.)

(Special on LOUIS. Everyone else disappears.)

LOUIS: And then I wake up.

(Perhaps daylight through a window, and songbirds chirping.)

(LOUIS closes his eyes and breathes deeply, tries to focus on his breath. In. And out. In. And out.)

(MR. HEINEMANN enters behind LOUIS in a corduroy blazer. He holds the manila card. He looks at LOUIS with great pride and wonder.)

(LOUIS does not see him.)

End.

DO YOU TAKE THIS WOMAN?
LOLLY WARD

BEST 10 MINUTE PLAYS 2019

THE PLAY:

Do You Take This Woman?

THE PLAYWRIGHT:

Lolly Ward

SYNOPSIS:

Every person is a work of art, and everyone's a critic. A writer married to an art critic leaves her mark with one final creation.

ABOUT THE PLAYWRIGHT:

Lolly Ward's plays include *Mate* (The Actors' Gang; California Institute of Technology), *Black Press in the White House* (Smith and Kraus, 105 Five-Minute Plays), and *The Ethel Party* (*Silk Road Review*). She received her Bachelor's and Master's in English and Creative Writing from Stanford University. As a member of The Actors' Gang in Los Angeles, she took on many roles, toured nationally and internationally, and acted in both the stage and film versions of *Embedded* at the Public Theater. After several years in Los Angeles as a member of the Playwrights Union, she moved to Portland, Oregon, where she cofounded LineStorm Playwrights.

CONTACT:

forwardwriters@gmail.com

WEBSITE:

lollyward.com
linestormplaywrights.com

314

THE THEATRE:

> Mildred's Umbrella Theatre Company
> 4617 Montrose Blvd. #100 Houston, TX 77006

MISSION:

> Mildred's Umbrella Theater Company seeks to challenge audiences and theatre artists by creating and performing bold, innovative, and fresh theatrical works grounded in the best traditions of the dramatic arts. With a strong feminine presence in our artistic vision, we strive to feature the work of female playwrights, actors, and directors, which promotes the empowerment of women through the performing arts.

ABOUT:

> Mildred's Umbrella began in 2001 when local actress, Jennifer Decker, and playwright, John Harvey, brought together a group of artists and actors to create a collaborative theatrical piece written by Harvey and directed by Decker. Since then, the company has grown into a fixture of Houston's performing arts community. Known for bringing edgy, new work to Houston and pushing the envelope of theatre, Mildred's Umbrella uses the art form to explore our world and present audiences with thought-provoking works. Now in its thirteenth full season, the company has produced a variety of pieces including mainstage, full-length plays, theatrical works in conjunction with lectures at the University of Houston, Fringe Festival pieces, and a popular festival showcase of short originals ("Museum of Dysfunction"), currently in its tenth iteration.
>
> Since 2008, Mildred's Umbrella has celebrated the dark, quirky, and absurd with a collection of short pieces submitted by emerging and established playwrights. Now in its tenth year, Museum Of Dysfunction has become a fun collaboration of Houston theater artists, a venue for playwrights to test new work, and a highlight of the summer festival season.

CONTACT:

> Rebecca Ayres or Jennifer Decker
> info@mildredsumbrella.com
> 832-463-0409

WEBSITE: https://mildredsumbrella.com

PRESENTING THE PLAY:

Do You Take This Woman?

CHARACTERS:

CARRIE: 30s

WILL: 30s

SETTING:

Will and Carrie's bedroom. Evening.

(Lights up on Carrie in the bedroom. She wears white night-clothes. She is — or used to be — a writer.

She rereads a note, signs and folds it. It is made of white paper, and she places it among a bevy of colorful origami swans on the bedside table.

She picks up a bottle of pills and shakes it. Several left. She checks the warning on the side. She opens the bottle and takes a few pills. Then a few more. One more.

She looks at the room, saying goodbye to favorite things.

She lies down on the floor.

She's startled by the sound of the front door opening. Will calls out from the living room.)

WILL: Hi, Lover!

(Carrie struggles to get up quickly and into bed.)

CARRIE: Hello, Bear.

WILL: You can't be in bed again.

CARRIE: I'll prove it to you.

WILL: I bought some ice cream. It's chocolate chip, and it's melting because I stopped to get a coffee.

CARRIE: Now?

(He comes into the bedroom.)

WILL: You can have some.

CARRIE: I can't.

WILL: It's a Venti. It's huge.

(He pushes her origami and note aside to put down his things.)

WILL: Did you get up at all today?

CARRIE: I got up.

WILL: I'm not accusing you, Carrie; I just saw the mail in the slot.

CARRIE: I didn't get the mail.

WILL: I know. I don't care. I got the mail. There's a credit card bill.

I'll take care of it tomorrow.

CARRIE: I didn't get the mail.

WILL: Right. We could watch TV. Want to watch TV?

CARRIE: I don't want to watch TV.

WILL: Someone big is on the late show tonight. Who is it?... It's... that...girl...who used to be on...

CARRIE: I don't want to watch TV.

WILL: Well, no one's going to force it down your throat.

CARRIE: You're home too early. Why aren't you at the gallery?

WILL: Because the show was crap, of course. The kid is twenty and he's famous and he can't paint a straight line. He understands color but that's it. He's tedious. In two years he'll be called a hack.

CARRIE: "He's a hack." Now you don't have to wait.

WILL: He should go back to painting houses. He was probably better. He's no artist like you.

CARRIE: Right.

WILL: I mean, no origami artist like you.

CARRIE: That's enough.

WILL: Bright hues, bold lines. Elements of cubism and strangely erotic. This visionary artist translates an ancient technique into a vital message for our times.

CARRIE: Stupid, meaningless, not worth the pot to piss in.

WILL: I wouldn't say that.

CARRIE: Because I'm your wife.

WILL: No, because I have to candy-coat it for my reviews.

CARRIE: You want to know something? Pam Anderson got a star on the Walk of Fame.

WILL: What? When?! It doesn't matter. You could get a star if you took off your shirt.

CARRIE: No, I — I don't think I could. I'd take it off and people would shove me aside to get their hands on Pam Anderson's star.

WILL: Is there dinner left over?

CARRIE: No dinner.

WILL: That's all right. I'll get jacked up on coffee and come find you in bed. Did you take your pill?

CARRIE: Yeah.

WILL: You took your pill.

CARRIE: Yes. I. Took. My.

WILL: All right, all right! *(A beat.)* Babe, isn't there anything to smile about?

CARRIE: I wrote a story.

WILL: Really? Today?

CARRIE: I've been working on it. People might think it's crap.

WILL: Come on.

CARRIE: I wish I could have read it to my mother. I think my mother would have — my mom could always find something of value — something to love even —

WILL: You know, your early work —

CARRIE: *(With bite.)* Had such promise. So much potential. Why don't you strangle me with those words? I'm already crippled by them. What happened to Carrie? Where did she go? Did she stop or did the world forget about her? Published at seventeen. A first novel at twenty-six. What did the critics say? Oh, yes, "Carrie Mullen's debut novel sends aloft a sad tale with such eloquence and deft humor that the reader forgets it's a tragedy until the final line." And then two years later, "Although Ms. Mullen won't reveal the subject of her follow-up novel, she hints that the topic of redemption will give readers a taste of hope." But instead, after a few more years, Mullen goes insane and falls into a pit of despair! "So early fans must seek solace in rereading her first and only novel, *The Swan Song*, having lost faith that a second will take flight."

WILL: Well, what do critics know anyway?

CARRIE: I am the Ugly Duckling in reverse. I was small but brave, and the world said, "Look at those feathers; look at those wings. This may be the finest swan we've ever seen." And then nothing happened. I floated away on the water, turning dull and ordinary.

WILL: You could try again.

CARRIE: You could paint again. *(A beat.)* I'd like to be caught in a still life that lasts forever. But with my luck, I'd be abstract, and critics like you would say, "Is that supposed to be a bird? It's hideous." Of course, I'd probably sell for $20 million dollars. I wonder... Will?

WILL: I'm still here.

CARRIE: If you had $20 million dollars, would you choose me again?

WILL: Don't take this the wrong way, but you look very pretty right now.

CARRIE: What's the wrong way to take that?

WILL: There's something different. You look translucent.

CARRIE: You can see through me.

(They look at each other.)

CARRIE: Do you want to hear what I wrote?

WILL: Now? Not now, Sweetie.

CARRIE: You're busy.

WILL: You're tired.

CARRIE: I'm tired.

WILL: Yeah.

CARRIE: I'm so tired.

WILL: And I'm wired. I was going to climb in there and kiss you but —

CARRIE: No...

She moves farther under the covers.

WILL: I think I'll watch a few minutes of the news.

CARRIE: Venti.

WILL: Venti Vidi Vici. I caffeined, I saw, I conquered. You want anything? Ice cream?

CARRIE: Nothing. *(A beat.)* I love you, William.

WILL: I barely understood you. It sounded like, "Buff the kitten."

CARRIE: Will —

WILL: What?

CARRIE: Buff the kitten.

WILL: I will.

> *He kisses her.*

WILL: I will, I will, I will.

> *(She's fading. He adjusts the covers.)*

WILL: Keep the bed warm.

> *(He takes his coffee, turns off the light, and leaves.)*
> *(The TV goes on in the next room.)*

End of play.

THE BOOK OF RUTH
JOSEPH SAMUEL WRIGHT

BEST 10 MINUTE PLAYS 2019

THE PLAY:

The Book Of Ruth

THE PLAYWRIGHT:

Joseph Samuel Wright

SYNOPSIS:

In 1930s Appalachia, a woman comes home to her secret lover so they can run away together. But she finds that their plans may have gotten complicated while she was gone...

ABOUT THE PLAYWRIGHT:

Joseph Samuel Wright is a queer writer, comedian, and producer whose works explore gender, the people pushed to the fringes of society, and folks trying to get their chance. A tenth-generation Tennessean, Joseph's passion for representation through storytelling inspired him to take his dog-and-pony-show to New York City. There he founded a theatre company to create a community of diverse, emerging artists and produce an annual festival of new works, Duct Tape and a Dream. His plays were also produced in NYC and regionally during this time. After six years, Joseph moved to Los Angeles to tackle TV and screenwriting, and the Duct Tape and a Dream festival continued under a new artistic director.

Joseph is currently a staff writer for the Facebook Watch series TXT Stories where his highest episode has 10 million views and counting! Wright's series concept JOCKSTRAP PALACE was optioned and developed by New Form. His pilot HOME TO ROOST was a Sloan Grant recipient, and his feature script THE FALL placed at Austin Film Festival. Joseph has performed as a stand up comedian all around Los Angeles, including at The Comedy Store.

CONTACT:

josephsamuelwright@gmail.com

THE THEATRE:

Barrington Stage Company
122 North Street, Pittsfield, MA 01201

MISSION:

Barrington Stage Company (BSC) is a not-for-profit professional theatre company with a three-fold mission: to produce top-notch, compelling work; to develop new plays and musicals; and to find fresh, bold ways of bringing new audiences into the theatre, especially young people.

ABOUT:

Barrington Stage Company (BSC) is a regional theatre company in The Berkshires of Western Massachusetts. It was co-founded in 1995 by Artistic Director, Julianne Boyd, and Managing Director, Susan Sperber, in Sheffield, Massachusetts. In 2004, BSC developed, workshopped and premiered the hit musical The 25th Annual Putnam County Spelling Bee. Following the successful Broadway run, which nabbed two Tony Awards for Best Book and Best Featured Actor, BSC made the move to a more permanent home in Pittsfield, Massachusetts. 10x10 New Play Festival: 10 Ten Minute Plays X 10 Playwrights = 100 Minutes Of Pure Joy.

CONTACT:

Megan Nussle
mnussle@barringtonstageco.org
413-499-5446

WEBSITE:

barringtonstageco.org

PRESENTING THE PLAY:

The Book Of Ruth

CHARACTERS

GRACE, early twenties, pleasing, sweet, grounded

RUTH, mid twenties, strong, loyal, earnest

SETTING:

The late 1920s. Tennessee. The Cumberland Plateau. A small wooden house perches at the top of a holler between Jamestown and Allardt.

(Lights up. GRACE sits on a hard stool with a bowl in her lap and a bowl at her feet. She strings beans. Behind her a pot boils on the fire stove. Two buckets of water rest in front of the fire. To one side, the counter is covered with empty mason jars. To the other, a wooden table is crowded with full, sealed jars of canned vegetables. RUTH stomps into the room brandishing a tightly-clutched purse.)

RUTH: Lo! Yer hero returns triumphant!

GRACE: Ruth! Didn't expect ya til tomorrow!

RUTH: Ten whole dollars, can ya believe it?

(RUTH tosses the purse to GRACE then plops down on the floor to pull off her shoes.)

RUTH: I told you that trip to Knoxville'd be worth it.

GRACE: You was right.

RUTH: Ain't I always right?

GRACE: Now don't go getting the big head. We can't afford new hats.

(RUTH scrambles up.)

RUTH: Can ya believe I got ten dollars for my mama's locket? In cash! Imagine what we can get for yer granny's ring?

(GRACE tosses the purse back to RUTH.)

GRACE: You figuring on selling my granny's ring now?

RUTH: Grace, just listen. I know where we can go. You and me are gonna sell everything that ain't nailed down and get ourselves out to Hollywood.

GRACE: Hollywood? You must've hit yer head galloping back up the mountain so fast. Hollywood's clear 'cross the country!

RUTH: But that's where they shoot the movies. And with yer face, you can make a bundle.

GRACE: I don't reckon I need to make a bundle. You and I talk about just getting out of Fentress County, and next thing I know you're trying to sweep me all the way to the Pacific? When'dya make that leap?

RUTH: When I saw the picture at the Bijou and thought, well shoot, my Grace is twice as pretty as that gal up on the screen. Three times!

(GRACE gets up, moving the bowl from her lap to the stool so she can cross away.)

GRACE: What's the point of getting outta this town and everybody prying into our business just to wind up in front of a camera with the whole country watching me?

(RUTH looks around the room.)

RUTH: I thought you was gonna wait for me to start canning.

GRACE: I was afraid if I waited any longer, everything in the garden'd go bad.

RUTH: So ya lugged all that water up from the crik by yerself? You could'a hurt yerself!

GRACE: I used the pulley.

RUTH: The pulley's broke.

GRACE: Willy fixed it.

RUTH: Willy Byrd? Fixed our pulley?

GRACE: Well he was just stopping by to say hi—

RUTH: Of course he was. He's had his eye on you since the—

GRACE: *(talking louder)* I offered him water, and somehow or 'nother it came up our pulley'd broke. He didn't want me trudging buckets up and down that holler any more'n you do, so he offered to take a look.

RUTH: Yeah? What else has Willy been takin' a look at 'round here?

GRACE: It was a real easy fix, and since I could just pull water up with the rope as need be now now, I decided to get started canning. Got through all the maters and the corn.

RUTH: Did Willy stick around and help ya with that, too?

GRACE: *(attempting to be gay)* 'course not! What does Willy Byrd know 'bout canning?

RUTH: Well here I 'bout killt myself comin' back from Knoxville, and you ain't 'even missed me.

GRACE: Don't be daft, Ruth. Course I missed ya. You've been gone almost a week!

RUTH: And all week long ya been with Willy?

GRACE: I told you. I've been pickin' and cannin'.

RUTH: 'Fore I left, you was as ready as I was to get outta here. Find a place we could be...invisible together.

GRACE: I didn't know "outta here" was gonna mean the whole other side of the country.

RUTH: It's not just California. Now you're hanging on to yer granny's ring. Carrying on with Willie Byrd. Lettin' him fix things 'round here. I coulda fixed that pulley, ya know. If you'd'a waited.

GRACE: I didn't wanna wait.

RUTH: I see that. I do see that, Grace.

GRACE: Oh Ruth, don't go getting into one of yer moods.

RUTH: *(an accusation)* You're thinking about staying.

GRACE: Ruth, I've never been off'a this mountain. Never even been to Knoxville—

RUTH: I wanted you to come with me—

GRACE: Maybe I'm happy like this.

RUTH: So ya do wanna stay.

GRACE: I don't know what I want.

RUTH: And you want Willy Byrd?

GRACE: I'm tired, Ruth. I'm tired of people whispering at church. I'm tired of Mama asking when I'm getting married. If I'm ever gonna use Granny's ring or if she should give it to cousin Mary. Of worrying about making folks suspicious.

RUTH: I thought that's why we was gonna go away.

GRACE: Is that easier? Movin' clean 'cross the country?

RUTH: People are freer in California. We'd blend right in. Shoot, we'd probably be too boring.

GRACE: And that's supposed to be easier? Running to some strange place is easier?

RUTH: We can stay here. If ya want.

GRACE: Is it so wrong to think it would be easier to just marry Willy Byrd? Live here like my sisters? I know he'd have me. And he's a nice man.

RUTH: So ya do want to marry Willy.

GRACE: I told him I had to think about it.

RUTH: He asked you?

GRACE: And when he did, I could see a life with him. I won't lie to ya. A life that wouldn't raise a single eyebrow. And maybe having that life would be the easiest thing.

RUTH: How could that be the easiest thing?

GRACE: I'm not. . . strong like you, Ruth. I couldn't go to Knoxville on horseback to sell a locket. And I couldn't go to California to be in pictures. And I don't know how much longer I can live on this bluff with you, knowing people are starting to talk.

RUTH: Oh.

GRACE: When we—. Nobody was supposed to say anything. Remember? Two spinsters livin' together. Sharin' a place. But it ain't been so invisible. People noticed. People notice we ain't interested in none'a the men who come 'round. People notice we're real close. And they notice… I don't know what all they notice! We're so careful, but—. But they're talkin'. And I can't stand it!

RUTH: So come with me to California! I will leave right this minute if you want. This ten dollars'll get us pretty far. We'll sell what we need along the way.

GRACE: I'm not running off in the night like a fugitive. Prove them all right.

RUTH: I would do anything, sell anything, scrub floors and warsh smelly drawers and cook for strangers, to keep you safe and comfortable and happy.

GRACE: What if what I need to be happy is to be let alone? To marry Willy Byrd or some other man. To have a few kids. To can beans and potatoes and soup and be simple?

RUTH: What you need to be happy is me. You know it's me.

GRACE: You may well be the thing that makes me happiest in this world. But this thing's also—I can't. I'm caught up, like a little sparrow sent up on a gust of air. Soaring higher than she ever meant to. But I wanna be on the ground, Ruth.

RUTH: This ten dollars is our freedom.

GRACE: It's yer freedom. You always been able to do things I couldn't do. And I think you should go. To California or wherever you can fly.

RUTH: You want me to leave?

(GRACE doesn't answer. RUTH picks up a string bean.)

RUTH: You ever looked at these bean plants?

GRACE: All afternoon while I was picking 'em.

RUTH: In every garden everywhere you go, the rows of bean plants look the same. Everybody puts their sticks in the same triangle, and the vines grow right up it. By September, every garden has a little wall of reaching bean vines. But that ain't the bean plants shape, Grace. That's just the direction we told it to grow. You understand what I'm saying?

(GRACE scoops up the bowl of beans and sets it out of RUTH's reach.)

GRACE: I understand. But you ever seen a bean vine growing without those sticks?

RUTH: It could. It always did before man tried to put it in a garden. Them bean vines used to find their own way.

GRACE: Well they sure look a lot stronger all stuck together in a garden.

RUTH: Just until we eat 'em.

GRACE: We ain't talking about beans, Ruth. And nobody's gonna eat me.

331

RUTH: I just don't know how things could'a changed so much in one week.

GRACE: They didn't. They changed over a long time. Until I couldn't deny it no more.

RUTH: Is this because I asked ya to move to Hollywood?

GRACE: No.

RUTH: Because I could be happy here in this house with you forever.

GRACE: I think Hollywood sounds like a fine plan. And I'm probably a fool to pass it by. You should still go. I think you can find yer way anywhere you set yourself to going.

RUTH: You really wanna get rid of me, huh?

GRACE: I'll miss you more'n you'll ever understand.

RUTH: You'll have Willy to distract you.

GRACE: Don't be like that.

(RUTH strings the bean in her hand. She drops the string in the bowl on the floor and sets the ready bean pod on the chair where the bowl used to be.)

RUTH: I better get outta here.

GRACE: Wait!

(GRACE rushes over and digs in a drawer. Ruth starts gathering her stuff to go.)

RUTH: If I stand here much longer I think I might bust.

(GRACE pulls out a ring and hurries to RUTH. She presses the ring into RUTH's hand.)

GRACE: Take my granny's ring.

(RUTH tries to hand the ring back, but GRACE won't take it.)

RUTH: The ten dollars will be enough for just me.

GRACE: It's not to sell. It's to keep. For you.

(RUTH pockets the ring.)

RUTH: I'll never sell it. No matter how desperate I am.

(RUTH puts on her shoes.)

GRACE: Write to me once you're settled.

RUTH: I will.

GRACE: But don't ask me to come.

RUTH: You know I'm gonna ask.

GRACE: Don't. It'll just hurt us both.

(GRACE walks with RUTH to the door.)

RUTH: You make sure Willy treats ya good.

GRACE: Ruth.

RUTH: I mean it.

GRACE: He will.

RUTH: Not as good as I could.

GRACE: Goodbye, Ruth.

(GRACE closes the door behind RUTH.)

END OF PLAY

THE BEAST IN YOUR WOODS
JONATHAN YUKICH

BEST 10 MINUTE PLAYS 2019

THE PLAY:

The Beast in Your Woods

THE PLAYWRIGHT:

Jonathan Yukich

SYNOPSIS:

A couple wakes to the sound of a doorbell at 3am. Who could it be? The possibilities mount, as the malaise of the suburban paradigm begins to seep through.

ABOUT THE PLAYWRIGHT:

Jonathan Yukich's plays receive over 200 full productions each year, and have been produced across the U.S. and Canada, as well as in Australia, New Zealand, South Africa, China, India, and throughout Europe and the Middle East. Jonathan's plays are published with Broadway Play Publishing, Playscripts Inc., Smith & Kraus, Applause Theatre & Cinema Books, Eldridge Publishing, Heuer Publishing, Pioneer Drama Service, and Meriwether Press. He is the recipient of a number of awards and honors, including the Kennedy Center's Paula Vogel Award for Playwriting. He lives in Connecticut and teaches at the University of New Haven.

WEBSITE:

jonathanyukich.com

The Theatre:

Trembling Stage
South Hadley, MA

Mission:

As a company we strive to explore and develop the relationship between author, actor and director in order to create compelling and visceral works of art. As artists, we are dedicated to theatre as a craft rather than a commodity, to collaboration with younger theatre professionals, and to our belief that theatre has the unique ability to be a conduit for humanity's most profound experiences.

About:

Trembling Stage was formed by Noah Tuleja and Jonathan Yukich after meeting each other as graduate students at Indiana University. They began their work together as playwright/director with the world premiere of Jonathan's play THE ALIEN FROM CINCINNATI, and continued to collaborate after graduating, forming Trembling Stage in 2007. Their first production, a joint collaboration with the Montana Repertory Theatre, was Jonathan's adaptation of Mary Shelly's "Frankenstein," FRANKENSTEIN UNPLUGGED. More recently, we presented AMERICAN MIDGET at the NYCFringe (called a "psychological gem" by the NY Times) and ALICE@WONDERLAND, first premiered as a partnership with Trembling Stage, won the 2014 Shubert Fendrich Award.

Contact:

Noah Tuleja: Co-Artistic Director
noahalexis@gmail.com

Website:

tremblingstage.com

PRESENTING THE PLAY:

The Beast In Your Woods

CHARACTERS:

KAREN, the wife

JOHN, the husband

SETTING:

Suburbia. A bedroom.

AT RISE: A doorbell is heard, then lights up sharply as KAREN sits up, with a jolt, from her sleep. She is in bed, wide-eyed, rattled, and suddenly alert, with her husband JOHN still asleep next to her. A bedside clock reads 3:04am.)

KAREN: John?

JOHN: Mm.

KAREN: John?

JOHN: Huh?

KAREN: Did you hear that?

JOHN: Hear what?

KAREN: The doorbell.

JOHN: What doorbell?

KAREN: Our doorbell.

JOHN: Are you –

KAREN: Someone rang our doorbell.

JOHN: *(Sitting up, half asleep.)* It's 3am.

KAREN: I heard the doorbell.

JOHN: You dreamt it.

KAREN: Wait. Listen.

(They listen. Stillness. Silence.)

JOHN: Go back to sleep.

KAREN: I know I heard it.

JOHN: This is Spring Meadow. Doorbells don't ring at 3am.

(KAREN gets out of bed and begins to throw on her robe.)

Karen?

KAREN: I'm going to see what it was.

JOHN: Honey, come back to bed.

KAREN: I know what I heard.

JOHN: You'll wake Abby.

KAREN: Abby sleeps like a log.

JOHN: You've had a troublesome day.

> *(Pause.)*

KAREN: Troublesome?

JOHN: It's been –

KAREN: Did you say troublesome?

JOHN: You know what I meant.

KAREN: It's a dumb choice of words.

JOHN: Okay, now –

KAREN: Back acne or slow internet – those things are troublesome, but not –

JOHN: I'm sorry. It's just, you've got a lot weighing on you.

KAREN: You think I'm delusional.

JOHN: Of course not. But you didn't say anything about – not a word, the entire car ride home. And all afternoon you locked yourself in your studio.

KAREN: I was working.

JOHN: And I totally understand if you're not ready –

KAREN: You think this is related to –

JOHN: You don't?

KAREN: That I'm imagining things as a way to express myself.

JOHN: Maybe.

KAREN: Gee-whiz, Sigmund fucking Freud.

JOHN: Karen, I'm here for you.

KAREN: Then believe me when I say I heard the doorbell.

JOHN: Even the doctor said –

KAREN: John.

JOHN: It hasn't spread.

KAREN: This is so condescending.

JOHN: Very treatable.

KAREN: I'm not a child.

JOHN: We'll survive this.

KAREN: I'm going downstairs.

JOHN: There's nothing there.

KAREN: I won't be able to sleep until I check. What if it was some lunatic?

JOHN: Lunatics don't ring doorbells at 3am. Besides, even if there was someone, they're gone by now.

KAREN: Maybe they were seeing if anyone was home, and now they're looking for a way to break in.

JOHN: Then I'll turn on the lamp. If someone is outside, they'll see the light and go away. Can we do that?

> *(Pause.)*

KAREN: Okay.

JOHN: Okay.

> *(JOHN turns on the bedside lamp. They wait in still silence for several seconds.)*

JOHN: See? Nothing but the quiet desperation of sleeping suburbanites.

> *(KAREN smiles. JOHN smiles.)*

Come back to bed?

KAREN: Okay.

JOHN: Yeah?

KAREN: (*Satisfied, removes robe and begins to climb back into bed.*) Yeah.

JOHN: (*Joking.*) This wasn't some elaborate attempt at foreplay, was it?

KAREN: (*Joking back.*) You wish.

JOHN: Because I could really get into that.

KAREN: Dream on.

JOHN: Just saying.

(They share a loving snicker. Pause.)

KAREN: I shut down today, after the doctor. I'm sorry.

JOHN: You have nothing to apologize about.

KAREN: I wasn't expecting to be dealing with this. Not now. Not this soon.

JOHN: We're going to get through this.

KAREN: You're good to me.

JOHN: You're good to me.

(Affectionately, they join hands. A moment.)

KAREN: I can't help but think of that episode of the The Twilight Zone.

JOHN: That show was before my time.

KAREN: Mine too, thank you very much. But my dad was a fan. There used to be marathons, in syndication. I'd watch them with him, as a kid. There was one – I forget what it was called – but the episode was about this old lady who wouldn't leave her house. She was afraid that Death would "get her." And she wouldn't let anyone inside either. But this man shows up on her doorstep. A wounded policeman, I think, asking for help. But she won't open up. She won't let him in. The policeman was played by Robert Redford.

JOHN: He must've been young.

KAREN: He was. Anyway, he pleads, and begs – the wounded hero in need – until finally she lets him in.

JOHN: Who can resist a young Robert Redford?

KAREN: I wouldn't kick him out of bed.

JOHN: And let me guess: she nurses him back to health and realizes that compassion overcomes fear?

KAREN: No, that's just it. He is Death. Mister Death, as she calls him. He tricked her. He's come for her, and now he's won.

JOHN: Mister Death – bummer.

KAREN: But the episode wasn't sad. It was sweet, tender.

JOHN: She dies?

KAREN: Yes, but the Redford character, even as Death, is kind, gentle, accepting. In the end, the old lady realizes she's ready, and he leads her off by the hand.

JOHN: Off where?

KAREN: I don't know. The beyond? Somewhere fuzzy. There's a line toward the end: "There's nothing in the dark that wasn't there when the lights were on."

JOHN: So you think maybe that was Robert Redford at our front door?

KAREN: John, I'm serious.

JOHN: Sorry.

KAREN: It was the first time I saw death as something binding, something – imminent.

JOHN: It's going to be okay.

KAREN: I believe you.

JOHN: Can I turn out the light now?

KAREN: Yeah, sure. Goodnight.

JOHN: *(He gives her a peck on the cheek.)* Try to stop thinking about all this. Get some sleep.

> *(JOHN turns off the lamp and lies back down. KAREN lies back down as well. There is stillness again. Silence. Then, the sound of the doorbell. JOHN sits up, KAREN does not.)*

JOHN: Hey.

> *(No answer.)*

Karen?

KAREN: John?

JOHN: I heard it that time.

KAREN: You heard what?

JOHN: What do you think? The doorbell.

KAREN: *(Sitting up.)* Are you messing with me?

JOHN: I wouldn't do that. The doorbell – it rang.

KAREN: I didn't hear anything.

JOHN: Were you asleep?

KAREN: I don't think so. We should check downstairs.

JOHN: It'll go away. Let's just keep still.

KAREN: Keep still? Aren't we too old for boogeymen?

JOHN: We'll wait it out.

KAREN: Maybe we should call someone?

JOHN: Like who?

KAREN: The police.

JOHN: It's not a crime to ring the doorbell.

KAREN: What if it doesn't go away?

JOHN: It'll be light soon.

KAREN: Abby!

JOHN: Karen, Abby's fine.

KAREN: I'm going to check on her.

JOHN: Karen!

> *(Throwing on her robe, KAREN rushes out. Pause.)*

Karen?

> *(Pause. Quiet.)*

Karen?

> *(Pause. Quiet.)*

> *(JOHN waits in bed, sitting on his knees, looking out toward where KAREN exited, anxious. He waits. Finally, she returns and stands still before him.)*

KAREN: She's okay.

JOHN: Still sleeping.

KAREN: Like a log. What now?

JOHN: Whatever it is, I think it's gone.

(*Long pause.*)

KAREN: (*Getting back into bed.*) I won't be able to sleep.

JOHN: Me either.

KAREN: It'll be light soon.

JOHN: Good.

KAREN: Another day begins.

JOHN: It's my morning to take Abby to school.

KAREN: Then I'll make breakfast. I'll make eggs.

JOHN: I made eggs yesterday.

KAREN: Something else then?

JOHN: Eggs are fine.

KAREN: Then I'll make eggs.

(*Pause.*)

JOHN: To be honest, I'm weirdly shaken by all this.

KAREN: Me too, but we'll recover. The day's monotony will erase it all.

JOHN: What if it returns? Tonight? Tomorrow?

KAREN: It may.

JOHN: Then what?

KAREN: We hope it goes away.

JOHN: And if it doesn't?

KAREN: We'll wait for the light.

JOHN: And begin another day.

KAREN: And try to forget again.

(*Pause. The doorbell rings again. They look at each other.*)

(*Blackout.*)

END OF PLAY

IN FULL BLOOM
PAIGE ZUBEL

THE PLAY:

In Full Bloom

THE PLAYWRIGHT:

Paige Zubel

SYNOPSIS:

Roger and Beth struggle to agree on the details of the most consuming event of their lives.

ABOUT THE PLAYWRIGHT:

Paige Zubel is a Philadelphia-based playwright and producer. Her plays have been staged internationally, with notable productions in her hometown of Houston, TX ($12.50/Hour, Sunday Flowers, Gel Us), NYC (In Full Bloom, The Pull of the Moon, Dead Meat), and Scotland (Under Covers). Her plays and prose have been published in One Act Play Depot, Every Day Fiction, and Hashtag Queer. She is the Artistic Associate of Shakespeare in Clark Park, National New Play Network Producer in Residence at InterAct Theatre Company, and a member of The Foundry, an emerging playwrights' lab partnered with PlayPenn. You can read more of her work on the New Play Exchange.

WEBSITE:

paigezubel.com

The Theatre:

Nylon Fusion Theatre Company
192 Lexington Ave. Suite #2009, New York, NY 10016

Mission:

Nylon, born of a fusion of New York and London creativity, is a theatre company committed to giving voice and perspective to established and emerging artists. We develop and produce plays that explore political, social and cultural awareness.

Contact:

Ivette Dumeng, Artistic Director
nylonfusion@gmail.com
646-883-5764

Website:

nylonfusion.org

Presenting the Play:

In Full Bloom

Characters:

ROGER

BETH

Time:

Now.

Place:

A dining room/living room combination. A modest home. You know this place.

BETH and ROGER sit on opposing ends of a dining table. Papers are formulaically spread out on the table and coffee table in columns and rows.

BETH is visibly pregnant. She is in jeans. They are too tight to wear.

ROGER fidgets with the papers, diverting all of his attention to them. BETH holds her stomach, fixated on it.

ROGER: *(Pulls two papers closer to him.)* What do you think about flowers?

> *(No response.)*

Beth?

> *(No response.)*

Beth?

BETH: *(Looking up from her stomach.)* Yeah?

ROGER: *(Holds up the two pieces of paper.)* Flowers.

Lilies or roses?

Come on, baby, lilies or roses?

BETH: I don't know, Roger.

ROGER: Just pick one.

BETH: I don't know.

ROGER: Whichever one you like the best. Do you like the lilies? These are orange. You like orange.

BETH: I guess.

ROGER: You wanna go with these?

BETH: Okay.

ROGER: Okay. Lilies it is.

ROGER puts the lily paper into one stack, the rose paper into another.

ROGER: *(Pulling more papers towards him.)* All right, next is—

BETH: Wait.

ROGER: What?

BETH: Not lilies.

ROGER: You don't want lilies?

BETH: No.

ROGER: *(Trying to find the rose paper.)* You want the roses?

BETH: No, I—

ROGER: No roses?

BETH: No.

ROGER: Then what flowers do you want?

BETH: Do we need flowers?

ROGER: I mean—yeah, we need / flowers.

BETH: Because I don't think we do.

ROGER: Beth, I already found them, all you have to do is pick—

BETH: They would be pretty, I know they'd be pretty. But do we need them?

ROGER: I just—you just have flowers, Beth. We can't not have flowers.

BETH: Okay.

ROGER: So, lilies?

BETH: No. Not lilies.

ROGER: Then roses?

BETH: No.

ROGER: We need flowers, Beth.

BETH: Well, I don't want lilies or roses.

ROGER: Then what do you want?

BETH: I don't know.

ROGER: Just pick from—

BETH: No, I don't want to. They're not right. They're not / right.

ROGER: We need to pick something.

BETH: I know that.

ROGER: We don't have a lot of time to—

BETH: I know that.

ROGER: Okay.

BETH: It's just all happening really fast and I need time to—

ROGER: Okay.

So what flowers do you want?

BETH: I don't know.

ROGER: Beth.

BETH: What? I'll decide later. Okay?

ROGER: Okay. Then...

ROGER puts the flower papers in a different stack than before. He grabs a few new papers from a different part of the table and drags them towards him.

ROGER: I was taking a look at some local caterers—there's this one, they even say 'serving great smiles.' What is that? / I've got some sample menus.

BETH: Food? We're having food?

ROGER: Yeah.

BETH: Why?

ROGER: Because, you—you get flowers, you have food, it's just what you do.

BETH: We don't need to have food.

ROGER: Yes, we do.

BETH: No, we don't. Make everyone go somewhere else afterwards. Make them pay for it.

ROGER: We can't do that.

BETH: Says who?

ROGER: You just—that's not what you do.

BETH: I don't care.

ROGER: And we can pay for it.

BETH: It's not about the money, Roger.

ROGER: Then what is it?

BETH: It's just—if there's food… people will stay longer.

BETH unbuttons her pants.

ROGER: We should get you some dresses.

BETH: What?

ROGER: You know, the ones with the empire waist? Your jeans—

BETH: I like my jeans.

ROGER: They're getting a little tight.

BETH: So?

ROGER: So, you look uncomfortable.

BETH: It's okay.

ROGER: And summer's coming. You could get those—you know—in the window at the mall, with those shoulder straps you like?

BETH: I don't need them.

ROGER: Yes, you do. Look at you.

BETH: I'm fine.

ROGER: You should get something for yourself. We can go tomorrow.

BETH: I'm not going to buy something I'll only use for two weeks.

ROGER: It's longer than that.

BETH: Its two weeks, Roger.

ROGER: Okay.

BETH: *(Off his look.)* What? Are you trying to make me feel bad?

ROGER: No.

BETH: I don't want a dress, okay? I don't need you to make me feel guilty about it.

ROGER: I'm not trying to make you feel guilty.

BETH: Really? Because you say shopping and I say no and suddenly I'm the bad guy.

ROGER: You're not the bad guy.

BETH: You look like a victim. That makes me the bad guy.

ROGER: I was just trying to do something fun.

BETH: Fun? How is that fun?

ROGER: I don't know.

BETH: That's not fun. That's torture.

ROGER: I'm sorry.

BETH: How can you not see that?

ROGER: I'm sorry.

BETH: Stop saying you're sorry.

ROGER: Then what do you want me to say?

BETH: Just stop apologizing.

ROGER: I'm sad. All right? You're not the only one who gets to be sad, Beth. I'm allowed to be sad, too.

BETH: I want to pick the casket now.

(Looking through the papers.)

There aren't any caskets here. Where are the caskets, Roger?

ROGER: I didn't print any out.

BETH: You didn't look for any caskets? We're talking about flowers and food and you haven't found any fucking caskets?

ROGER: Jesus, Beth, I didn't know you'd—

BETH: What?

ROGER: Want to.

BETH: Of course I don't want to. You think I'm doing any of this because I want to?

ROGER: You think I want to?

BETH: Telling me I should get an empire waist dress—

ROGER: I just thought you should have something nice.

355

BETH: Nice?

ROGER: To have, to remember—

BETH: I don't want to remember any of this.

ROGER: I know.

BETH: Do you?

ROGER: What, you think I enjoy this?

BETH: You keep talking about lilies and roses—

ROGER: Because one of has to. We can't both just fall apart.

BETH: I am not falling apart.

ROGER: You aren't helping me, Beth, you aren't helping me—

BETH: Because I don't want to do any of this. You do.

ROGER: He's my son, too, okay? I'm losing him, too. And I know it's different for you. That your grief and my grief look and feel and smell different but that doesn't mean I don't feel it just as much as you do. And I'm trying to help my grief, by printing out pictures of lilies and roses and fucking catering menus and organize them into rows that when you look at them, they make sense, because nothing about this makes sense. That's all I can do. This is all I can do, and it's nothing. Do you know what that feels like? To watch you sit there and hold your stomach and all I can say is, let's get you some dresses, because I don't know what you want. I don't know what his skin feels like in my arms, what his laugh feels like when his body rumbles against my chest. I don't know if he likes the color orange, like you. I always thought he'd love orange. You know his weight. You know his kicks. You know more about him than I ever will.

   (An apology:)

   If you want, I can do it myself.

BETH: No. I need to…

ROGER: What?

BETH: I didn't get to pick his crib. I want to pick his casket.

ROGER: I saw one that was nice. Just wood. Just plain wood.

BETH: How much was it?

ROGER: It doesn't matter.

BETH: How much was it?

ROGER: Infant caskets don't cost that much.

BETH: Okay.

> *BETH goes back to holding her stomach.*

BETH: We can go with the lilies.

ROGER: Are you sure?

> *BETH still stares at her stomach. She nods.*

ROGER: Okay. Lilies it is.

> *(ROGER rearranges the stacks of paper once more. Lights down on them at the table.)*

END PLAY

2ND PLACE

The Circle of Excellence Award

The Play:

Pudding

The Playwright:

Mark Andrew

Synopsis:

A woman leaves the home she shared with her partner for twenty years, and reveals her part in his release from pain.

About The Playwright:

Mark's short plays have been performed in Australia, England, Malaysia, the USA and New Zealand. His longer plays have been performed at Dantes (Seven of Hearts, directed by Wayne Pearn), Carlton's Courthouse Theatre (Time's Arrow, directed by Shannon Woollard) and as part of The Melbourne Fringe (Bomb the Base, directed by Louise Howlett).

Contact:

mark@scenario.net.au
+61 419 183 113

Website:

scenario.net.au

THE PLAY:

Something's Gotta Give

THE PLAYWRIGHT:

Paul Barile

SYNOPIS:

Pops will do anything to not be alone today. Sarge understands the problem, but is helpless to fix it.

ABOUT THE PLAYWRIGHT:

Paul Barile is a writer/storyteller working and playing in Chicago. His debut novel "My Brother's Hands" is out now. His audio-book "Chasing Happy" is available wherever fine mp3s are sold. His poetry blog is thepoemguy.wordpress.com. His coming-of-age novel-blog "Hercules the Lesser" is available at herculessquared.com. In his spare time, he writes.

CONTACT:

PaulBarile@gmail.com

WEBSITE:

Iampaulbarile.com

THE PLAY:

Say Goodbye to Hollywood

THE PLAYWRIGHT:

Bruce Bonafede

SYNOPSIS:

In this affectionate satire on the movie business, a writer goes to interview a former film star and learns that in the land of illusion success may not be what it seems.

ABOUT THE PLAYWRIGHT:

Bruce Bonafede's first produced play, ADVICE TO THE PLAYERS, won the Heideman Award at Actors Theatre of Louisville's Humana Festival in 1985, and was published in "The Best Short Plays—1986." His play QUARANTINE was an award-winner in the 2017 One-Act Playwriting Competition at the Little Theatre of Alexandria in Virginia. Bonafede studied at New Playwright's Theatre in Washington DC where he was a founding member of the Washington Playwrights Unit. He is a long-time member of the Dramatists Guild. He lives in Palm Springs, California.

CONTACT:

bruce@bonafedecommunications.com
760-831-5080

WEBSITE:

brucebonafede.com

THE PLAY:

Really Adult

THE PLAYWRIGHT:

Rachel Bublitz

SYNOPIS:

Julie would love to have a great first day working the Customer Service desk at Target, but maybe not as much as flirting with Frank, the employee assigned to train her. As the two discuss a possible date their personal lives become more and more clear, which leads to awkward territory.

Another Winning Play by Rachel Bublitz

Mom's Ham

Synopsis:

A ten-minute adaptation of Charles Dickens' *A Christmas Carol*, "Mom's Ham" follows a woman's desperate attempt to make a perfect Christmas feast in honor of her mother's recent passing.

About The Playwright:

Rachel Bublitz is an award winning and internationally produced playwright. Her full-length "Ripped" will have its World Premiere Production with Z Space in 2019. She's been produced by Plan-B Theatre, PlayGround, This Is Water, Custom Made Theatre Company, and many others. Awards include: 2018 Detroit New Works Festival Winner ("Ripped"), Playwrights Foundation's 2018 Bay Area Playwrights Festival Finalist ("Let's Fix Andy"), Actors Theatre of Louisville's 2017 Heideman Finalist ("Really Adult"), and PlayGround's June Anne Baker Prize. When she isn't writing, she's chasing after her two viking like children.

Contact:

Rnbublitz@gmail.com

Website:

RachelBublitz.com

THE PLAY:

Beds

THE PLAYWRIGHT:

Susan Cinoman

SYNOPIS:

Two couples in two beds tangle and untangle, in this contemporary short, and slightly surreal farce.

ABOUT THE PLAYWRIGHT:

Susan Cinoman is a playwright, published and produced internationally. For television, she is the creator of the recurring character, Miss Cinoman on ABC's, The Goldbergs, and wrote the story for Mama Drama , featured on the comedy. Her one-act play, Fitting Rooms, Applause Books, Best Short Plays of 1996 is produced internationally. Off Broadway productions include, Cinoman and Rebeck, Gin and Bitters and Out of the Blues all produced at Miranda Theatre. One acts include Beds at City Wrights, Miami. And Sweet Sand produced by Ensemble Studio Theatre. Cinoman's first published prose, McKenna on the Half Shell appears in Seven Deadly Sins published by Harvardwood/The Harvard Review. Her new play, Guenevere received the Guilford Performing Arts Award and will be presented in 2019. Cinoman is also the recipient of the Maxell Anderson Playwright's Prize, Theatre Ariel Award, Best Connecticut Filmmaker 2008, Best Narrative Screenplay, New England Film and Video Festival, Selection Berkshire International Film Festival, Aristos Scholarly Prize.

CONTACT:

Michael Moore Agency
450 West 24th Street, Suite 1C
New York, NY 10011

WEBSITE:

susancinoman.com

THE PLAY:

Admittance: A Letter to Northwestern University

THE PLAYWRIGHT:

Elijah Cox

SYNOPIS:

Mackenzie and Sydney are best friends ready to graduate high school. But when Mackenzie gets her decision letter from her top choice college, tensions flare as the girls debate the nature of success and what we owe to others.

ABOUT THE PLAYWRIGHT:

Elijah Cox is an actor, playwright and teaching artist in Chicago, where he has worked with companies including Steep Theatre, Theatre Momentum, and Windy City Performs. He is a proud graduate of Loyola University Chicago.

CONTACT:

elijahqcox@gmail.com

WEBSITE:

newplayexchange.org/users/20943/elijah-cox

THE PLAY:

Swimming in Captivity

THE PLAYWRIGHT:

Brandon M. Crose

SYNOPSIS:

A married couple's intimate night in takes a sharp left turn when their thirty-something live-in son "transforms" into an inflatable orca whale.

ABOUT THE PLAYWRIGHT:

Brandon M. Crose's plays have appeared at various theatre festivals all over the world. In addition to writing short, usually comedic theatrical works, Brandon also writes and produces the fantasy adventure audio dramedy podcast The Ordinary Epic (the-ordinaryepic.com). Brandon holds degrees from Emerson College and Trinity College, Dublin, is the author of several nonfiction books

CONTACT:

brandon.crose@gmail.com

WEBSITE:

brandoncrose.com

THE PLAY:

The Art of Tea

THE PLAYWRIGHT:

Daniel Damiano

SYNOPIS:

Centered thinking is put to the test when two English women share a polite cup of tea.

ABOUT THE PLAYWRIGHT:

Daniel is an Award-winning Playwright and Award-nominated Actor and Voice-Over Artist, based in Brooklyn, NY. Recent notable productions of his work include the acclaimed and extended run of his solo play, AMERICAN TRANQUILITY at the East Village Playhouse in NYC (fandango 4 Art House, 2018), the World Premier of HARMONY PARK (Detroit Repertory Theatre, 2018), as well as the recent publication of his acclaimed play DAY OF THE DOG with Broadway Play Publishing. Other recent productions include THE DISHONORABLE DISCHARGE OF PRIVATE PITTS (Iati Theatre/fandango 4 Art House, NYC), the World and NYC premiers of DAY OF THE DOG (St. Louis Actors' Studio/59E59 Theatre) and THE GOLDEN YEAR (workshop Theater, NYC.)

CONTACT:

damiano_daniel@yahoo.com

WEBSITE:

danieldamiano.com

THE PLAY:

The Women's Follow Your Dream Club

THE PLAYWRIGHT:

Jack Feldstein

SYNOPIS:

A comic glimpse into a meetup where three women plan to follow their dreams.

ABOUT THE PLAYWRIGHT:

Jack Feldstein is an award-winning writer and neon animation filmmaker. His playscripts including A House Like Any Other, The Confessions of Peter McDowell and The Process have won prizes in Australia, Britain and the USA. His playscript of Three Months with Pook was a finalist in the BBC International Play Competition. His plays have been staged with many productions in Australia, New York and all over the USA. Falling in Love with Mr Dellamort, his first foray into the world of musical theater was produced in NYC in December 2017. Originally from Australia, he lives in New York City and developed many of his plays at Workshop Theater in Midtown where he was an artist member.

CONTACT:

jack.feldstein@gmail.com
347-586-8437

THE PLAY:

The Phlebotomist

THE PLAYWRIGHT:

Charlie Edwin Fisher

SYNOPIS:

A young woman donates blood for the first time on the day of Sept 11th.

ABOUT THE PLAYWRIGHT:

Charlie holds a BA in theatre for playwriting from Marymount Manhattan College. His plays have had readings and performances in one act festivals in several cities in the United States including NYC as well as in Sydney Australia.

CONTACT:

charlieedwinfisher@gmail.com
646-320-7789

THE PLAY:

Camping Out

THE PLAYWRIGHT:

Anne Flanagan

SYNOPIS:

New Jersey State Park, 1978. Three pre-teen Girl Scouts suffer through an overnight under the stars, each facing her future and budding sexuality with equal parts excitement and dread.

ANOTHER WINNING PLAY by Anne Flanagan:

Three Ghosts of Elizabeth Bathory

SYNOPIS:

Sixteenth century Hungarian Countess Elizabeth Bathory allegedly tortured and murdered up to 600 girls, then bathed in their blood. The ghost of Elizabeth Bathory attempts to revamp her reputation, however, her vehicle for redemption is an apathetic teenager.

ABOUT THE PLAYWRIGHT:

Anne Flanagan Anne Flanagan's plays include Lineage, Artifice, First Chill, Skirts, Dark Holidays and Death, Sex & Elves. Her work has been produced throughout the US and internationally. Anne is the recipient of several writing awards and zero sports trophies. Publications include her comedy Artifice (Dramatic) as well as many short play and monologue anthologies. Anne has worked as a private investigator, actor, and pelvic model – none of which were as exciting as one might think.

CONTACT:

AngryTimmyPresents@yahoo.com

WEBSITE:

AnneFlanagan.net

THE PLAY:

Ailurophobia

THE PLAYWRIGHT:

Scott Gibson

SYNOPIS:

Kate brings her date Bret back to her place for a romantic evening. However their tryst is continually interrupted by Kate's cat Jinx.

ABOUT THE PLAYWRIGHT:

A Colorado native, Scott has had a number of plays produced around the country, including New York City, Los Angeles, Miami, St. Paul, Tampa, Dallas, Seattle and Denver. His play "Someone Else's Life" won the Steven Dietz Original Playwriting Competition in 2005.

CONTACT:

scottconundrum@hotmail.com

The Play:

Longshot

The Playwright:

Aren Haun

Synopis:

The day after her father's death, Christine finds a notebook containing her father's final horse racing picks. When every pick begins to win, she decides to bet everything she has on a longshot.

About The Playwright:

Aren Haun received his MFA in Playwriting from Columbia University. Short plays include Standing Room Only and A Walk in the Park, both published by Smith & Kraus. He currently teaches playwriting at the Ruth Asawa School of the Arts in San Francisco.

Contact:

arenhaun@gmail.com

Website:

arenhaun.com

THE PLAY:

Talking Points

THE PLAYWRIGHT:

Steven Hayet

SYNOPIS:

Mike holds a press conference during his family's Thanksgiving dinner, to announce his recent separation.

ABOUT THE PLAYWRIGHT:

Steven Hayet is a New Jersey playwright whose work has been performed from Los Angeles to London and New York to New Zealand. His short plays include Talking Points (City Theatre Winter Shorts), George Orwell's 1989: A "Swift" 10 Minute Adaptation (Week 1 People's Choice Winner, Short+Sweet Hollywood), Everlasting Chocolate Therapy (Audience Choice Runner Up, The Oakville Players TOP 10 Festival), and Stage Mom. He also co-wrote the short film Frame of Reference (Bronze Remi Award for Best Romantic Comedy, Worldfest Houston). He is a graduate of the College of William & Mary and Rutgers University.

CONTACT:

stevenhayet@gmail.com

WEBSITE:

stevenhayet.com

THE PLAY:

Face Time

THE PLAYWRIGHT:

Donna Hoke

SYNOPIS:

A play for this social media age: when high school friends Angela and Kelly bump into each other at a brick-and-mortar store, they discover that too much connection has driven them apart.

ABOUT THE PLAYWRIGHT:

Donna's work has thus far been seen in 46 states and on five continents. Plays include BRILLIANT WORKS OF ART (2016 Kilroys List), ELEVATOR GIRL (2017 O'Neill, Princess Grace finalist), TEACH (Gulfshore New Works winner), and SAFE (winner of the Todd McNerney, Naatak, and Great Gay Play and Musical Contests). She has been nominated for both the Primus and Blackburn Prizes, and is a two-time winner of the Emanuel Fried Award for Outstanding New Play (SEEDS, SONS & LOVERS). She has also received an Individual Artist Award from the New York State Council on the Arts to develop HEARTS OF STONE, and, for three consecutive years, she was named Buffalo's Best Writer by Artvoice—the only woman to ever receive the designation. Donna also serves on the Dramatists Guild Council and is a blogger and moderator of the 12,000+-member Official Playwrights of Facebook.

CONTACT:

donna@donnahoke.com
Agent: Samara Harris
samara@robertfreedmanagency.com

WEBSITE:

donnahoke.com

THE PLAY:

Phone Friend

THE PLAYWRIGHT:

Jonathan Josephson

SYNOPIS:

Returning to the light after descending to the depths of personal tragedy can be a dark, difficult chore… but, when a chance wrong number links two complete strangers in the middle of the night, their common humanity may just help them survive their personal demons.

ANOTHER WINNING PLAY by Jonathan Josephson:

The Play: The Tale of Dakota Dawson

SYNOPIS:

Wilbur Wyoming is perturbed. His agency has been getting blasted all over social media for unfair business practices, and he's gunnin' for the no-good ad man whose responsible... who happens to be Dakota Dawson, and she's not exactly gun shy. Enjoy this modern day Western-spoof set in a San Francisco ad agency.

ABOUT THE PLAYWRIGHT:

Forty-one of Jonathan's plays have been produced at site-specific locations, schools and theatres around the world including Actors Theatre of Louisville (Humana Festival), Milwaukee Rep (RepLab), the Samuel French Off-Off Broadway Play Festival (Festival Winner), San Jose Rep (SJREAL), Chance Theater, NY SummerFest, Mountain View Mausoleum, and the LA County Arboretum. As the founding Executive Director of Unbound Productions, he is also one of the creators of the perennially sold out theatre events Wicked Lit, History Lit and Mystery Lit. He is a five-time Finalist for the Heideman Award, and also a Finalist for the O'Neill National Playwrights Conference and the City Theatre National Short Play Award. His plays have received staged readings at the Great Plains Theatre Conference, Seattle Rep/Northwest Playwrights Alliance, and The Huntington Gardens in San Marino. His plays are published by Samuel French, Stage Rights, Playscripts, YouthPLAYS, and Original Works Publishing. B.A. Theatre: Playwriting, UCSD. DG, ALAP.

WEBSITE:

jonathanjosephson.com

THE PLAY:

Low & Away

THE PLAYWRIGHT:

Demetra Kareman

SYNOPIS:

A couple struggles to teach their young daughter how to play baseball.

ABOUT THE PLAYWRIGHT:

Demetra Kareman is a born and bred New Yorker, a Catholic School survivor, and a published and internationally produced playwright.

CONTACT:

demdemk@gmail.com

THE PLAY:

Hiccup

THE PLAYWRIGHT:

Stacey Lane

SYNOPIS:

An over-confident teenager waits for her turn in a speech contest when she develops a bad case of hiccups. Her brother and the contest facilitator try to come up with inventive ways to cure her before she must deliver her speech.

ABOUT THE PLAYWRIGHT:

Stacey Lane's plays have been seen at over a thousand theatres on six continents. Her scripts are published with Smith and Kraus, Dramatic Publishing, Playscripts Inc., Pioneer, Heuer, Eldridge, Brooklyn Publishers, YouthPLAYS, Applause Theatre & Cinema Books, Meriwether, Routledge, Infinity Stage, Sound, and Film, JAC Publishing, and in forty anthologies and literary magazines. She is the recipient of the Helene Wurlitzer Foundation Residency Grant, the Montgomery County Arts & Cultural District's Literary Artist Fellowship, and winner of the Unpublished Play Reading Project Award at the American Alliance for Theatre and Education.

CONTACT:

Stacey@StaceyLaneInk.com

WEBSITE:

StaceyLaneInk.com

THE PLAY:

When Songs Meant Something

THE PLAYWRIGHT:

Matt Martello

SYNOPIS:

Marisa is stumped with a music assignment concerning the Vietnam era. While offering help on the assignment, Marisa's grandpa is reminded of an unpleasant moment in his life.

ABOUT THE PLAYWRIGHT:

Matt has been involved with the various aspects of theatre (acting, directing, playwriting and producing) since 1986. He was a high school English, Speech and Drama teacher for schools in Michigan and Ohio for 15 years, from 1997-2012. During his time as a drama director, he produced several of his works, including "A Touch Of Class," "Back To Reality," and "(She Was) Maid To Order." He now heads his own theatre company in Las Vegas, M-Wil Productions of Las Vegas. His works have been included in the Las Vegas Little Theatre's Fringe Fest, including "Theatre Roulette" (2014), "Ex-Dating" (2014), "Soundtracks" (2017) and "Time Capsule" (2018). In 2013, his short play "Wasted Words" was featured in the Theatre Madness Festival in New York City. His play "Ex Dating" earned 3rd Place in the Original Works Competition for Las Vegas Little Theatre. His plays have been produced throughout the country, including New York, Chicago, Ann Arbor, Cleveland and Las Vegas. He is also a consistent contributor to the $2/10 Minute Series at Cockroach Theatre in Las Vegas.

CONTACT:

matt_martello11@yahoo.com
702-321-3610

THE PLAY:

A Little Magic

THE PLAYWRIGHT:

Scott Mullen

SYNOPIS:

A woman in a bus stop is stunned when a stranger claims to have created a man for her. She tries to determine whether or not this "new man" is real – and represents the potential for happiness – or is just a trick.

ANOTHER WINNING PLAY by Scott Mullen:

THE PLAY:

The Man In The Hat

SYNOPIS:

A woman is surprised when a man tells her that they are just characters in different ten minute plays. He tries to convince her to run away with him.

ABOUT THE PLAYWRIGHT:

Scott Mullen is a longtime Hollywood screenplay analyst and screenwriter, a two-time winner of Amazon Studios' screenwriting contest, whose thriller THE SUMMONING aired on TV One. His short plays have been performed hundreds of times around the world. An evening of his comic plays, A NIGHT OF S.M., recently had a two-week run in Hollywood.

CONTACT:

scottmullen9@sbcglobal.net

THE PLAY:

Someone Else's Eyes

THE PLAYWRIGHT:

Barry M. Putt, Jr.

SYNOPIS:

A downtrodden woman has been on her share of monotonous blind dates. When she goes out with a visually impaired man, he helps her to see life in a new and exciting way.

ABOUT THE PLAYWRIGHT:

Barry M. Putt, Jr.'s plays have been performed in Canada, the United Arab Emirates, and throughout the United States. They include productions of TRIANGLE and THE PORCH at the Samuel French Off-Off Broadway Short Play Festival and THE LOLLIPOP LADY and DEAD BODY by Turtle Shell Productions. Mr. Putt's children's plays, A NUTTY TALE and ALL IS FAIR IN SHOW BUSINESS, have been published by Drama Notebook. His audio-drama credits include adaptions of THE HOLLY TREE INN and MYSTERIOUS ISLAND for Colonial Radio Theater. Mr. Putt wrote the screenplay for the VR film MAREN'S ROCK. BearManor Media published his book entitled ALICE, THE TV SERIES: LIFE BEHIND THE COUNTER IN MEL'S GREASY SPOON. Mr. Putt is a member of the Witherspoon Circle, American Renaissance Theater Company, the Dramatists Guild, and the Authors Guild.

CONTACT:

bmputt@aol.com

WEBSITE:

barrymputtjr.com

THE PLAY:

Appetizers, or "On an Island Somewhere"

THE PLAYWRIGHT:

Scott C. Sickles

SYNOPIS:

Alice and her husband host a farewell party celebrating Tamara and her husband moving back to the Mainland after years on the Island have cured them all of being homosexual. Or has it?

ABOUT THE PLAYWRIGHT:

SCOTT C. SICKLES in an LGBT playwright of Asian descent whose plays have been performed in New York City, across the U.S., and internationally in Canada, Australia, the UK, Hungary, Singapore, and Lebanon. His bioplay Nonsense and Beauty will receive its world premiere at The Repertory Theatre of St. Louis next spring. His play Composure was a 2018 Lambda Literary Award finalist. He has received four consecutive Writers Guild of America Awards for General Hospital and six Emmy Award nominations.

CONTACT:

ScottCSickles@gmail.com
The Barbara Hogenson Agency
bhogenson@aol.com
212-874-8084

WEBSITE:

ScottCSickles.com

THE PLAY:

Miss Irrelevant

THE PLAYWRIGHT:

Jeff Stolzer

SYNOPIS:

Retired NFL star CHARLIE WEEMS has just published his autobiography as a prelude to a run for the U.S. Senate. But everything changes when the charismatic Charlie is approached at a book signing by AMY STERLING, a woman who confronts him about a sexual encounter they had in college twenty years earlier.

ABOUT THE PLAYWRIGHT:

Jeff Stolzer is the author of 7 full-length plays and 18 one-act plays. His full-length plays include SURVIVORS (Arts Club of Washington National Playwriting Award); UNSPORTSMANLIKE CONDUCT (Woodward/Newman Drama Award finalist); STORAGE LOCKER (Pickering Award for Playwriting Excellence finalist); and PARALYZED (Ohio State-Newark New Play Contest third prize). His short plays have been produced at festivals in New York, across the US and in the UK. EMERGENCY ROOM, a one-act about the dysfunctional American health care system, received the Upstage Playwright Award from Houston's Upstage Theatre. His short play CUSTOMER SERVICE will receive its world premiere at Smock Alley Theatre in Dublin, Ireland in February, 2019.

CONTACT:

jeffardy@outlook.com

WEBSITE:

jeffstolzer.com

The Play:

Three Syllables of Shame

The Playwright:

Rom Watson

Synopis:

Charlie and his pregnant wife Angela play a game to see who can think up the worst possible name for the baby. In between coming up with names like Marmaduke, Levitra and Cholera, they also discuss how they're going to raise their child.

About The Playwright:

Rom Watson is the author of the full-length plays LYING BENEATH THE SURFACE, IMAGE AND LIKENESS, THE NORMA CONQUESTS, PICKLE JUICE and PINOCCHIO IN THE BRONX. 12 of his 27 short plays have been produced, including THREE SYLLABLES OF SHAME, THE BEAUMONT TECHNIQUE, CURB YOUR URGES, CELEBRITY DEATH WATCH and MR. CUDDLES. His full-length plays have had readings at The Road Theatre, Moving Arts, The MET Theatre, Alliance Repertory Company, Unknown Theatre, Celebration Theatre and Neo Ensemble Theatre. He is a member of The Dramatists Guild of America and The Alliance of Los Angeles Playwrights.

Contact:

romwatsonwriter@gmail.com
310-625-7374

Website:

romwatson.com

THE PLAY:

The Boy on the Beach

THE PLAYWRIGHT:

Matthew Weaver

SYNOPIS:

Three mysterious women happen upon a young boy sleeping on a beach. They plot to give him his first kiss.

ABOUT THE PLAYWRIGHT:

Matthew Weaver is a Spokane, WA playwright. He has been produced in Washington State, Canada, New Jersey, Massachusetts, Ohio, Texas, West Virginia, New York, Pennsylvania, Michigan, Virginia, Indiana, Kentucky, Colorado, Florida, California, Ireland, Japan, Oregon, Illinois, Maryland and Missouri. Full-lengths include BED RIDE, GLUTTONY AND LUST ARE FRIENDS, ACES ARE FEVERISH, TIMMY'S BIG KISS and an evening of very short plays in alphabetical order, AND SOMETIMES Y.

CONTACT:

WeaverRMatthew@gmail.com

WEBSITE:

newplayexchange.org/users/9069/matthew-weaver

THE PLAY:

The One

THE PLAYWRIGHT: SHERI WILNER

SYNOPSIS:

Amy has invited her former high school sweetheart Chris and his fiancé Jake to dinner in honor of their recent engagement. Chris arrives first to warn Amy that Jake will be searching for signs that they still harbor feelings for each other... a notion Amy protests is ridiculous given their relationship ended twenty-five years ago when Chris acknowledged he was gay. Yet when they examine the evidence behind this accusation, they're forced to admit the profound dissatisfaction they've had with all subsequent romantic partners and their futile attempts to replicate the profound connection they once shared with each other.

ABOUT THE PLAYWRIGHT:

Sheri Wilner's plays include Kingdom City, Father Joy, Relative Strangers, Labor Day, Joan of Arkansas, and Hunger, and have been performed and developed at such major American theatres as the La Jolla Playhouse, Guthrie Theater, Actors Theatre of Louisville, Williamstown Theatre Festival, the O'Neill Playwrights' Conference and Primary Stages. She co-wrote the libretto for the musical, Cake Off (based on her ten-minute award-winning play Bake Off), which was workshopped at the Old Globe in San Diego and produced by both the Signature Theatre in Washington, D.C. (nominated for a Helen Hayes Award for Outstanding Original Musical Adaptation) and the Bucks County Playhouse. Playwriting awards include a Bush Artist Fellowship, two Playwrights' Center Jerome Fellowships, and two Heideman Awards, granted by the Actors Theatre of Louisville. Her work has been published in more than a dozen anthologies, which has led to over four hundred productions of her plays worldwide. Also an established playwriting teacher, Sheri is a faculty member of the Dramatists Guild Institute and is the 2017-19 Master Playwright for the Miami-Dade Department of Cultural Affairs Playwrights Development Program.

CONTACT:

Ben Izzo, Abrams Artists Agency
ben.izzo@abramsart.com
646-461-9383

3rd Place

The Spotlight Award

THE PLAY:

That Water Moment

THE PLAYWRIGHT:

Sara Jean Accuardi

SYNOPSIS:

Two frustrated parents struggle to be optimistic about the future as they clean up the aftermath of their developmentally disabled son's fourth birthday party. A 10-minute play about parenting and facing the unknown.

ANOTHER WINNING PLAY BY SARA JEAN ACCUARDI:

THE PLAY:

Off Duty

SYNOPSIS:

Two police officers on their lunch break try to make sense of the world and proceed as normal on the sidelines of a catastrophic event. A 10-minute play about how life goes on, even when that seems impossible.

ABOUT THE PLAYWRIGHT:

Sara Jean Accuardi's plays have been produced, read, and work-shopped at Theatre Vertigo (Portland, OR), The Blank Theatre (Los Angeles, CA), Portland Center Stage, Seven Devils Playwrights Conference, Victory Gardens (Chicago, IL), and Chicago Dramatists. She is a member of the Dramatist Guild and LineStorm Playwrights, and she holds an MFA in Writing for the Screen and Stage from Northwestern University.

CONTACT:

sjaccuardi@gmail.com

WEBSITE:

sarajeanaccuardi.com
newplayexchange.org/users/8661/sara-jean-accuardi

THE PLAY:

Christopher's Voyage

THE PLAYWRIGHT:

Sam Affoumado

SYNOPSIS:

High school sophomores, Emma and Chris, must choose hero-worthy, historical figures for a class project. Their inability to see the other person's point of view begins to jeopardize their budding relationship.

ABOUT THE PLAYWRIGHT:

Sam Affoumado has written six full-length plays and over a dozen short pieces. His play, Peanut Butter Patty, was a semi-finalist in the 37th Annual Samuel French OOB Short Play Festival. His one-act, One-Way Ticket, was presented at the William Inge Festival (2018). His plays have been performed in festivals in North Carolina, Washington, DC and New York. Published work: The Bully's Eye, (2015), More 10-Minute Plays for Teens, edited by Lawrence Harbison. Sam directed his jury-selected play, Doctor Truth, (2017) as part of the Village Playwrights' "Loud and Proud" Festival and again at the MRT Spring Festival in NY. He is a proud member of the Dramatists Guild, Actors' Equity, SAG-AFTRA and Theatre Resources Unlimited.

CONTACT:

Saffu@aol.com

WEBSITE:

samaffoumado.com

THE PLAY:

Out of Gas

THE PLAYWRIGHT:

Cynthia Faith Arsenault

SYNOPSIS:

In a race against time, a whistleblower rushes to get to a critical on-air interview, when her driver runs out of gas in a deserted area. Who do you trust when you can't trust anyone?

ABOUT THE PLAYWRIGHT:

Cynthia Arsenault, psychologist by day, writer by night, is a former director, whose playwriting group, aptly named Group, encouraged her to take up the pen. Five years later, she is published in "Best of 5 Minute Plays for Teens," "Best 10 Minute Plays of 2017," "A Solitary Voice," and multiple times at Monologuebank,com. There have been over 80 productions of her short plays in the US, Canada, London and Australia.

CONTACT:

Cynthiafaith@comcast.net

WEBSITE:

newplayexchange.org/users/2521/cynthia-faith-arsenault

The Play:

Siren

The Playwright:

Sarah Elisabeth Brown

Synopsis:

An experienced Masters and Johnson's sexual surrogate and her long-term client, an adult virgin man, wrestle with boundaries, their feelings for each other, and the nature of sex.

About The Playwright:

Sarah Elisabeth Brown is an award-winning playwright/screenwriter based out of New York City and Ann Arbor, Michigan. She is currently a company member of Workshop Theater in New York, and founder of Ann Arbor Playwrights, a collaboration with Theatre Nova. In the past, she has served as Playwright-in-Residence for Theaterwork in Santa Fe, New Mexico, and is an original member of Chicago's Theater Oobleck. She studied scriptwriting at The Jacob Krueger Studio, Hampshire College, Interlochen Arts Academy, and North Carolina School of the Arts. Successful productions of her play, "Bermuda Triangles: The Non-monogamy Experiment," lead to the film version, "Mango Kiss," distributed by Wolfe Video.

Contact:

selisabrown@gmail.com
929-777-0658

THE PLAY:

Under a Watchful Eye

THE PLAYWRIGHT:

John Busser

SYNOPSIS:

A few weeks before Christmas, a young woman visits her comatose father in the hospital and tells him why she will always be there for him.

ABOUT THE PLAYWRIGHT:

John Busser is a Cleveland-based actor and writer. He is a regular cast member of Flanagan's Wake, celebrating it's tenth season starting January 2019. Recently, Blank Canvas Theatre presented Children's Letters to Satan (and Other Horrible Scribblings), a collection of 7 of his original short plays.

CONTACT:

johnbusser@hotmail.com
216-470-9793

THE PLAY:

Leading Players

THE PLAYWRIGHT:

Scott Carter Cooper

SYNOPSIS:

Two actors meet at an audition for an upcoming production of Hamlet and try to convince each other of their success.

ABOUT THE PLAYWRIGHT:

In the Chicago theatre community Cooper has worked as a producer, writer, director, actor, and singer for some of the most prominent companies, including Steppenwolf, The Lyric Opera of Chicago, Theo Ubique, Prop Thtr, Circle Theater, Bailiwick Repertory, CityLit, and many other small storefront theatres. His plays are intended for small professional companies with diverse ensembles looking for economical plays to produce. His casts are small, and the plays require one set with minimal production demands. In 2018 recordings of six of his short works were released in podseries form titled Flash Radio Theatre.

CONTACT:

ScotCoop@aol.com

WEBSITE:

scottcartercooper.com

THE PLAY:

Socialite Networking

THE PLAYWRIGHT:

Nicky Denovan

SYNOPSIS:

In 1930s London, bright young socialites Gertie and Duch must keep up with a fast-changing high society. So when Upper Circle magazine goes instant, the pair get to grips with a strange new world of selfies, status updates and social shaming.

ABOUT THE PLAYWRIGHT:

Nicky Denovan is a writer based in Berkshire, UK. Her work has been performed in playwriting, theatre and comedy festivals in the US, Dubai, Australia and the UK, including the finals of the Snow-dance® 10-Minute Comedy festival. She was the overall winner of the Pint-Sized Plays 2017 international writing competition and was shortlisted for the prestigious British Theatre Challenge in 2018

WEBSITE:

nickydenovan.com

THE PLAY:

Overachiever

THE PLAYWRIGHT:

Dean Donofrio

SYNOPSIS:

A slippery reality show producer manipulates a teenage girl into saying bad things about her mother on camera. But the saavy young girl has a far more despicable plan of her own...

ANOTHER WINNING PLAY by Dean Donofrio:

THE PLAY:

All The Decorations

SYNOPSIS:

When an aspiring romance novelist catches her husband in the act of watching pornography, she confronts him about their failing relationship.

ABOUT THE PLAYWRIGHT:

Dean has been writing short plays for over a decade, as well as TV pilots and screenplays. His plays have been produced all over Los Angeles.

CONTACT:

Dean726@gmail.com

THE PLAY:

Tonka Mom

THE PLAYWRIGHT:

Bonnie Milne Gardner

SYNOPSIS:

At a Midwest mega-store, a teenage Mom and a tenacious Grandmother battle over the right to buy the only remaining "Cyborg City Tonka Truck." A funny and touching tale of connection between strangers.

ABOUT THE PLAYWRIGHT:

Gardner's work has appeared in theatres around the country, including the Cleveland Play House, Edward Albee's New Frontier Conference, Contemporary American Theatre Company, New School for Drama, John Houseman Theatre, and San Diego's Human Rights Theater Festival. She is a lifetime member of Dramatist's Guild, and her awards include two Excellence in Playwriting grants from the Ohio Arts Council.

CONTACT:

bmilnegardner@gmail.com

WEBSITE:

bmgardner.weebly.com

THE PLAY:

A Sound Came Flashing

THE PLAYWRIGHT:

Michael G. Hilton

SYNOPSIS:

Marlon travels with his son, Jacob, to Princeton University to meet with an Admissions Officer. On the way, Jacob has a profound and transcendent experience in a roadside port-a-john, one which transforms his ideas of happiness and personal fulfillment yet will lead to a total breakdown of communication with his father.

ABOUT THE PLAYWRIGHT:

Michael G. Hilton's plays include "Blue Sky Somewhere" (Manhattan Repertory Theatre), "The Mountaineers" (T. Schreiber Studio), "Dance With Winter" (Finalist for Best Original Script, F.E.A.T.S. International Festival Luxembourg 2014), "The Weary" (RPW & Stories About Humans 2018), and "Light Below Us" (New English and American Theatre, Stuttgart). He won the Governor's Award for Best Play in the State of New Jersey in 2004 and 2005. He studied playwriting at Fordham University. He holds a Master of Arts from the University of Tübingen. His plays have been developed and produced in the United States, Luxembourg, and Germany. He lives with his family in Germany.

CONTACT:

Michael.g.hilton@gmail.com

WEBSITE:

newplayexchange.org/users/21182/michael-g-hilton

THE PLAY:

Happy Baby

THE PLAYWRIGHT:

Susan Jackson

SYNOPSIS:

Mrs. Willian visits her daughter, Fanny, at Meridian Center—a retreat for people dealing with various mental challenges. The form of therapy is different; the "clients" are asked to re-create a happy past.

ANOTHER WINNING PLAY by Susan Jackson:

THE PLAY:

Tending to Other Things

SYNOPSIS:

Phyllis Rentner, wife of a famous sportscaster accused of molesting boys, is recovering from a broken ankle after a drunken fall down the stairs. Rejected by her friends, Phyllis attempts to be-friend a reluctant inhouse care nurse, Miriam: based on a true story.

ABOUT THE PLAYWRIGHT:

Jackson received the Bay Area Theatre Critics Circle Award for Best Original Play. Her works have been staged- read/produced in New York City—Off-Broadway, Bay Area, Eugene O'Neill Foundation, William Inge New Works Festival, Sydney, London and South Carolina. Her plays—finalists and semi-finalists: Fusion Theatre Company, 3Girls Theatre Company, Creede Repertory Theatre, South Carolina Centre Stage, Little Black Dress Ink Women's Theatre Festival and SAMARITAN was a finalist for the Henley Rose Competition for Female Playwrights. She's a Resident Playwright for 3Girls Theatre Co. She's won Best of Capital Fringe.

CONTACT:

> susjcks5@aol.com
> 415-505-2151

WEBSITE:

> southernrailroadtheatrecompany.com

THE PLAY:

Scattered Shower

THE PLAYWRIGHTS:

Deborah Ann Percy and Arnold Johnston

SYNOPSIS:

Kevin and Marigold drive to a baby shower while discussing the quirky and somewhat presumptuous language of the invitation. The comic discussion exposes their own tensions about family planning and parenthood and, as they arrive at their destination, we see that the annoying invitation has actually moved them toward resolution of their dilemma.

ABOUT THE PLAYWRIGHTS:

Married writers Deborah Ann Percy and Arnold Johnston live in Kalamazoo and South Haven, MI. Their individually and collaboratively written plays have won some 150 productions, as well as numerous awards and publications across the country and internationally; and they've written, co-written, edited, or translated some twenty books, including Debby's short fiction collections Cool Front: Stories from Lake Michigan (March Street Press) and Invisible Traffic (One Wet Shoe Press). Arnie's poetry, fiction, non-fiction, and translations have appeared widely in literary journals and anthologies. His books include two poetry chapbooks—Sonnets: Signs and Portents (Finishing Line Press) and What the Earth Taught Us (March Street Press)—and The Witching Voice: A Novel from the Life of Robert Burns (Wings Press). A full-length collection of Arnie's poems—Where We're Going, Where We've Been—will appear soon from FutureCycle Press, and his new novel—Swept Away—is forthcoming from Caffeinated Press.

CONTACT:

arnie.johnston@wmich.edu
269-870-0703
dajohnston2@gmail.com
269-870-0704

THE PLAY:

Noir Man

THE PLAYWRIGHT:

Ken Levine

SYNOPSIS:

A modern day Philip Marlowe tries to solve the biggest mystery of all — the plot of "the Big Sleep."

ABOUT THE PLAYWRIGHT:

Ken Levine is an Emmy winning writer/director/playwright/ major league baseball announcer. Full-length plays include A or B?, Going Going Gone, Our Time, Upfronts and Personal, America's Sexiest Couple, and Guilty Pleasures. They've been performed in New York, Los Angeles, and throughout the country. His many short plays have been produced around the world and have won numerous festivals and competitions. Ken has written over 200 episodes of television for such shows as MASH, Cheers, Frasier, the Simpsons, and Wings. He has directed over 60 TV episodes and has been the play-by-play voice of the Baltimore Orioles, Seattle Mariners, and San Diego Padres and hosted Dodger Talk for eight seasons.

CONTACT:

KenLevinePlays@gmail.com
310-849-9990

WEBSITE:

kenlevineplays.com

THE PLAY:

Table in the Air

THE PLAYWRIGHT:

Rex McGregor

SYNOPSIS:

Marie Curie prides herself in being a rational scientist. Tonight, she confronts the notorious "medium" Eusapia Palladino.

ABOUT THE PLAYWRIGHT:

Rex McGregor is a New Zealand playwright. His short comedies have been produced on four continents from New York and London to Sydney and Chennai. His most popular play, *Threatened Panda Fights Back,* has had over a dozen productions. Rex has a Master of Arts (Honors) in Languages and Literature from the University of Auckland and is currently a senior collections librarian at Auckland Libraries.

Agent: Playmarket playmarket.org.nz

CONTACT:

rex.mcgregor@xtra.co.nz

WEBSITE:

rexmcgregor.com

THE PLAY:

Formerly Known As

THE PLAYWRIGHT:

Alyson Mead

SYNOPSIS:

A 10-year high school reunion brings Barry, a former football God, more than he bargained for when all is not as it seems. As his past and present merge, he's forced to consider a brand new ways of looking at things.

ABOUT THE PLAYWRIGHT:

Alyson Mead studied at Yale, the Slade School of Art in London, NYU's Tisch School of the Arts and with iO West, UCB and Tectonic Theatre Project. Her plays include THE FLORA AND FAUNA (Princess Grace Award finalist, Henley-Rose Award winner, Bridge Initiative New Work winner, WAM Theatre, Magnolia Theatre, Cherry Lane Theatre, Project Playwright semi-finalist), THE PULSE PROJECT (Steppenwolf, Emerald Theatre, Stage Q), THE QUALITY OF MERCY (Urban Stages Emerging Playwright Award finalist, Bay Area Playwrights Festival semi-finalist, Elephant Theatre, Skylight Theatre), THE HONOR SYSTEM (Cimientos/IATI Theater finalist, Manhattan Theatre Works' Newborn Festival semi-finalist, Pasadena Playhouse), THE FLOWER (Kenneth Branagh Award for New Dramatic Writing finalist, NEWvember New Plays Festival finalist, Rough Writers New Play Fest), and PUNK ROCK MOM (Venus Theatre), among others. Alyson was awarded residencies and fellowships through Ragdale, the Tyrone Guthrie Centre in Ireland, Can Serrat and the Women's International Study Center, and her work has been developed and commissioned by Kenyon Playwrights Conference, Playwrights Center San Francisco, 360repco, Ensemble Studio Theatre, and the 365 Women a Year Playwriting Project. She's published by Original Works Publishing and Smith & Kraus, and is a member of the Dramatists Guild, Ammunition Theatre's Writing Workshop, the

Ensemble Studio Theatre's Playwriting Unit and the Los Angeles Female Playwrights Initiative.

CONTACT:

admin@pageturnermedia.com

WEBSITE:

AlysonMead.com

THE PLAY:

Cancelled

THE PLAYWRIGHT:

M. Rowan Meyer

SYNOPSIS:

Preparations for a new baby come to a sudden and tragic halt, forcing Geoff and Dominic to ask what comes next. Or if there can even be a next.

ABOUT THE PLAYWRIGHT:

Rowan is the showrunner of the multi award winning series "Patient", set for release in Spring of 2019. His plays have been produced all across the country. He is the author of "Tiny Fiction" and co-author of "Freak Week" with two time New York Times Bestselling author Grace Helbig. MFA in Acting, Rutgers University.

WEBSITE:

mrowanmeyer.com

THE PLAY:

The Dog in the Woods

THE PLAYWRIGHT:

Cayson Miles

SYNOPSIS:

Parker is being interviewed by the police over the murder of his dog while his friends Katie and Alison are lost in the woods. Who murdered Lola the lazy dog, and why?

ABOUT THE PLAYWRIGHT:

Cayson Miles is a playwright from Ocean Springs, Mississippi. They are an alumnus of the Powerhouse Training Company, and runner up of the Mississippi Theatre Association's Adult Playwriting Competition for 2018.

CONTACT:

caysonmiles@gmail.com

THE PLAY:

Window Shopping

THE PLAYWRIGHT:

Alexander Millington

SYNOPSIS:

At what point does a fascination become an obsession? Can one person truly fall in love with another without even seeing their face?

ABOUT THE PLAYWRIGHT:

Alexander Millington set up his own theatre company, Conceptual Arts Theatre Company Ltd, in 2015 specialising in producing new writing and encouraging young writers to get their work produced. Since 2015, Alexander has worked on various new productions across England including musicals, comedies and dark dramas and has also had his work selected to be performed at fringe venues in London.

CONTACT:

alexander1992@live.co.uk
07882 453434

THE PLAY:

And Everything Was Perfect

THE PLAYWRIGHT:

Monte D. Monteleagre

SYNOPSIS:

Five identically dressed men work at five identical desks completing identical task. They internally mark each other as the odd one out while wondering why they each turned their own back on the moon.

ABOUT THE PLAYWRIGHT:

When Monte D. Monteleagre was young, he wanted to be an astronaut. Then, he found theatre, writing, and music in high school. He's been on a trip to the moon ever since. Monte is a graduate of Nebraska Wesleyan University with a BFA in Theatre Studies.

CONTACT:

montedmonteleagre@gmail.com

WEBSITE:

montedmonteleagre.com

The Play:

Girl Scout Cookies

The Playwright:

Patricia Montley

Synopsis:

A friendly Pothead tries to do business with an entrepreneuring Girl Scout at her cookie table outside a marijuana store.

About The Playwright:

Dramatists Guild member Pat Montley has 20 plays published (French, Playscripts, Meriwether, Heinemann, Applause, Dramatic Publishing, Prentice-Hall, ICWP, HaveScripts, Dramatics). Her plays have enjoyed readings at the Kennedy Center, Baltimore Center Stage, Rep Stage (MD), Abingdon Theatre (NYC), and productions at Nebraska Repertory Theatre, Manhattan Theatre Source, Harold Clurman Theatre, Nat Horne Theatre, and the Edinburgh Fringe Festival. Her work has been supported by a Kennedy Center Playwrights' Intensive, residencies at the Millay Artists' Colony (NY) and the Djerassi Resident Artists Program (CA), and grants from the Deutsch Foundation, Maryland's and Pennsylvania's Arts Councils, Shubert Foundation, Mary Roberts Rinehart Foundation, and Warner Brothers.

Contact:

pat_montley@msn.com
410-252-6074

Website:

newplayexchange.org/users/24016/pat-montley

THE PLAY:

Ted and Margaret

THE PLAYWRIGHT:

Fred Pezzulli

SYNOPSIS:

Margaret (a "Rosie Riveter"} and Ted (a U.S. Army private) meet at Penn Station in New York in 1943 during Thanksgiving. They get married after Christmas and Ted is shipped overseas. He returns home permanently scarred.

ABOUT THE PLAYWRIGHT:

Born and raised in West Virginia. Plays include: Rattlesnake, Ginny, The Iron Horse Cafe, The Doubling Time, The Trial of Klaus Barbie, A Small Inconvenience, The Encounter, Hampton Harbor.

CONTACT:

fpezzulli@nyc.rr.com
646-478-7332

THE PLAY:

Emily and Henry

THE PLAYWRIGHT:

Gary Richards

SYNOPSIS:

A chance meeting between Emily Dickinson and Henry David Thoreau.

ABOUT THE PLAYWRIGHT:

Gary Richards is a director, actor, producer, and teacher as well as a writer. His plays, include The Root (five Drama-Logue Awards, four Carbonell nominations), Children at Play, Slambook, Social Studies, Dividends, Stag, Shiva, Tropical Depression, Second Summer (Best Play Award, Colleagues Theatre Company), Two Piece, Scrambled Eggs, Somebody's Somebody, and A Chip in Time. He also has several one-act plays to his credit. His screenplays include In Scoring Position, To Go, The Root, Beating Hearts, Doin' Time, Two Regular Guys, Butch and Kiki, Garage Band, Second Summer, Continuing Ed, and The Florida Room, among others.

Mr. Richards is currently on the faculty of the School of Visual Arts where he teaches screenwriting and storytelling. He lives with his wife, children's book author/illustrator, Karen Katz, and their daughter, Lena, in New York City and Saugerties, N.Y.

CONTACT:

grichardsnyc@aol.com

THE PLAY:

Good Meeting

THE PLAYWRIGHT:

Julia B. Rosenblatt

SYNOPSIS:

In the midst of a financial crisis at The Ferber Foundation for Equity and Justice, Community Engagement specialists Judy, Brian, Sariya and Megan try their damnedest to keep everything civil, progressive and "woke," as they battle for their jobs.

ABOUT THE PLAYWRIGHT:

Julia B. Rosenblatt, is a playwright, director, actor and adjunct theater professor at Capital Community College. She was the Co-Founding Artistic Director of the award winning HartBeat Ensemble for 16 years, where she wrote her acclaimed plays, Flipside and Gross Domestic Product among others. In 2018, Julia was a Graustein Memorial Fund Playwriting Fellow and a Connecticut Women's Hall of Fame "Women Center Stage" Honoree. In 2015 and 2016, Julia was the Playwriting Consultant at the Harriet Beecher Stowe Center. Julia is a Theater of the Oppressed (TO) practitioner and has taught TO workshops throughout the United States, Nicaragua and Mexico. Julia holds a BA from UCLA School of Theater, Film and Television and an MFA in playwriting from Spalding University.

CONTACT:

juliabrosenblatt@gmail.com

The Play:

What You Don't Know

The Playwright:

Brian Shnipper

Synopsis:

Beth and Rachel meet for coffee to discuss their friend's intervention, but Beth's husband keeps interrupting. A play about dark secrets and the lengths we go to to cover them up.

About The Playwright:

Brian Shnipper conceived and directed the world premiere of STANDING ON CEREMONY: THE GAY MARRIAGE PLAYS (Los Angeles Drama Critics Award) at the Coronet Theatre where it was hailed in the Los Angeles Times as "a burgeoning phenomenon" and a "vital achievement". It has since been performed in over 100 theatres around the world. Off Broadway: New York Theatre Workshop, EST, Negro Ensemble Company, New Dramatists. Regional: Ensemble Theatre Company, Colony Theatre, Pasadena Playhouse, Profile Theatre, Broadway Rose, Luna Stage. He served as Artistic Director for 12 Miles West Theatre Company in New Jersey. Plays include IT'S NOT UNUSUAL, DIARY OF A LOST BOY with Connie Congdon (adapted from the novel by Harry Kondoleon), FAMILY COMMITMENT, WHAT I LEARNED IN KINDERGARTEN.

Contact:

Susan Gurman. Susan Gurman Agency
susan@gurmanagency.com

THE PLAY:

English Majors

THE PLAYWRIGHT:

Donna Spector

SYNOPSIS:

Paul and Lisa meet through eHarmony.com in an Upper West Side café. Former English majors and devout iconoclasts, they have an astonishing amount in common until they land on the subject of baseball.

ABOUT THE PLAYWRIGHT:

Off Broadway: Golden Ladder (Women Playwrights: Best Plays of 2002) and Another Paradise. Short-Term Affairs (35 in 10: Thirty-Five Ten-Minute Plays, Dramatic Publishing), Acrosstown Repertory's Sunwall Comedy Prize, Eileen Heckart Drama. Award, Two N.E.H. grants to study theater in Greece, Grants from the Geraldine Dodge Foundation and the New York Council for the Arts.

CONTACT:

donnaspector@optonline.net

WEBSITE:

donnaspector.net

THE PLAY:

Vintages

THE PLAYWRIGHT:

Chloë Whitehorn

SYNOPSIS:

Elizabeth's bedroom mirrors show every threat of impending wrinkles and reflect the carefree youth she wasted on a man. How can she live in the moment when the future looks bleak and the past is so seductive?

ABOUT THE PLAYWRIGHT:

A graduate of Queen's University's (Kingston, Canada) theatre program, Chloë Whitehorn is a playwright, actor, and underwater photographer. Chloë's work often examines taboo moralities, tragic love, and the licentious desires and imaginative reasoning of human beings. Her plays include "Love, Virtually", "Divine Wrecks", "Mourning After the Night Before", "The Pigeon", "Clarissa on her Deathbed", "Dressing Amelia", "The Frank Diary of Anne","The Deepest Trench", and "How to Not Die Horribly in a Fire".

CONTACT:

chloe.whitehorn@gmail.com

WEBSITE:

chloewhitehorn.com